THE PRINCETON
FUGITIVE SLAVE

THE PRINCETON
FUGITIVE SLAVE

THE TRIALS OF JAMES COLLINS JOHNSON

LOLITA BUCKNER INNISS

Empire State Editions
An imprint of Fordham University Press
New York   2019

Visit us online at www.fordhampress.com/empire-state-editions.

Library of Congress Control Number: 2019945353.

Printed in the United States of America

21 20 19   5 4 3 2 1

First edition

Contents

Preface

> I am intrigued and amazed to learn all of this
> about my family. In my heart, this is a sad
> conversation, but we all own who we are. The
> Wallises were not on the right side of history
> in the case of James Collins Johnson. But this
> case helped to get a lot of people thinking
> about the wrongfulness of slavery, and for
> that much we can be happy.
>
> *—Philip Severn Wallis, a member of*
> *the Princeton class of 1981 and a direct*
> *descendant of Philip Wallis (1793–1844),*
> *the enslaver of James Collins Johnson*

James Collins fled slavery in Maryland in August 1839. He changed his name to James Collins Johnson along the way, apparently to obscure his identity. A few days after he fled, Johnson reached Princeton, New Jersey, where he obtained a job at the College of New Jersey, now known as Princeton University. Johnson worked on the college's campus without incident until 1843, when disaster struck: Johnson was arrested on suspicion of being a fugitive slave after a student recognized him and alerted Johnson's owner. Johnson's owner came to Princeton and had Johnson seized and detained for trial as a runaway slave. Johnson was adjudged a slave and slated for return to slavery. However, he was redeemed from slavery by a local white woman who had significant ties to Princeton.

Johnson spent the next several years repaying the funds advanced for his purchase. He went on to become one of the best-known vendors over his six-decade career on campus. At his death, Johnson was described as "the oldest Negro in Princeton." He was buried near what was then the whites-only section of the local cemetery, lying only a few feet away from some of the region's and the country's most prominent citizens. Alumni

Gravestone of James Collins Johnson, Princeton Cemetery. (Photo credit: Daryl Inniss.)

and students took up a collection for Johnson's burial and erected a grave-stone whose epitaph pays tribute to him as "the students' friend."

This is the story that I heard from a Princeton graduate as I sat sunning in the plaza in front of Firestone Library early in my freshman year at Princeton in 1979. As a stereotypical Los Angeles native, I was friendly, relaxed, and eager to talk to anyone who approached me. I was also a black woman who was the first in her family to attend college, and I had come to Princeton sight unseen. I wanted to learn all that I could about the university, and about the town surrounding it. So when the elderly white man in a vivid orange-and-black-striped reunion jacket asked if I wanted to hear the story of an "old-time colored man" at Princeton, I smiled and said, "Yes!" The story that I heard that day stayed with me for decades. A lover of fairy tales, I enjoyed the story's happy ending. Then, as now, I relished the generative force of the tale to convey a particular sense of Princeton history and belonging, and I turned it over and over in my head.[1] But understanding that few people's lives can be so neatly summed up, I vowed to someday learn more about James Collins Johnson.

My research has shown that the truth of Johnson's life both before and after his arrival in Princeton was likely far less sanguine than most stories suggest. While his life as an ostensibly free man was clearly an improvement over slavery in Maryland, neither the association of his Mid-Atlantic enslavement with oppression nor the association of his escape north to Princeton with freedom is likely accurate. Johnson's life in Princeton was one of tremendous vicissitudes. In one interview he evidenced bitterness when he complained about a white Civil War veteran who had been given a campus vending permit, thus encroaching into his fiefdom. When told that his anger was misplaced because the white veteran had fought for Johnson's freedom, Johnson sharply retorted: "I never got no free papers. Princeton College bought me; Princeton College owns me; and Princeton College has got to give me my living."[2] If Johnson was in fact unhappy at Princeton, one might wonder why he remained in the shadow of the university from his arrival in 1839 until his death in 1902. The answer lies perhaps in an observation of Lea VanderVelde, in writing about Dred Scott and his family: slavery and freedom are not clearly opposite poles. Instead, there are "gradations of liberty, security, and autonomy."[3]

The story of Johnson's trial, known at the time as the Princeton fugitive slave case, captured local and national popular imagination. Most accounts of Johnson's trial and fuller life story agree on the basic details. Students, alumni, and other college figures framed Johnson as a puckish, picayune, and relatively minor figure who lived a humble, respectable life of service. For these narrators, Johnson symbolizes a fondly remembered earlier time at Princeton. His life is seemingly a counterparadigm for the so-called Great Man Theory that was popularized in the 1840s just as Johnson reached Princeton. According to this theory, history can be explained in substantial part by the impact of "great men": highly influential individuals who are historically meaningful because of their power, intelligence, charisma, or wisdom. But the counternarrative argues that the people who constitute the broader society, the lesser-known individuals, are at the heart of the historical moment. By this reckoning, Johnson is much more than a minor historical glyph that appears in the background of better-known figures in the larger panorama of Princeton University history.

Princeton University was founded in Elizabeth, New Jersey, in 1746 as the College of New Jersey. This is the name by which it was known for 150 years, through its move to the town of Princeton in 1756 and until 1896. From its inception, it served the sons (and, beginning in 1969, the daughters) of America's social, political, and economic elite. Through the generations, Princeton University became a site of memory and part of the American patrimony. Princeton was the alma mater and the ideological home of many of the nation's founding fathers and of other key political and social figures in U.S. history. From June through November 1783, when the Continental Congress met at Nassau Hall, Princeton was the capital of the United States. Scholars at Princeton helped foster the growth of American ideals of political, intellectual, and religious freedom from the mid- and late eighteenth centuries until the early nineteenth century. At the same time that these ideals of freedom were flourishing at Princeton University, James Collins Johnson and other persons of African ancestry, both slave and free, lived in narrowly circumscribed social and political spaces in its shadows. Johnson's presence at Princeton is a reminder that slavery and universities, though seemingly disparate topics, have long been intertwined. This book is part of a burgeoning area of inquiry: slavery and the memory of slavery in the context of universities.

The impact of the African slave trade and the enslavement of African-ancestored people in relation to institutions of higher education in the Atlantic world is an especially contentious thread in history. This contention occurs because the values and high ideals of academe are often framed in implicit but substantial contraposition to the horrors of human bondage. Enslaved people were often the backbone of the laboring class at eighteenth- and nineteenth-century college campuses.[4] Related to the presence of this enslaved workforce, scholars at such institutions often shaped the content of proslavery thought and ideas, doing so in a manner that was coherent, organized, and evidence-based so as to legitimize the practice of slavery.[5] Some educational institutions, such as the University of North Carolina, Brown, Harvard, the University of Alabama, the University of Virginia, Columbia, and the College of William and Mary, have in recent years considered their own involvement in the institution of slavery. Many of these institutions have united in a group of over three dozen colleges and universities called the Universities Studying Slavery consortium.

In addition, a growing number of scholars have also begun to address slavery in the higher education context. In one book, *Ebony and Ivy: Race, Slavery, and the Troubled History of America's Universities*, Craig Steven Wilder discusses how leading colleges and universities in the United States depended on slavery for economic sustenance and how these academic centers sometimes promoted proslavery ideas.[6] A set of edited volumes, *Scarlet and Black: Slavery and Dispossession in Rutgers History*, offers essays on Rutgers University's (earlier known as Queen's College) involvement with slavery, providing valuable discussions of slavery and higher education in New Jersey.[7] A recent volume of the journal *Slavery and Abolition* discussed various aspects of slavery at several colleges and universities.[8]

Besides the way in which it centers the engagement of colleges and universities with slavery, Johnson's story of emancipation by purchase is also part of a larger story of slave redemption. Antebellum manumission of slaves is often framed as the magnanimous act of a kind slave master. However, some research shows that a large number of emancipations occurred when owners were paid to free their slaves, with the payment often coming from slaves themselves. In 1839, the same year that Johnson escaped from Maryland slavery, over 40 percent of the free blacks in Cincinnati, Ohio, purchased their own freedom. In traditional accounts of his story, Johnson is framed as the fortunate beneficiary of a series of generous and just actions crowned by the indulgence of owners willing to accept a price for Johnson's liberty. However, for James Collins Johnson the man, these acts of "generosity" and "justice" may have been part of the harsh reality of a world where slavery was a vital economic engine and where every enslaved person represented an investment.

As Edward Baptist shows in *The Half Has Never Been Told: Slavery and the Making of American Capitalism*, U.S. slavery, beyond being a brutal system of physical, social, and psychological oppression, was also crucial to the country's geographic and economic growth.[9] Johnson's owners, the Wallises, were in a financially precarious situation at the time of the case. The family had descended from one of the wealthiest families in Maryland, one with roots in the early colonial history of the state. In 1843, at the time of Johnson's fugitive slave trial, the family patriarch, Philip Wallis, lived on a farm in Yazoo City, Mississippi. The purchase of the farm was funded by the sale of the remnants of a greatly diminished family empire of slaves and land in Maryland. Rather than an act of generosity, the

Wallises' act of allowing Johnson to achieve emancipation by purchase is perhaps better seen as an act of economic pragmatism.

The nature of buying freedom is two-sided. While some slave owners such as the Wallises may have felt an economic compulsion to accept money for a legally enslaved James Collins Johnson, it is also the case that the antislavery activists who often funded emancipations by sale saw the practice as a way to quickly conclude what might otherwise have been a long and contentious battle with aggrieved slave owners. However, while emancipation by purchase was a potent tool for effecting freedom, it raised moral concerns: Did not paying the slave owner both validate and perpetuate the institution? The moral and ethical dilemmas such purchases evoke also arise in the context of modern-day human trafficking. While buying freedom is often framed as an antebellum phenomenon that lost its coherence as a legal and moral undertaking in the postemancipation world, contemporary slavery has made it relevant again.

One question raised in this book is the extent to which Johnson may have dissembled to hide his true feelings or engaged in strategic relationships with those around him. Some accounts reported that Johnson was a jovial, beloved campus friend to all. The seeming ordinariness and easy-going nature of those relationships is remarkable when one considers that many of the students at Princeton were slave owners, often heartfelt pro-slavery sympathizers from the South. Indeed, the claims of ongoing warm relations between Johnson and the white students he was surrounded with in the middle and late nineteenth century seem incredibly unlikely in what was then small-town, semirural Princeton.

That Johnson was a perennial good fellow who engaged in mirthful, warm relations with students may have been part of what James C. Scott has termed a public transcript: the visible, open interaction between the oppressed and those who dominate them.[10] Johnson's public persona may have been a stylized public performance crafted to negotiate the perils of an antebellum and, later, a postbellum world. Johnson appeared to embrace the respectability politics described by Cheryl D. Hicks in *Talk with You Like a Woman*, her account of black women in the criminal justice system in New York in the late 1800s.[11] These efforts at uplift often dominated the lives of striving freedmen and their children, efforts, sometimes strained, and not always successful, to live better, do better, and be better. Indeed, a closer look suggests that all was not well between Johnson and the students. The students on their part often acted out a barely disguised disdain for Johnson through the rough jocularity that they aimed at him. As for Johnson, it is possible that he was a beleaguered, overburdened man who wore a mask of good-natured bonhomie to cover fatigue, bitterness, and anger. The process of unmasking Johnson to expose his real thoughts and feelings offers a look at the larger function of "Happy Negro" myths that were part of the social and legal justification for slavery and for the postslavery subjugation of blacks.[12]

Another intriguing question that research into Johnson's life raises is the identity of Johnson's betrayer. Several accounts identify one man as the person who revealed Johnson's whereabouts to his master. However, there is a substantial amount of evidence, including details offered by Johnson's owner and purportedly by Johnson himself, that the man most commonly identified as the betrayer was not, in fact, the betrayer. This part of Johnson's story not only makes for an engaging whodunit in the context of his life but also addresses the broader questions of informant narratives, vulnerability, heroism, and culpability. Are those who expose persons who may be wrongdoers under the letter of the law but innocent victims in moral terms (such as escaped slaves or, in a contemporary context, undocumented aliens) to be lauded as good citizen whistleblowers or reviled as ill-motivated informants or collaborators?[13]

Perhaps one of the most intriguing questions this book addresses is whether Theodosia Ann Mary Prevost acted alone when she paid Johnson's slave price. Most accounts agree that Johnson was redeemed from slavery by purchase and suggest that Prevost advanced the funds, either in whole or in part. But at an institution filled with the sons of many of the wealthiest men in the United States, it is curious that an unmarried woman of unexplained means would play so significant a role in such a matter. Prevost and her family had a long and close association with Princeton and with many of its principal figures. Even long after Johnson's trial and redemption, she easily accessed and seemingly commanded persons in power at the college. Might Prevost have been a straw person in the transaction between Johnson and his owners, the public face of a college that, for numerous reasons, did not wish to involve itself directly with slavery? Johnson's redemption thus addresses some of the ways that gender, race, and class governed institutional and legal interactions and cultures.

Research about James Collins Johnson reveals information about black food vendors who plied their wares at or near Princeton University in the nineteenth and early twentieth centuries. Crucial figures in and around Princeton, these men dwelt in the margins between the black and white communities. Black vendors like Johnson and those who came before and after him were often seen as motley fools and framed as the butt of cam-

pus and community jokes. Johnson was certainly not the first; men such
as Cezar Trent and Peter Scudder were two predecessors of Johnson who
were well known in their time.

In the early decades of the college, Trent cut and hauled wood and
performed other tasks for students, faculty, and administrators. In 1787,
for example, Trent received money from Princeton for scrubbing the en-
trances to campus housing areas and cleaning the "back campus" and
"necessary house"—the campus outhouse. Trent was a longtime resident
of the town of Princeton and lived on what was known as African Lane,
or more pejoratively, Nigger Lane, and now called Witherspoon Street.
Trent was described in one account as a "native of Africa" and was remembered by one college figure as a jovial clown who entertained the
public at holidays.[14]

Most such "natives of Africa" in the United States arrived as slaves in
the antebellum period; Trent was born in Africa and was likely a slave
for some period in his life. Given his close association with Princeton,
one wonders whether Trent was the same enslaved Cezar purchased by
Princeton president Aaron Burr Sr. in 1755 and who served him at his
campus home when Burr took up residence in 1756. Trent in turn may
have himself held slaves; advertisements in the 1790s show him as the
advertiser in an advertisement seeking a runaway and as the seller of
an enslaved person in another advertisement.[15] Scudder, another late
eighteenth-century Princeton servant, was sometimes called Peter Polite.
He worked at the undergraduate college near the time of its founding and
by 1801 was employed at the seminary. Scudder was described as a former
slave. It seems that he was with the college for several decades; an 1827
note shows a Peter Scudder acknowledging receipt from John Maclean
for $22.67 in satisfaction of "all demands."[16]

Partly because he was the first of these vendors to live in the age
of photography and widely disseminated media accounts, James Collins
Johnson was by far the best known of these men. Much Princeton University history notes Johnson as such, and it is Johnson's story that is at the
center of the present book. But for all his notoriety, Princeton history has
in many respects treated Johnson as an amalgam of what could be called
the black Princeton vendor archetype: a lovable, laughable, and inter-
changeable cog in a system that valorized black obeisance in the guise of
wandering food purveyor. Hence, in filling in the details of Johnson's life,
this book performs a conscious process of disaggregating him from and
dismantling a facile archetype. The lives of Johnson and other black food
vendors, especially those who came after Johnson, showed these men to
be less fools than the idiomatic antithesis: sages or savvy knaves.

Johnson standing with basket over his arm in posed scene with painted backdrop; circa 1872s. (Historical Photograph Collection: Individuals series, Box AC067. SP001, Folder 040; Princeton University Archives, Department of Rare Books and Special Collections, Princeton University Library.)

One vendor who came after Johnson was Archibald Campbell "Spader" Seruby, born some sixty years after Johnson on August 5, 1877, in Pennington, New Jersey.[17] Seruby's nickname, Spader, was said to grow from his similarity to a black vendor named Conover Spader who had visited the Princeton University community to sell foodstuffs sometime in the 1880s.[18] Seruby was believed to have been attached to university service from his early youth; a photograph from around 1890 was said to show Johnson as an old man posed alongside a teenager said to be Spader.[19]

Archibald "Spader" Seruby, 1920. (Historical Photograph Collection: Individuals series, box AC067.SP001, folder 080.001; Princeton University Archives, Department of Rare Books and Special Collections, Princeton University Library.)

Seruby was clearly viewed as Johnson's successor, as an item in the February 14, 1903, *Princeton Alumni Weekly* noted:

> We have the pleasure in introducing to the alumni and all Princeton visitors Mr. Archibald Campbell Seruby. He stands under the west arch of the University library, ready to sell you peanuts, and anxious to prove a worthy successor—as much as anyone can be—to the late Jimmy Johnson, Purveyor in Ordinary to the sweet tooth of Princeton, whose stutter and caramels will long be affectionately remembered by all old graduates of Nassau Hall.[20]

Like Johnson, Seruby was regularly present at athletic events at Princeton University.[21] However, Seruby had a wider reach than Johnson and worked at public and private venues throughout central and southern New Jersey and beyond. Reports about Seruby often described him as a good-natured clown, much as Johnson was described.[22] But Seruby's public persona as a fun-loving harlequin was often belied by a more somber public presence. He was, for instance, known as an astute man with cash holdings and real estate who deftly avoided fully disclosing details of

William Taylor, undated, Nassau Street, Princeton, New Jersey. (Historical Photograph Collection: Individuals series, box LP1, image no. 294; Princeton University Archives, Department of Rare Books and Special Collections, Princeton University Library.)

his financial status. More archly, Seruby was involved in frequent minor conflicts with police, courts, and other legal authorities. He was on several occasions arrested, charged, fined, or jailed for unlicensed food sales, disorderly conduct, and other infractions.[23] Accounts of Seruby's lawbreaking show him to be a man acting with an air of pleasant and pliant defiance, determined to succeed in the face of myriad barriers. Seruby died on September 24, 1935, leaving yet another void for Princetonians seeking itinerant food vending services.[24]

Seruby's absence was filled by William Taylor, also known as the Jigger Man. Taylor also served in the dual role of mascot and food vendor to members of the Princeton community. Born around 1872 in Virginia, Taylor served the Princeton community from 1904 until his death in 1949. Taylor and his predecessor black vendors were frequently compared, sometimes confused, and often linked.[25] Like Johnson and Seruby, Taylor plied his wares from a pushcart that he wheeled throughout the town when not stationed at the university. And like both Johnson and Seruby, Taylor's genial "Jigger Man" university persona obscured a serious and more reserved demeanor that is little revealed in most writings about him.

These black vendors, Johnson chief among them, served as models of success for the wider black community. Forays in entrepreneurship provided blacks in Princeton with some measures of economic independence and dignity from the mid-1800s until the dawn of the twentieth century. This sense of pride was sorely needed, for the twentieth century brought as many downs as ups for Princeton's blacks.

Princeton University came into a new era of national and international renown at the end of the nineteenth century. Around the same time, the town of Princeton attained fame as a place of genteel social sensibilities, and large spacious homes and esteemed new residents (such as former U.S. president Grover Cleveland) appeared in the town.[26] But while blacks in Princeton were well ingrained in the life of the town and at the university at the beginning of the twentieth century, relatively few blacks thrived. In the shadows of the noble buildings of the college and of the fine homes and residents of the town, black Princeton residents had few educational opportunities, were employed at scarcely better than subsistence wages, and frequently lived in squalid housing.

Five years after the death of James Collins Johnson, a 1907 *Princeton Alumni Weekly* article noted plans to provide bathing facilities for black servants employed in the dining halls and to make workplace bathing compulsory because "not ten percent of the two thousand negroes of Princeton have access to ordinary bathing facilities."[27] However, it appears that these plans never came to fruition and that blacks were fired on a mass scale; the premise was that they presented a danger of contaminating students.[28] In 1917, fifteen years after Johnson's death, Arthur Evans Wood, a University of Michigan sociologist, portrayed the Princeton black community as one where disorder, poverty, and illness were rampant.[29]

Wood conducted a house-by-house inspection of the black and immigrant white communities and chronicled what he described as conditions of extreme poverty, filth, allegations of immorality, and contagious disease. Wood's study followed investigations conducted by David C. Bowen, the sanitary inspector for the state of New Jersey; Andrew C. Imbrie (Johnson's principal biographer), a Princeton alumni trustee and financial secretary; and Lucy F. Friday, sanitary inspector of the university. All three reports were based on surveys that included areas of the town where black residences were clustered.[30] Bowen's report focused on the living conditions of black employees of the university.[31] Perhaps most dismaying about the early nineteenth-century residential conditions for many blacks in Princeton was the way in which conditions had markedly declined since 1855, when Ann Maria Davison surveyed the living conditions of several black Princeton families and found that many lived in comfortable, clean, and even relatively prosperous conditions.[32]

Despite the attention to housing in the black community, little improvement occurred over the next ten years. In 1929 Baker Street, the core of Princeton's black neighborhood, was demolished to make way for the Palmer Square development project. Some blacks who dwelt in this central area were relocated to other black areas of town.[33] Though contemporaneous accounts of the 1929 removal highlighted efforts to find new homes for those dispossessed, a few decades later it was clear that this alternative housing had left some black Princeton dwellers in more dire straits. In the 1950s, after several months of investigation of the black community that had been partially relocated when the Baker Street area was razed, student reporters from a Princeton University magazine decried the crowding and decrepit housing.[34] Some of these poor conditions abated in the next several years, but part of this improvement was tied to the influx of wealthier and often white residents.

The inexorable march of "progress" over the last few decades has caused significant erosion to Princeton's historic black community. By the early 1980s there were clear signs of gentrification, as white families purchased homes in what had been a principally black area for decades.[35] In the mid-1980s the black population in the town of Princeton was 15 percent, down from 20 percent in the 1970s.[36] At the beginning of the twenty-first century, blacks in the town of Princeton were the only demographic group to see a loss of population.[37] This loss occurred because of increasing taxes, pressure to sell from people seeking what were some of the last affordable housing units in town, and the ongoing spread of commercial interests.[38]

With the decline in the number of blacks in the town of Princeton in the past few decades has come some acknowledgment of the important role that people like James Collins Johnson played in the Princeton community and of the ways that historic and ongoing racist practices limited opportunity for blacks in the town and at the university. The Presbytery of New Brunswick researched historic racially animated harms to the traditionally black Witherspoon Presbyterian Church and in February 2015 promulgated a report recommending efforts at reconciliation and making financial amends.[39] In November 2015 the Presbyterian Synod of the Northeast gave $175,000 to the Witherspoon Presbyterian Church so the church could redeem mortgages on the Robeson House, the birthplace of Paul Robeson and the parsonage occupied by his father, the Reverend William Drew Robeson, when he was pastor of the church.[40] The Presbytery of New Brunswick also issued a formal apology for asking black members of the congregation to leave the predecessor of what is now Nassau Presbyterian Church in 1836 and expressed regret for the removal of Reverend Robeson from his post in 1900.[41]

The city has also taken actions to acknowledge the historic and contemporary importance of the black community in Princeton. In 2016 the Princeton City Council created the Witherspoon-Jackson historic district in order to help preserve a traditionally black section of town.[42] The Princeton City Council also that year reinstated a long-dormant Civil Rights Commission and charged it with seeking informal resolutions to complaints of discrimination.[43]

Like the town of Princeton, Princeton University has also made efforts to offer address, if not redress, for some of its history of antiblack racism. Princeton enrolled no black undergraduates until the late 1940s. A handful of black students were enrolled in the 1950s and early 1960s. One such student, Dr. Robert Rivers, class of 1953, was the son of parents and grandparents who had worked at Princeton in the generations before he enrolled.[44] In January 1962 there were only seven "American Negroes" enrolled on campus.[45] Princeton articulated a plan to seek out a critical mass of black students beginning in 1967 and nine years later awarded 8.5 percent of bachelor's degrees to black students. But despite a stated commitment to admitting black students, the percentage of blacks declined in subsequent years.[46]

Besides admitting black students, Princeton also made attempts to address the historic exclusion of black students once they arrived on campus, and what some have considered the historic diminution of black student concerns. For instance, on June 4, 2001, Judge Bruce Wright was awarded an honorary degree at Princeton as part of what was termed an apology for Princeton's 1939 revocation of Wright's admission after learning that he was black.[47] In 2015 black students engaged in a series of protests over racist practices and conditions on the campus. One claim of the student protesters was that retaining Woodrow Wilson's name on campus buildings constituted endorsement of Wilson's role in maintaining the bar on black students at Princeton, and of his other racist actions. Princeton undertook a study to consider whether Wilson's name should be removed.[48] Although the Board of Trustees ultimately declined to remove Wilson's name, the process of considering Wilson's legacy led to some changes.[49] A wall-sized portrait of Wilson in one of the dining halls was, for example, removed after being noted as "unduly celebratory" in view of Wilson's mixed legacy.[50] Perhaps the greatest achievement of this study was a statement by the trustees, however understated and subtle, acknowledging the fraught history of race relations at Princeton: "The committee acknowledges that over the course of Princeton's 270-year history, there have been people connected to the University—influential alumni, generous benefactors, and celebrated professors—who have espoused views that are antithetical to our values today."[51]

Besides efforts to address the historic exclusion of black students, Princeton also incorporated blacks into the faculty during the twentieth century. In 1955 Princeton appointed its first black tenure-track faculty member, Charles Twitchell Davis.[52] In 1964 Carl Fields came to Princeton as a student aid administrator and in 1968 became the university's first black dean. In the late 1960s Princeton hired Henry Drewry and Cecilia Hodges Drewry, a married couple, to serve as administrators and to offer black studies seminars. In 1973 Princeton hired Howard F. Taylor as a tenure-track professor in the sociology department. Taylor remained on the faculty until his retirement some twenty-five years later, and during those decades Princeton saw an increasing number of black faculty members, including renowned faculty figures such as Cornel West and Toni Morrison, esteemed university administrators such as Ruth Simmons and Valerie Smith,[53] and the creation of a department of African American studies.[54]

A recent example of addressing historic racial injustice at Princeton was the creation of a course on Princeton University and slavery taught by the history department.[55] The course was a precursor to the 2017 unveiling of the Princeton and Slavery Project, launched to investigate the university's involvement with the institution of slavery.[56] Most striking of all, Princeton University added the name of two formerly enslaved persons to campus architecture, including naming an arch after James Collins Johnson.[57]

Perhaps one of the most poignant and unanticipated aspects of this book on Johnson's life has been the identification of some contemporary direct descendants of Johnson's enslaver, Philip Wallis (1793–1844). Johnson also had direct descendants, but the trail runs relatively cold after the death of his youngest child, a daughter named Emily, and the early deaths of two of her children. Part of this absence of information is due to the paucity of public and private documents recording the lives of Johnson's family. In contrast, the descendants of Johnson's enslaver are relatively easier to trace, for, as one of the early settling European families in the United States, Wallis family history is discussed in several public and private sources. Among the numerous descendants of Philip Wallis are at least three Princeton alumni.[58] In a trenchant irony, one of the youngest of those descendants, Philip Severn Wallis, class of 1981, shares the names of Johnson's enslaver Philip Wallis and Wallis's co-enslaver, son Severn Teackle Wallis. Though I did not know him at the time, Philip Severn Wallis was a schoolmate of mine, having been on campus for two of my Princeton undergraduate years.[59] Near the end of my research on this manuscript, I had the chance to speak with him. While he knew something of his family's history, he was unacquainted with much of his family's Maryland connection and with the story of James Collins Johnson. The twenty-first-century Philip Wallis expressed dismay at learning the role that his ancestors had played in Johnson's story. But he looked forward to sharing the story with his family and with incorporating this new knowledge into his thinking about issues of U.S. culture and race more broadly.

These efforts at recognition and reconciliation are hopeful signs for black-white relations in Princeton's contemporary town and gown climate. These changes may be harbingers of hope well beyond Princeton University and its environs, in much the same way that the story of James Collins Johnson is a tale that exceeds its own boundaries. Johnson's story is one of slavery in the Mid-Atlantic, of slavery in the context of universities, of antebellum black life in New Jersey and the northern United States, and of justice and law more broadly.

Timeline

1600s–1700s

1696   The town of Princeton is settled.

1746   The College of New Jersey is founded in Elizabeth, New Jersey, by the Presbyterian Synod.

1747   Jonathan Dickinson is appointed first president of the College of New Jersey in April.

The college moves to the Newark parsonage of Aaron Burr Sr. after Dickinson's death in October.

1748   Aaron Burr Sr. becomes the college's second president.

1756   Nassau Hall and Maclean House (the president's house) are completed.

The College of New Jersey moves from Newark to Princeton.

1758   Jonathan Edwards becomes third president of the College of New Jersey.

1768   Rev. John Witherspoon is installed as sixth president of the College of New Jersey. Witherspoon is a direct ancestor of Johnson's benefactor, Theodosia Prevost.

1777   George Washington drives the British from Nassau Hall at the College of New Jersey.

1783   The Continental Congress meets in Nassau Hall, which served as the capitol of the United States from June to November.

1793 The Fugitive Slave Act of 1793 is enacted.

1795 Samuel Stanhope Smith, the maternal grandfather of Johnson's rescuer Theodosia Prevost, becomes seventh president of the College of New Jersey.

1798 Betsey Stockton is born a slave in Princeton, New Jersey. Her owner is Robert Stockton (1703–1805), a quartermaster in the Revolutionary War.

1800s

1801 Theodosia Ann Mary Prevost is born in New York City on January 10.

1802 Nassau Hall is gutted by fire and rebuilt.

1804 A New Jersey law provides that children of slaves born after July 4, 1804, are nominally free but must serve their master or the master's agent for several years.

John Bartow Prevost, the father of Theodosia Prevost, becomes the first judge of the Superior Court of the Territory of Orleans. He serves from 1804 to 1808. Prevost and his family move to New Orleans.

1812 Samuel Stanhope Smith resigns as president of the College of New Jersey after an acrimonious battle with the trustees. He is given a house and a pension.

Ashbel Green, the enslaver of Betsey Stockton, is installed as eighth president of the College of New Jersey. Stockton lives with Green and his wife, Elizabeth Stockton Green (possibly a half-sister of the enslaved Betsey), on the Princeton campus.

1816 Severn Teackle Wallis, the son and co-owner of Johnson, is born on September 8 in Maryland.

James Collins, later James Collins Johnson, is born on October 2 in Maryland.

1818 John Bartow Prevost is appointed as an American commissioner to examine the state of Spanish colonies in South America. He moves to Peru, taking his two sons with him but leaving his two daughters, Theodosia and Frances, in the United States.

1819 Samuel Stanhope Smith dies on August 21.

1822   Betsey Stockton, one of the best-known enslaved people to live on the Princeton campus, is freed and allowed to travel to the Sandwich Islands (later Hawaii) as the first unmarried woman of any race to serve as a missionary there.

1823   James Carnahan becomes ninth president of the College of New Jersey.

1831   Nat Turner leads a rebellion of slaves in Virginia. In response, Maryland enacts a greater number of laws to control slaves and slavery.

1835   The Snow Riot, cited as the first race riot in Washington, D.C., takes place in August, incited in part by the man who was dispatched to arrest Johnson.

1836   Johnson marries for the first time to a woman named Phillis, who lived in Church Hill, Maryland.

1837   Philip Wallis, James Collins Johnson's co-enslaver and father of Severn Teackle Wallis, moves to a plantation near Yazoo City, Mississippi, taking many of his Maryland slaves with him.

1839   James Collins Johnson escapes from slavery in Maryland and travels to Princeton, New Jersey, in early August.

1842   U.S. Supreme Court decides *Prigg v. Pennsylvania* on March 1, which narrowed the procedural rights of escaped slaves on trial.

1843   James Collins Johnson is captured on July 28 in Princeton.

Johnson's trial takes place on August 1.

1844   Philip Wallis, one of Johnson's enslavers, dies on October 23 in the explosion of the steamboat *Lucy Walker*.

1846   First Presbyterian Church of Princeton (Colored) is formed for black Princetonians

1850   The Fugitive Slave Act of 1850 is passed on September 18 as part of the Compromise of 1850.

1851   Johnson purchases a house at 32 Witherspoon Street in Princeton.

1852   Johnson's first wife, Phillis, dies, likely on July 17.

Johnson marries Catherine McCrea on December 23.

1854   John Maclean Jr. installed as tenth president of the College of New Jersey.

1855   Nassau Hall is gutted by fire again and rebuilt again. James Collins Johnson establishes himself as a campus vendor after the fire.

1857   U.S. Supreme Court rules on *Dred Scott v. Sandford* on March 6.

1861   Civil War begins.

1864   Theodosia Prevost, Johnson's benefactress, dies on December 13 in Englewood, New Jersey.

1865   Civil War ends.

1868   James McCosh of Scotland elected eleventh president of the College of New Jersey.

1880   Catherine McCrea Johnson dies on June 22.

1888   Francis L. Patton becomes twelfth president of the College of New Jersey.

1895   James Collins Johnson marries Anetta Webb Warden.

Emily Johnson Sorter Gordon, daughter of James Collins Johnson, dies.

Alexander Dumas Watkins becomes the first black instructor at Princeton University.

1896   The name of the College of New Jersey is changed to Princeton University. Professor Woodrow Wilson provides Princeton's informal motto: "Princeton in the Nation's Service."

1898   Scholar, athlete, actor, and political activist Paul Robeson is born in Princeton on April 9. Robeson's father, William Drew Robeson, was, like James Collins Johnson, a fugitive slave.

1900s

1901   Belle Da Costa Greene, born Belle Marion Greener, begins working at the Princeton University Library. Greene, who later gained fame as the librarian for J. P. Morgan, was from an African-ancestored family and passed for white during much of her adult life.

1902   Woodrow Wilson, class of 1879, elected thirteenth president of Princeton University in June.

James Collins Johnson dies on July 22.

But perhaps the black man best known to the longest list of graduates is the now celebrated Jim Johnson. He will be found on the campus to-day, in silver spectacles and golfing-stockings, and he was there 50 years ago. He has bought the cast off clothes of the students for a half-century. When the author of this volume was in college, Jim used to furnish oyster suppers, and many a good pair of trousers has passed into his shop to square an account for a feast already eaten. Jim stuttered badly, and still stutters; and the students used to give him a shilling to say "Philadelphia" and other long words which threatened to suffocate him. Jim remembers every graduate, and called him by name; a shade of sorrow passes over his ebony face, fringed with gray beard, if the old friend does not "come down with a quarter."

—*James Waddel Alexander,* Princeton—Old and
New: Recollections of Undergraduate Life

Introduction

> You would find daily on the walk between
> Whig and Clio Halls, a little old Negro with
> his push cart and his offering of molasses
> candy. He was small, shabby, insignificant,
> but not at all deserving of his malodorous
> sobriquet, Jim Stink. No one knew his real
> name or where he lived, but he was always
> there and in his day a pattern of industry
> and humility. There was always a smile under
> his battered derby. But when your mouth
> watered for his sweets and you asked the
> price just to hear his stuttered reply, it was
> always—"Ppppppenny pppppppiece Sir."
>
> —*William H. Hudnut, class of 1886*

The story of James Collins Johnson, like that of many lesser-known historical figures, suffers from the problem of factual scarcity. This paucity of information is especially true for enslaved persons. As the historian Annette Gordon-Reed wrote in describing the difficulties of seeking to "know" enslaved persons and the institution of U.S. slavery, a complex set of sources is required to paint a full picture: recollections of the enslaved, records of white enslavers, and information about the larger historical context.[1] Little is known, for instance, of Johnson's life in Maryland before he reached Princeton. Although some accounts tell us that Johnson had a "kind" master and that his enslavement was of the gentler sort, few facts about Johnson's pre-Princeton past come across in most accounts. As for Johnson's life after his arrival at Princeton, several stories describe him as a contented, jovial soul who reveled in his role as campus

1

food purveyor and mascot. Johnson was creatively if not well dressed, often sporting the clothes of students who had sold or traded their attire to him.[2] However, Johnson was also a much-changed man near the end of his life. By the end of the nineteenth century, Johnson was a familiar presence on campus, but one about whom little was known except the offensive nickname that followed him throughout his relationship with Princeton University: "Jim Stink."

Although Johnson could apparently read and write, he appears to have left behind no writing of his own about himself.[3] Thus Johnson's life in Maryland before arriving in Princeton must be drawn from the broader social and legal context of life for enslaved persons in Maryland. Information may also be gleaned from drawing inferences about Johnson from the lives of his Maryland enslavers. Like Sally Hemings and her family, who were enslaved by Thomas Jefferson, Johnson was kept in bondage by the Wallises, a family well known within and outside Maryland.[4] Johnson's story after arriving in Princeton is far better documented. However, information about Johnson during this period is seen in the writings of persons who frequently had only scanty knowledge of the close details about Johnson, so again, the broader social and legal context must be used to construct what Johnson's life was like in Princeton. Not surprisingly, even where there are archival materials, it is difficult to find first-person accounts of Johnson there. As Erica Armstrong Dunbar wrote about her search to document the life of Ona Judge, the escaped enslaved woman held by George Washington, it is difficult to find our subjects in the archives.[5] Instead, powerful white men often gave voice to these subjects only incidentally through their own self-reflections. Because there is an absence of primary writings and material artifacts that Johnson generated or that originated with him, it is necessary to give existing written sources a close, critical, and often interlineal reading. It also calls for focused methods and the use of framing themes that help elucidate the life of James Collins Johnson.

Sources, Methods, and Themes

This work draws on a plethora of documentary materials: the minutes of Princeton college trustee meetings, federal and local census records, newspapers, photographs, family records, local histories, and other documents to reveal Johnson's life story. Perhaps the most crucial source of information is records left by students themselves. Many Princeton students left direct and indirect references to James Collins Johnson in their student records. Student information sheets containing family information preface most of these records. These sheets, so painstakingly completed by Varnum Lansing Collins, help link students to each other and to Johnson. Collins was a graduate of Princeton, class of 1892, and served as the university's secretary from 1917 to 1936. Collins had a lifelong passion for Princeton's history and wrote several works on that theme.[6] A significant number of undergraduate files contain handwritten notes and typed letters from Collins requesting that graduates and their families complete the biographical data forms. These forms and the letters that often accompanied them are a treasure trove of information.

Although the material records of the past found in archives, demographic materials, and published narrative accounts are presented in different rhetorical styles and may be interpreted through several methodologies, two methods are especially valuable: viewing Johnson's story as a slave narrative and using a genealogical approach.

In addition to materials compiled during their student days and as part of student records, several students wrote nonfiction accounts of Johnson that offered a look at his life. Some of these, such as George R. Wallace's *Princeton Sketches: The Story of Nassau Hall*, make passing references to Johnson.[7] Two other nonfiction accounts, however, give vital information about him. The first is Andrew C. Imbrie's biographical article on Johnson that appeared in 1895.[8] The other is Marion Mills Miller's 1948 "Jimmy Johnson, D.C.L.," in which he recounts anecdotes about Johnson.[9] Both of these student biographies of Johnson, though short, may be said to constitute slave narratives.

What counts as a slave narrative has been the focus of much debate over the years. Generally stated, slave narratives recount the personal experiences of African-ancestored people who escaped in antebellum North America.[10] Although some accounts focus on Caribbean or Latin American slavery, for the most part the genre is centered on enslaved blacks in the southern United States who escaped slavery and made their way to free territory, typically in the northern United States or Canada. Some of the best known of these accounts are autobiographical in nature; perhaps the best known and most influential is *Narrative of the Life of Frederick Douglass, an American Slave* (1845).[11] Other accounts consisted of stories that former slaves told to others, sometimes years after their enslavement. While these narratives typically centered on the enslaved person, they were often framed by the words of white interviewers or biographers and validated by testimonials, letters of reference, or other documents attesting to the veracity and reliability of the black subject and of the authenticity of his or her claims. The story of James Collins Johnson, especially as told to some interviewers later in his life, could be viewed as a slave narrative.

Sometimes validations by whites occurred not only at the time of publication but also many years after the account was written, as in the case of the 1968 republication of Solomon Northup's 1853 narrative, *Twelve Years a Slave*, which details his 1841 kidnapping and enslavement and the dozen years he spent in servitude.[12] The republication of Northup's narrative was framed by the validation of white editor David Wilson at the time of its original publication, and over one hundred years later, it was validated again by Sue Eakin and Joseph Logsdon, who researched and retraced Northup's account and pronounced it accurate. Similarly, an 1861 memoir by an escaped slave named Harriet Jacobs, *Incidents in the Life of a Slave Girl*,[13] was not only supported by appended references from prominent whites at the time of publication but was also closely studied and validated by Jean Fagan Yellin in her 2004 publication, *Harriet Jacobs: A Life*.[14] This confirmatory testimonial framing of many slave narratives was often deemed necessary because of concerns about the truth of such narratives and, especially in earlier times, about the intellectual capacity of the enslaved or formerly enslaved people who related these narratives. While the scholarly genre of the slave narrative is often enriched by such endeavors, the original work is altered by the double narrative.[15]

A subset of the genre of slave narratives, fugitive slave narratives, has been subjected to even closer scrutiny than the narratives of slaves who remained in the South until the general emancipation of slaves during the Civil War and after. There were sometimes similarities in the accounts of formerly enslaved persons who fled slavery, and it is possible that some fugitive narratives were influenced by others' narratives. Johnson's account of his flight from Maryland, for example, bears some similarities to accounts seen in the work of Frederick Douglass. Johnson's narrative as it appears in the accounts of Imbrie and Mills also bears some resemblance to claims made in the account of another Maryland fugitive slave, Samuel Ringgold Ward, the author of *Autobiography of a Fugitive Negro: His Anti-Slavery Labours in the United States, Canada, & England*.[16] Though Johnson's story varies from Ward's in many respects, there are some similarities. Both men described a three-day journey from Maryland to New Jersey in August, though Ward escaped in 1826 and Johnson in 1839. Like Johnson, Ward and his family escaped from Maryland and spent many years in New Jersey.

The narrative of two other Maryland fugitive slaves, James Watkins and

Alexander Helmsley, also resembles Johnson's narrative in some respects, such as leaving on a weekend and going in the middle of the night to bid good-bye to family and friends.[17] These types of similarities sometimes caused critics to doubt the veracity of some slave narratives. However, similarity in certain details may simply be the result of common methods of escape. Moreover, even where some details in the accounts of fugitive slaves may be subject to challenges regarding veracity, intentional obfuscation was likely necessary to protect not only the escaped slave but also those who provided assistance and those who followed the escapee into freedom. Such intentional ambiguity may also have been used to preserve any truce, however uneasy, that may have been reached between the escapee and his enslaver or their heirs. This may be the reason that while many escape narratives portrayed the harshness of slavery and the crisis that fueled the narrator's decision to escape, other narratives, like Johnson's (who is known to have reached a freedom settlement with his enslavers), avoid describing specific details of servitude and painting it in a harsh light. Despite ambiguities, similarities, or missing details, many accounts of formerly enslaved persons have been deemed authentic and worthy of historical regard, even where some details may be subject to challenge.[18]

The story of James Collins Johnson is also revealed in fictional accounts by former Princeton students. It has often been the case that the stories of escaped or former slaves are explored through the medium of fiction.[19] Samuel Bayard Dod wrote one of these novels, *Stubble or Wheat?*, in 1888. Dod was a member of the Princeton class of 1857. The book focuses on the undue pessimism of its Princeton-educated hero. In the book, a character called James, who closely resembles Johnson, is described as "easily located in his true ethnic relation to the second son of Noah. He was Hamitic without any doubt."[20] Another such book was *His Majesty, Myself* (1880) by William Mumford Baker, class of 1846.[21] Baker's book includes an account of the arrest of Caesar Courteous, a fictional character with close similarities to the real-life James Collins Johnson. The arrest of Caesar Courteous was said to draw on actual details about Johnson's arrest that many nonfiction accounts omitted.[22] Jesse Lynch Williams (Princeton class of 1892) wrote *The Adventures of a Freshman* (1899) and *Princeton Stories* (1916),[23] both of which described James Collins Johnson. Other fictional books that included references to characters that resembled or were based on Johnson are *A Princetonian* (1899),[24] by James Barnes (class of 1891); *Mr. Christopher Katydid* (1864), by Joseph Tuisco Wiswall (class of 1851);[25] and *Deering at Princeton* (1914), by Latta Griwald (class of 1901).[26]

That James Collins Johnson, or characters closely based on him, lived in both the nonfictional and fictional renderings of these former students speaks to the role Johnson played in the realities and the imaginations of many students.

One important mechanism I use for learning about Johnson and the people who surround him is a genealogical approach. Here I am not referring to the methods of Michel Foucault and other critical theorists and philosophers. For Foucault, genealogy is not the search for origins or the identification of a linear historical development; his genealogy seeks to show the plural and sometimes contradictory pasts that reveal traces of the influence power has had on truth.[27] Although this sort of critical methodology could be useful and indeed applicable in my work here, I mean genealogy in the more traditional sense: understanding and mapping the family lineage of James Collins Johnson and other figures in this book.

To do this work, I looked at the direct biological antecedents of many persons in this book along with biological collateral figures where it was relevant to do so, drawing chiefly on sources of demographic data such as censuses, birth and death certificates, immigration records, and other administrative records. The aim of genealogical research is to establish the origins and relationships of families and persons, who are often metaphorically depicted as trees and branches of trees. Some genealogists prefer the term *family history* to *genealogy* because the latter term implies a genetic connection that may not be real because of questionable parentage. While much contemporary genealogy is done by amateurs and purely for self-knowledge and amusement, the historical point of departure for detailed genealogical work was the nineteenth century, when it became clear that property transfers based on familial relationship were legitimate only in a context where there was certainty of ancestry. As people moved beyond small towns in circumscribed regions, such certainty could not be assumed. The irony of a genealogical approach here is that the biological antecedents of the book's principal figure, James Collins Johnson, are unknown.

Genealogy and kinship commonly play a crucial role in the structure of societies, determining both social relations and group relationship to the past. For example, using links of kinship determined by marriage and descent, I explored the lives of the persons who are suspected of having betrayed Johnson. Genealogical exploration of the figures surrounding the incident revealed them to be either in kinship relationships or other close social relationships with each other. Similarly, a genealogical background helps illuminate the life of Theodosia Ann Mary Prevost, the woman who is most commonly described as Johnson's primary benefactor.

Usages

In this work I refer to the College of New Jersey as the college and as Princeton or Princeton University. The College of New Jersey was the official name of the institution now known as Princeton University from 1746 until 1896, when it changed its name, underwent great physical and programmatic expansion, and officially became a university. Some historical documents cited also refer to the school as Nassau Hall after its iconic founding building, as Old Nassau, as Princeton College, and, more rarely, as New Jersey College. Because of the decision of Trenton State College to change its name to the College of New Jersey in 1996, the possibility exists for confusion with Princeton University's predecessor institution. However, because most of my work is in the context of the eighteenth and nineteenth centuries, well before the college now known as the College of New Jersey (formerly Trenton State) came into existence, there is little probability of confusing the two institutions.

Because I often refer to the original College of New Jersey as Princeton, I distinguish between the college and the town of Princeton when necessary. Though European settlement of what is now the town of Princeton occurred in the 1600s, the first official use of the town's name was in 1724.[28] For decades, many parts of the municipality now known as Princeton were seen as separate geographic locales such as Stony Brook settlement, an area in the southeastern part of town at the intersection of Princeton Pike / Mercer Road and Quaker Road. Similarly, portions of what is now the northeastern section of the town of Princeton were formerly known as Queenstown and as Jugtown.[29] As some early colonial documents cited in this book show, much of what is now known as Princeton was also referred to as Prince's town and Princetown.[30] In 1813 the borough of Princeton was incorporated as a municipal entity. In 1838 the contemporary geographic and governmental boundaries of Princeton began to take shape when Mercer County was formed from parts of Somerset and Middlesex Counties.

Some words recur with particular frequency in this book: *may*, *likely*, and *probably*. These words reflect some of the contingency of writing about history and law in a context where the book's main character, like many African-ancestored enslaved persons, has little personal documentary history and lives at the margins of the events and in the shadows of many better-known figures.

Many of the figures in this book are connected to each other through biological kinship or close social ties. This is unsurprising in an eighteenth- and nineteenth-century world in which the U.S. upper classes consisted of relatively few European-descended families, knowledge of black people's ancestry (especially of their white forebears) was often intentionally suppressed, and whites and blacks were strictly separated socially. Interestingly, while Johnson was apparently unrelated biologically to the elite white people surrounding him and was on the outside of their formal social circles, he was often the link between the people around him. This might have been a testimony to what was likely Johnson's charismatic personality and his intense desire for freedom and independence. Even more intriguingly, Johnson often seems no more than a few degrees away from some of the most renowned and written-about people in U.S. history.

Indeed, one might playfully yet earnestly hypothesize a game called Six Degrees of James Collins Johnson, a takeoff on the parlor game Six Degrees of Kevin Bacon.[31] In a hypothetical game of Six Degrees of James Collins Johnson, there is an inversion: naming any famous person who lived from the colonial period onward yields a link of only a few degrees to Johnson. Consider, for example, the first U.S. president, George Washington. Washington is linked to Johnson in a few ways: Washington's wife, Martha Dandridge Custis Washington, was a cousin by marriage of Johnson's enslaver Severn Teackle Wallis and his mother, Elizabeth Custis Teackle Wallis. In addition, Washington's step-grandson and adopted son George Washington Parke Custis attended the College of New Jersey during the term of President Samuel Stanhope Smith, who took a close personal interest in young Custis.[32] Smith was the grandfather of Johnson's benefactor Theodosia Ann Mary Prevost. A similar link of a few degrees exists between Johnson and King Edward VIII.[33] Yet another set of links exists between Johnson and Francis Scott Key and between Johnson and U.S. Supreme Court Justice Roger Taney.[34] While such links create a useful framework from which to draw information about Johnson, there is little choice but to remain in the realm of contingent language, speculating on the specific details of Johnson's mostly unrecorded life.

It should also be noted that I often eschew the more current expression *African American* in favor of *black* or *African-ancestored*. In keeping with the customs of the times, I sometimes use the words *Negro* (sometimes in lowercase) and *colored*. I also frequently use the word *black* to refer to people who themselves originated in or for whom a significant number of whose ancestors originated from the continent of Africa and who embraced contemporary social customs and norms associated with this ancestry. Just what to call such persons has long been a subject of some debate. The transition from *Negro* and *colored* to *black* and *African American* was the result of the efforts by persons of African ancestry in the 1960s to achieve a sense of racial pride.[35]

Ultimately, however, the word *black*, having become acceptable in public discourse, has remained as the most popular choice in written accounts and conversation. It has been estimated that *African American* is used only one out of three times over *black* by blacks themselves and even less often by nonblacks.[36] Two likely reasons for the preference for *black* are the relative brevity and discursive adroitness of the word. I choose *black* for these reasons and for a third reason: *black* is not as historically or geographically limiting as *African American*, yet it is equally as or more culturally defining than the term *African American*.

Similarly, I use the lowercase word *white* to designate European-ancestored persons in the United States, as many other scholars have.[37] The boundaries of whiteness are less stringently drawn in the contemporary United States as a result of the inclusion of pan-European identities. Racial mixing among whites and certain racial minority groups (chiefly Asians and Latinos) has also resulted in an expansion of whiteness, as these hybrid identities are embraced as white identities.[38] But in the main, *white* throughout this work refers to the people descended chiefly from European forebears.

I often use as ideological and material contrasts derivatives of the words *free* and *slave*. By free and its derivatives, I typically mean the absence of legally sanctioned physical restraints and compulsions (either in the property sense or in the criminal law sense). *Free* would seem to need little explanation in the context of the antebellum United States, where human captivity was a legal and social reality for millions of people. However, slavery and freedom in the context of the U.S. antebellum world were not always at distinctly opposite poles. Indeed, as with the case of James Collins Johnson during parts of his life, there were often varying degrees of liberty, autonomy, and security depending on age, geographic location, and the social class of the whites with whom he interacted. This was no less true after his emancipation than it had been before.

It is common for many recent writings to refer to slaves as "enslaved persons." This is a linguistic mechanism used to reinvest humanity in persons whose servitude often stripped them not only of autonomy but also of human dignity. I use both *slave* and *enslaved* interchangeably at times in this text. While "slave as chattel" was fundamental to the system of U.S. slavery, more crucial than the property aspects of slavery are the psychological and ideological factors embedded in the slavery system that dehumanized individuals. These factors acted to render the master authoritative and the slave subservient both within and outside the master-slave relationship. Understanding the enslavement and emancipation of James Collins Johnson thus requires an understanding that he ceased to be a "slave" not necessarily when his master ceased to pursue his claim over Johnson but when Johnson himself was able to control his own fate and forge a self-directed life of familial, civic, and social connections.

The word *slave*, which seems to need no explanation, is also subject to varying understandings, especially in a legal context. As Jean Allain notes, while there are many shared understandings of the legal definition of slavery in both historic and contemporary terms, especially centering on a property paradigm, the historic legal definition of slavery has nonetheless often been subject to numerous debates.[39] It is mostly used here to refer to persons of primarily African ancestry in the United States who were legally held in bondage without compensation. However, as some scholars have observed, in many systems of slavery, and that includes the system under which Johnson worked, key attributes are also natal, civic, and social alienation: a sense of kinlessness, rootlessness, and social ignominy.[40] These multiple forms of alienation often helped sustain and maintain the chattel relationship. Using the lesser status of "slave" as it appears in U.S. laws moves slavery away from its most facile description as a system wherein one person owns another.

Given the contested social acceptability and even morality of slavery, it is perhaps not surprising that many slave-owning whites in the North, especially at the college and in the town of Princeton, often referred to their slaves as "servants." The goal of this euphemized term was to alter or obscure the perspective of both the enslaved and the enslaver, causing the former to envision a liberty that did not exist and allowing the latter to deny an ongoing oppression that very clearly did exist. As is evident from the life of Johnson and other such enslaved and formerly enslaved persons, slavery was recognizable regardless of varying linguistic forms that were used to obscure its existence.

Outline of the Book

This book consists of a preface, an introduction, and seven chapters. The preface addresses the general topic and the goals of the book, and offers an "ending at the beginning" view of life in and near Princeton University after the death of James Collins Johnson. The introduction frames the text by comparing similar genre works, defining some terms, discussing limitations and scope of the book, and describing methodologies and approaches to the materials. Chapter 1 discusses the life of James Collins Johnson in Maryland, along with the how and why of his escape. Chapter 2 details Johnson's arrival in Princeton and his engagement at the college, providing a rarely seen picture of antebellum life at Princeton. This chapter also addresses the harrowing slave-like conditions of some aspects of life at the college and in the town of Princeton. Chapter 3 addresses the major conflict of Johnson's young life: his betrayal and arrest. Although the typical story told identifies one student as the culprit, there are at least two other persons who may have been responsible for or involved in Johnson's betrayal. Chapter 4 considers Johnson's fugitive slave trial and offers a look at the lawyers and jurors who participated. Johnson's young co-enslaver Severn Teackle Wallis was himself a lawyer, one who became one of the most prominent public figures in the South, and this fact may have helped shape the proceedings of the trial. Chapter 5 discusses Johnson's redemption from slavery and seeks to shed light on how Johnson achieved his freedom. Particular attention is given to the woman typically described as Johnson's benefactor. An enigmatic figure, she was affiliated with some of the most illustrious persons and families in the country. Chapter 6 describes Johnson's life after the trial, filling in biographical details and challenging the image of Johnson as a happy-go-lucky figure with little existence independent of the college. Finally, the conclusion summarizes some of the book's main points.

1

James Collins of Maryland, and His Escape from Slavery

For fifty-six years this old negro has been a familiar figure about the Princeton campus; he is known by nearly every living alumnus, and hundreds whom he saw graduate have long ago passed away. Myths and traditions have clustered about him, rumors have sprung up which in after years have been accepted as true, and stories are told which I fear cannot always be "mentioned in the presence of Mrs. Boffin" as Dickens would say. And yet, no one has ever undertaken the task of "writing him up."

"Now wh-wh-wh-what d' yo' want?"

"Your history, Jim—your personal history. I have no doubt, Mr. Johnson, that there are few men in this country who can point to a career more interesting than yours, few men who can look back upon a life more adventurous and romantic—" "Ye-ye-ye-yes, sah," he replied slowly, scratching his head reflectively. "But I neber tol' nobody 'bout dat. Hones'ly, sah, I neber did." "Will you tell me, then?" "Ye-ye-ye-yes, sah. I guess, den, I'd better begin at 'bout de time I was b-b-b-born." I quietly assured him that such would be a very satisfactory starting point.

—*Andrew C. Imbrie, from his 1895 interview with James Collins Johnson*

13

Who was James Collins before he arrived in Princeton and became James Collins Johnson, and why and how did he flee Maryland in 1839? Details about Johnson's Maryland life are sparse. As was true for many enslaved persons, few contemporaneous writings described his life during servitude. Even in the stories written about Johnson after his escape, including writings where he was interviewed, little was said of his early life. Though many enslaved families passed down oral histories, some of these stories tended to be lost due to forced family dissolutions after sales of the enslaved, escapes by the lucky few like Johnson, and by the even broader dispersal of some families after the general emancipation of enslaved blacks. Just as there is little information about Johnson's life in Maryland, it is also difficult to know the precise cause for Johnson's flight from Maryland and the details of his journey to freedom in New Jersey. Some indicators of Johnson's ancestry and about his escape do remain, however, and these clues, taken together with the broader context of what is known about the lives of his enslavers, and the lives of other enslaved persons in Maryland, help provide a picture of Johnson's early history and his flight.

Johnson's Origins

James Collins (he was known as Collins while in Maryland and later added the surname Johnson) was born near Easton, Maryland, on October 2, 1816. His parents' names are unknown. According to the account that Johnson gave to Andrew C. Imbrie, a member of the class of 1895, Johnson's parents were owned by "Colonel Wallace."[1] This is a reference to Philip Wallis, the family patriarch when Johnson was born. By this same account, James Collins Johnson was given as a "gift" to Severn Teackle Wallis, one of the sons of his owner.[2] Johnson apparently served the younger Wallis as both companion and body servant. Johnson's fate was not unusual; enslaved children were sometimes presented as gifts to young white children.[3] Though Johnson asserted that his parents were also owned by Philip Wallis, it is not clear whether his parents and other family members were in proximity in his childhood.[4] They may not have been, as it was not unusual for young enslaved persons to be far apart from their families.[5] As Frederick Douglass, also a native of the Eastern Shore of Maryland, noted in his writings about his own parentless childhood: "It is a common custom, in the part of Maryland from which I ran away, to part children from their mothers at a very early age. Frequently, before the child has reached its twelfth month, its mother is taken from it, and hired out on some farm a considerable distance off, and the child is placed under the care of an old woman, too old for field labor."[6]

There are few other clues to the identity of Johnson's family. A December 1839 article in the *Baltimore Sun* notes that Littleton and Emeline Collins, slaves of a P. Wallis, had escaped with "a quantity" of clothing.[7] Described as a boy and girl, it is not clear whether they were in fact children or young adults; even adult blacks were sometimes called boys and girls. Because of their common surname, the escapees may have been siblings, spouses, or related in some other degree. The pair might just as well have been unrelated to each other and to James Collins Johnson. Collins was a common enough name, and the pair may have owed their common surname to a shared enslaver. The reference to "P. Wallis," however, is a likely indicator of Philip Wallis, the elder.[8] Wallis appeared frequently in Baltimore papers of the time and was designated often by his first initial only in several listings. If the pair were escaping from Philip Wallis, the "boy and girl" might have been enslaved persons related to James Collins Johnson. Johnson had fled Maryland just a few months before in August 1839; these might have been relatives who, encouraged by Johnson's success, sought to follow. It is odd that Philip Wallis seems not to have advertised Johnson's flight. While Wallis appeared fairly frequently in local news stories and advertisements, no mention of Johnson's escape appears in news accounts until during and after his fugitive trial.

A more narrow clue about Johnson's family came from what appears to be James Collins Johnson himself. Decades after Johnson's escape from Maryland, in the aftermath of the U.S. Civil War, a James Collins of Princeton placed an advertisement seeking his brother Henry Collins, who had been owned by a Sarah Harris of Queen Anne's County, Maryland.[9] Perhaps one of the most significant emotional and practical burdens of formerly enslaved people after the Civil War was that of locating relatives from whom they had been separated. One common tool for seeking these family members was newspaper advertisements.[10] It is difficult to learn more of Henry Collins, as the name is so common as to yield hundreds of results in a search of records of persons from Maryland born between 1800 and 1830, a period that would likely cover the birth of a sibling of Johnson. Similarly, Sarah Harris is also a common name. There are two possible Sarah Harrises to whom the advertisement might have referred, one married to a Robert Harris and the other to an Edward Harris. Though it does not discount the possibility that either of the Sarahs may have owned Henry Collins, neither they nor their husbands are indicated in slave census records as slave owners in 1860.[11] There is also the possibility that Johnson may have misstated either the first name or the last name of his brother's enslaver. There are, for example, several Harrisons who enslaved laborers in and around Queen Anne's County.

Another possible clue to Johnson's ancestry is the 1900 decennial census report, which indicates that Johnson's parents were born in Africa.[12] It is not clear whether Johnson himself made this claim about his parentage or whether some other informant, or census takers themselves, provided this information. If Johnson did provide this information, it is impossible to know whether he was serious: Johnson was known to Princeton students and faculty as a joker. However, census enumeration was a crucial governmental function that few persons, including Johnson, would have treated with levity. Census inaccuracies did sometimes occur, especially around factors such as age, names of informants and their families, or place of origin. Sometimes informants misled demographers to protect their identities or to avoid legal trouble. Johnson was himself using a pseudonymous surname once he reached Princeton, going back and forth between Collins and Johnson in census reports over the decades. Nonetheless, it has been asserted that the decennial census of 1900 was more accurate than any had been up to that period, especially as it concerned age and other background information.[13]

Even if Johnson had been inclined to joke or give false information to census takers, it is perhaps less likely that he would have done so in the 1900 census, when he approached his middle eighties, was subject to ill health, and had little reason to obscure details of his identity. Moreover, though the 1900 census was the first to ask informants the precise place of their parents' birth, beginning in 1870 informants were asked if their parents were of foreign birth. While the 1880 census reports that Johnson's parents were born in Maryland, on the 1870 report the box for foreign parents appears to be checked next to Johnson's name. There is some ambiguity in these demarcations, however, as there is a check mark right on the line and not directly in the boxes for foreign born. Other persons in the area who indicated that they were born in England or Ireland (as were several persons in Princeton of the late 1800s) had clearly indicated tally marks placed directly in the boxes for foreign-born parents.

While it is possible that Johnson's parents came from Africa, it not probable that his parents were transported directly from Africa to Maryland. The vast majority of documented arrivals of enslaved persons from Africa to Maryland arrived before 1774.[14] However, it is possible that Johnson's parents arrived from Africa either in a later Maryland cohort or disembarked from Africa in another state and were transported to Maryland. Between 1790 and 1816, scores of ships transported African captives to the United States, with most ships landing in South Carolina, Georgia, and Florida.[15] Moreover, there is some evidence that as late as 1859, well after the 1808 ban on the importation of slaves into the United States, captured Africans were brought to the United States to be sold as slaves. The ship *Clotilde* (or *Clotilda*) is believed to be the last known U.S. slave ship to bring captives from Africa to the United States. The *Clotilde* arrived at Mobile Bay in Alabama in either 1859 or 1860 (sources are unclear) and carried somewhere over one hundred slaves.[16]

In 1836 Johnson apparently married a woman, Phillis, who had been manumitted by her enslaver and who lived nearby in a cottage at Church Hill, Maryland, about thirty miles from Easton.[17] Marriages between enslaved blacks and freed blacks were apparently not unusual, as parts of Maryland, especially urban areas, had high numbers of freed blacks.[18] Moreover, even when such couples married, they did not always cohabit the same household. This practice of marrying "abroad," or away from an enslaved person's primary residence, expanded the potential pool of marriage partners.[19] However, such relationships were often difficult to sustain, given the difference in status between spouses, the possibility that the enslaved spouse might be sold or hired out far away, and the logistics of maintaining a regular family life when couples lived apart even when in geographic proximity.[20] The little that is known of Phillis comes from Johnson's interview in 1895.

The identity of Johnson's family, and the details of his early life in Maryland, may be gleaned only by inference aided by limited clues, analogy, and reasoned conjecture. In contrast, much is known of the family of Johnson's enslavers, the Wallises. Even with the tensions stemming from the vast status separation between blacks in bondage and their white enslavers, there existed at the same time a requisite physical proximity, as enslaved blacks like Johnson sometimes performed intimate personal care for their white enslavers such as bathing and dressing. This enforced vassalage meant that details of the lives of enslavers were much more known to the enslaved than vice versa.

Johnson's Enslavers

James Collins was enslaved by the Wallis family, a Maryland Eastern Shore family with landholdings throughout the state. The Wallises were a prominent family with land in Kent, Talbot, and Queen Anne's Counties,

Maryland, and beyond.[21] Many Wallises resided in Maryland, though in the middle and late nineteenth century many began moving to the southern United States.[22] Samuel Wallis, the father of Philip Wallis, was a descendant of one of the early settlers of the colony of Maryland and one of its largest landholders.

Philip Wallis, the patriarch of the family when Johnson was born, was born May 17, 1793, in Baltimore, Maryland. On January 26, 1814, Philip Wallis married Elizabeth Custis Teackle. At the death of his father, Samuel Wallis, in 1807, Philip Wallis inherited a substantial amount of both real estate and personal property.[23] Though wealthy, Philip Wallis apparently did not inherit all of the family property that his father owned. Some have surmised that this was because Samuel Wallis was not married to Philip's mother, Bathsheba Eagle Cosden, the widow of a man named Jesse Cosden.[24] Samuel Wallis's will stipulated that his son Philip should not sell any of the land included in the estate until he was thirty years old.[25] This age stipulation may have been meant to prevent Philip Wallis from too rapidly consuming his inheritance. It is not clear that the stipulation did its intended work, however. Philip Wallis was a teenager at the 1807 death of his father. When he reached the age of twenty-one in 1814, and for the next several years, local newspapers were filled with advertisements for land that Philip Wallis had inherited from his father. One such advertisement mentioned that land would be "sold low, if immediate application be made."[26] Samuel Wallis's concern with his son's potential intemperate spending may have been well warranted. Records suggest that Philip Wallis was a sportsman with involvement in horse racing and breeding; his name appeared frequently in listings of thoroughbred horse owners and breeders in the early nineteenth century.[27] He was a participant in several races throughout the 1830s.[28]

Philip Wallis engaged in a variety of professional activities, but no single activity seemed to predominate. Wallis had studied law but never practiced. He was often involved in local and regional politics in roles such as Baltimore councilman for what was then the seventh ward, bank commissioner, and a member of various committees and delegations.[29] Wallis apparently felt grievances deeply, and he was frequently involved in lawsuits either to collect on debts, as in the case of foreclosures, or to vindicate himself. He was also apparently a man of sharp words, and on more than one occasion he was involved in legal or other official actions as a result.

For example, in the 1810 case *Wheatley v. Wallis*, Wallis's overseer sued him for slander after Wallis accused him of stealing corn and wheat.[30]

Wallis prevailed when the court found that an employee may be charged with stealing goods belonging to the employer even when the goods have been entrusted to the employee. In the years after the American Revolution, Wallis suffered financial losses that he felt were attributable to French seizures of cargoes in which he held an interest, and he spent years pressing for compensation. Wallis also sought government compensation for private losses occasioned by the War of 1812.[31] In 1839, a few months before Johnson's escape, the Baltimore City Council censured Philip Wallis for making threats against another council member.[32] An April 15, 1839, notice in the *Baltimore Sun* from Wallis indicated that he contested the censure entered against him by the council. Wallis indicated that he wished for the public to reserve judgment in the matter until he had the opportunity to fully refute the claims.[33]

It is unclear how many enslaved people Philip Wallis held over the course of his life. Besides those he inherited, there is some evidence of his purchase of the enslaved, such as a July 1814 advertisement through which Philip Wallis sought to purchase a "Negro man who has been accustomed to full charge of horses, etc."[34] Wallis offered a "liberal place" for such a slave.[35] However, this pledge of liberality may have been less an indication of kindness and more an acknowledgment of the fact that some Maryland enslaved people during this period were allowed a say in their own placements and would have sought fair if not pleasant working and living conditions before making a change.[36] In addition, skilled enslaved persons such as horsemen were especially valuable, and obtaining the services of such a person, even an enslaved person, would have required a conciliatory approach to engaging someone. For much of the eighteenth and nineteenth centuries, enslaved grooms and jockeys had relatively greater autonomy than other enslaved persons, and even sometimes traveled on their own to interstate venues.[37]

Wallis apparently came into some of his slave ownership through his father's will, which left slaves to him in 1807.[38] At least one of the slaves he inherited from his father fled bondage, as advertisements in April and May 1814 indicate. In these notices, Philip Wallis sought to recover an escaped slave named Abraham, whom he described as having been owned by Samuel Wallis.[39] Abraham had apparently escaped while being leased.[40] Philip Wallis also parted with some enslaved people by sale, as a May 1815 advertisement shows. The advertisement indicates that Clark Stone had purchased an enslaved man named Jacob from Philip Wallis. Jacob apparently fled captivity after Stone purchased him.[41] Besides those he owned, Philip Wallis leased enslaved laborers. In 1815 he had the "use of" an en-

Portrait of Severn Teackle Wallis by
Thomas Cromwell Corner, 1896.
(Owned by the Maryland Historical
Society Museum Department.)

slaved man, a girl, and a boy belonging to a Frederick Boyer and an enslaved man and woman belonging to a Stephen Boyer.[42]

Though Philip Wallis was the nominal head of his home and owner of
the enslaved persons in his home, his second child, Severn Teackle Wallis, was frequently listed as the owner or the co-owner of James Collins
Johnson in accounts about Johnson's fugitive trial, perhaps giving some
credence to Johnson's claims of having been presented to Severn Teackle
Wallis as a "gift." Born on September 8, 1816, in Baltimore, Severn Teackle
was just one month older than Johnson, and the two spent much of their
childhood as playmates. Though Johnson claimed an Easton birthplace,
he very likely spent much of his youth in Baltimore, as Philip Wallis and
his wife took up residence at their Charles Street home in Baltimore the
same year that Johnson was born, and all the Wallis children were born
there.[43] The 1830 census lists five enslaved people in residence at his house
on North Charles Street, opposite the residence of the Roman Catholic
archbishop of Baltimore.[44] One of these enslaved people could have been
a teenaged James Collins Johnson.

While there is no indication that Johnson fared better in servitude
than many of his fellow enslaved Maryland workers who were engaged
in agricultural or industrial concerns, the work of an enslaved household

worker was typically less onerous than that of enslaved people employed in agriculture or heavy industry. Indeed, many of the brief accounts of Johnson's life in bondage suggest that he had a "kind master." It is difficult to surmise whether Philip Wallis was an easy or harsh taskmaster. Too often, such accolades were from enslavers and not the enslaved. As the abolitionist Theodore Dwight Weld wrote in 1838, "The old falsehood that the slave is *kindly treated*, shallow and stupid as it is, has lullabied to sleep four-fifths of the free north and west."[45] Domestic enslavement in Maryland urban areas during the 1830s and 1840s could be as perilous and violent as any other setting of enslavement.

For example, Isaac Mason, an enslaved man owned by Wallis family kinsman Hugh Wallis, detailed horrific beatings while serving a term of leased enslavement as a domestic worker in Chestertown, Maryland, in the 1830s and 1840s.[46] Chestertown was the county seat for Kent County and was, according to Mason, "quite a thriving place, having five thousand or more inhabitants," many of them wealthy families.[47] In a counter to common understandings about the harshness of agricultural labor in rural settings relative to the ease of domestic work in urban environments, Mason did not achieve relief from constant beatings until he was allowed to return to rural farm labor.[48] After Mason was threatened with being sold south to Louisiana, he escaped, traveling first to Philadelphia (as had Johnson) and eventually making his way to Worcester, Massachusetts.[49]

However, even if Johnson experienced a relatively less onerous domestic or urban enslavement, this would not have altered the essential fact of being human chattel. Moreover, even if conditions within the Philip Wallis family made Johnson's enslavement less harsh than that of some other enslaved people, he still contended with wider practices of slavery all around him that, even though sometimes described as benign, were often anything but.

Maryland Slavery in the 1830s

Maryland slavery was a long-entrenched institution; it existed from before 1650 during the colonial period until the state abolished slavery in 1864.[50] Maryland slavery was frequently described as benign in comparison with slavery practiced in more southern states. Such descriptions belie the fact that even in its supposedly mild form, enslavement often involved physical violence, psychological trauma, forced separation from family, and the stripping away of identity. Frederick Douglass, a contemporary of James Collins Johnson, addressed the claims of benign enslavement in his autobiography, *My Bondage and My Freedom*: "It is generally supposed that slavery, in the State of Maryland, exists in its mildest form, and that it is totally divested of those harsh and terrible peculiarities, which mark and characterize the slave system, in the southern and south-western states."[51] Yet as Douglass pointed out, even in Maryland

> there are certain secluded and out-of-the-way places ... seldom visited by a single ray of healthy public sentiment,—where slavery, wrapt in its own congenial, midnight darkness, can, and does develop all its malign and shocking characteristics, where it can be indecent without shame, cruel without shuddering, and murderous without apprehension or fear of exposure.[52]

Moreover, slavery, as a system of multigenerational uncompensated labor, was often maintained not only by overt physical violence but also by the "soft" compulsions exerted by inducements to loyalty. These included attempts to promote within slaves "family feeling" for their enslavers, and appeals to the personal integrity or religious duty owed by "good slaves."[53] Enslaved persons like Johnson were often framed as "willing" participants in a well-ordered system in which whites held all the power, thereby making a choice to not serve impossible.[54] But even with these efforts to paint a pretty picture of slavery, many Maryland whites knew, even if they did not acknowledge, that Maryland slavery in the immediate antebellum decades could frequently be as harsh as any enslavement.

Some Maryland slaveholders were known to be especially cruel.[55] In describing the history of Talbot County, Maryland, the ancestral home county of some of Johnson's enslavers, Oswald Tilghman was careful to observe that domestic servitude at the home of the plantation owner Edward Lloyd, the owner of the plantation where Douglass worked during part of his youth,[56] was of the "mildest and least objectionable character" and that Lloyd was, in his domestic setting, "kindly almost to affectionateness" toward his slaves.[57] Nonetheless, Tilghman agreed that plantation slavery such as that practiced by Lloyd[58] was likely "rendered in a more heavy and galling manner than he wished them to be, or than they were elsewhere in the county."[59] As in most places where slavery was practiced in the United States, the chains of Maryland slavery were sustained by more than large-scale institutional practices; the quotidian social practices of ostensibly benevolent individual citizens also served to terrorize and subjugate enslaved blacks.

Other Eastern Shore slave owners were also known to be severe with their slaves. One such owner, Ezekiel Forman Chambers, had a particularly harsh reputation.[60] Chambers, a staunch proslavery advocate, was adamantly opposed to black freedom and played a major role in state and local efforts to suppress resistance to the continuation of slavery. One of Chambers's slaves, Harriet Fuller, managed to escape using the Underground Railroad. Of Ezekiel Forman Chambers, Fuller later said, "He is no man for freedom, bless you . . . he would hire them [slaves] to any kind of a master, if he half killed you."[61]

In the midst of the debate about the conditions of Maryland slavery, one fact spoke for itself: many enslaved people fled the state in search of freedom. Little is known of most of these escapees. Other Maryland slaves became the subject of some of the most famous slave escapes in history, with the two best-known escapees being Harriet Tubman and Frederick Douglass. Some of these fugitives, like Tubman and Douglass, offered written accounts of their lives and escapes.[62] With the possibility of black freedom visible all around him, Johnson may have longed to join the ranks of the emancipated.

Johnson's Escape from Maryland—Why, and How?

Johnson's motivations for escape from Maryland were likely highly unique to his own circumstances, even if his means of leaving were shared by some other enslaved persons. Even given the particular reasons for his escape, his flight from Maryland occurred near the beginning of what would become a steadily increasing exodus of slaves fleeing from the South to the North. Although there were exceptions, the mechanisms of flight, and the reasons for doing so, can be broadly categorized. Enslaved Marylanders in the 1830s found themselves in a peculiar space where enslavement was allegedly benign and where the free black population was growing steadily. Cities like Baltimore rivaled Philadelphia and New Orleans for the number of free people of African ancestry present.[63] Attitudes toward slavery often leaned toward emancipation in Baltimore, as some residents adopted the attitudes of some northern antislavery, free labor activists.[64] Even whites who supported slavery sometimes used freed and enslaved blacks in the same setting. As early as 1820 Johnson's enslaver listed both free and enslaved blacks in his household.[65] At the same time, Maryland's rural regions depended heavily on enslaved labor, and increasing numbers of enslaved blacks were being sent farther south to staff plantations cut out of recently opened lands in Mississippi, Louisiana, and Alabama.

The motivations for escape from slavery, while varying from person to person, often began with the slaves themselves. As one commentator wrote: "Among the many weak spots in the system of slavery, there were none like the locomotive power of the slaves."[66] While the fundamental basis of slavery was people as property, slaves were property like no other. Slaves were "things" who could observe freedom all around them, "things" who could dream of a better life, and "things" who could, ultimately, travel north and out of slavery.[67] However, some enslavers gave enslaved persons little credit for either envisioning or enacting their own freedom.

Instead, using rhetoric that was seen over a century later to blame black civil rights activism on "outside" agitators,[68] enslavers frequently blamed white abolitionists and free blacks for enticing enslaved people away from what enslavers often believed was a contented servitude. This image of the enslaved as pawns of outside forces was far from accurate, however. James Collins Johnson, like other enslaved people similarly situated, may have fled Maryland first and foremost in response to the possibility of unencumbered liberty. According to the U.S. Census, there were over 2.8 million free blacks in the United States in 1840.[69] Johnson may simply have wanted to join the rapidly increasing group of blacks living in freedom. Johnson may also have fled because of his fear of being sent farther South. Finally, Johnson may have fled Maryland to avoid the growing thicket of rules and norms that consigned even free blacks and blacks with liberal masters to harsh and immensely circumscribed social and civic lives.

The lure of northern freedom may have been the clearest incentive for Johnson's flight. As the practice of slavery was inconsistent with American ideals of freedom, it was largely abolished in most northern states well before the U.S. Civil War. Even in northern states such as New Jersey, where the practice of slavery continued in some form long after it had ended in other states above the Mason-Dixon Line, abolitionist pressures led to a drastic reduction in the number of slaves in the North by the 1830s. This diminution in slavery made New Jersey an attractive place for slaves from southern states, especially for Maryland slaves. Maryland slaves such as Johnson were daily confronted with the realities and possibilities of liberty thanks to the steady increase in abolitionist thought in Maryland and the ever-growing number of free blacks in the decades after the American Revolution. From the time of his birth, Johnson experienced the relative nearness of northern freedom and the liberty that local free blacks enjoyed. Johnson and other Maryland slaves like him navigated the tension between the present constraints of slavery and the future hope of freedom.

The fear of being sold farther South was a well-founded fear for many Mid-Atlantic slaves. This was in significant part because in the early and mid-1800s, an increasing number of slaves from the Eastern Shore of Maryland were sold to provide labor for the growing plantation economies of the Lower South.[70] While slavery diminished in the North and in the Upper South throughout the decades after the American Revolution, it continued in full force in most of the South and grew substantially in some parts of the Lower South in response to heightened demands for labor after the American Revolution. As many scholars have noted, after the Migration and Importation clause of the U.S. Constitution foreclosed additional slave imports from Africa in 1808, the only legitimate source for additional slaves was in U.S. domestic markets.

This closure of the African slave trade increased prices for U.S. slaves and began what Ira Berlin has called "the Second Middle Passage," the large-scale movement of slaves from the Mid-Atlantic and seaboard regions to states well below the Mason-Dixon Line and in the interior of the United States.[71] This vast movement of slaves helped transform both the economic aspects of slavery in Maryland and other states and the political and cultural milieu of slavery. Johnson may have had particular reason to dread being sent farther south; his owners had acquired land in Louisiana in the early 1830s.[72] Philip Wallis apparently complained of financial difficulties shortly after that land acquisition.[73] Soon thereafter the family established a Mississippi plantation.

Johnson, having been enslaved in the Wallis household for his entire life, may have been more aware than others of what appears to have been the family's steady financial decline. In 1828 Wallis sold one of the jewels of his inherited property, a Chesterton mansion that came to be known as the Wallis-Wickes House.[74] In 1837 Wallis began the move to a plantation he owned near Yazoo City, Mississippi, following his son and namesake Philip Custis Wallis, who had managed the Mississippi holdings for several years.[75] By 1840 the elder Wallis had apparently moved his remaining Maryland slaves south, as he indicated in a newspaper advertisement in March 1840.[76] In the advertisement Wallis sought to sell his five-hundred-acre farm called Secale Hall.[77] The 1840 census showed Philip Custis Wallis as the owner of twenty slaves of all ages at his Yazoo City farm. The youngest was a female slave under five and the eldest was a woman between the ages of thirty-six and fifty-four.[78] As nothing is known of Johnson's parents or other members of his family of origin, it is difficult to speculate about whether his siblings (if any) or parents are included in these numbers. By 1842 the elder Wallis had listed even his longtime Baltimore home on North Charles Street for sale.[79] In 1842 Wallis was also the defendant in a foreclosure suit against one of his Charles Street lots.[80] James Collins Johnson likely knew that many of those with whom he had been enslaved were being sent south and may well have sought to avoid this fate.[81]

Philip Wallis the elder died a little over a year after Johnson's fugitive slave trial, on October 23, 1844. Wallis was in transit to his Mississippi plantation when he died in the explosion of the steamboat *Lucy Walker* on the Ohio River.[82] At his death in 1844, Wallis had a 320-acre plantation and sixteen slaves.[83] Severn Teackle Wallis, as executor of his father's estate, placed the plantation, its equipment, and its slaves for sale, indicating that "all property, in preference, be sold together."[84] This proviso presumably included the sixteen slaves, who were described as young male and female slave hands, all of whom were of "likely and prime quality" and whose children were "very promising."[85] By 1850 Philip Wallis the younger owned only four slaves, and instead of listing his primary work as agriculture, he listed his occupation as steamboat captain.[86] But for his escape to Princeton, New Jersey, Johnson might have been one of the Mississippi slaves placed for sale at the death of his master in 1844.

Maryland Slavery and Law in the 1830s

Besides the lure of northern freedom and the fear of being sent farther south, perhaps another reason for Johnson's flight from Maryland was the fixedness of slavery and the growing morass of social and legal norms that governed black life in Maryland. When Johnson fled slavery in Maryland, he was leaving a place where he had no immediate hope of attaining freedom through a general emancipation of enslaved people. Maryland, like some other states in the Upper South, experienced turmoil between abolitionists and proslavery forces throughout its history. One result of this ongoing conflict between Maryland antislavery activists and those who embraced slavery was efforts to reduce the number of enslaved blacks in the state; a relatively large number of antebellum emancipations took place in Maryland compared with other slave states. Nonetheless, slavery remained firmly entrenched and widely pervasive until the Civil War, in both Maryland law and society.

Slavery in Maryland relied on legal norms that rendered human bondage conceptually clear and legally supportable. These norms, however, could not entirely eliminate what some viewed as the inherent conflict between slavery and democracy. Thus much formal regulation of slavery in Maryland depended on a Byzantine structure of locally codified practices that often reflected differing opinions on slavery. In this atmosphere of contention over slavery, escapes occurred with increasing frequency. In response, there was greater effort to put into place top-down, territory-wide legislative norms. Hence Maryland laws dating back as far as the 1700s attempted to curtail the number of runaways by restricting the movements of slaves and by levying penalties on those who provided assistance to runaways. By the 1830s the institution of slavery in Maryland, as in most southern states, was under even greater pressure from abolitionist agitation and from growing doubt about the moral and ethical rightness of slavery. Nat Turner's 1831 rebellion in Virginia raised fear throughout the slaveholding states of widespread slave uprisings, and this fear, coupled with the ever-increasing bans on slavery in nearby northern states, created an atmosphere in which Maryland slavery was under continual assault. To cope with the growing climate of insecurity surrounding slavery during this period, slaveholders first sought to develop what they believed to be a more humane system of slavery that employed sublegal social norms.

This new system allowed enslaved people more personal liberty in and around their places of employ. Some slaves routinely traveled between plantations on their own. Some, like Johnson, even had spouses who belonged to other owners or who were free.[87] This seemingly lax social milieu for slaves was constrained, however, by a hefty social counterweight. In this more liberal atmosphere, enslavers relied increasingly on trusted slaves and freed blacks to help police the boundaries of slavery and freedom by betraying blacks who sought to escape or who otherwise violated rules. Maryland slave owners also developed private mutual aid associations that helped protect slave property. One such example was a Kent County "Mutual Aid Society" whereby individual enslavers policed slaves and insured each other for possible slave loss.[88]

During the same period that enslavers sought more private, informal norms to govern slavery, however, Maryland lawmakers enacted increasingly detailed sets of measures covering a broad range of matters related to slaves and slavery, all of which were also designed to protect and sustain the institution of slavery. Many of these legislative norms were meant to punish infractions, while others sought to induce whites to comply in light of the fact that a growing number of whites were dubious about the institution of slavery. In 1831, in response to Nat Turner's rebellion, the Maryland legislature barred free blacks from carrying arms, fearing that Maryland free blacks might aid slave insurrections. That year the legislature also actively adopted African colonization as a policy for relocating freed slaves, thereby mollifying some antislavery forces and providing a release valve for freed slaves. Also enacted in 1831 was a law barring the importation of slaves from out of state. While seemingly a measure to ultimately limit slavery in Maryland, the act barring slave imports was subject to numerous exceptions, such as for nonresident slave owners who sought to bring their slaves to Maryland, for slave owners who brought in slaves who had previously lived in Maryland, and for out-of-state slaves married to Maryland slaves.[89] Indeed, the measure to limit slave imports into Maryland was so shot through with exceptions that only the barest threads of prohibition on entering slaves remained.

Subsequent Maryland legislation not only sought to penalize those who aided slaves but also offered monetary inducements to those who prevented escapes or helped recover slaves. Both law enforcement officers and private citizens could receive rewards for capturing runaway slaves.[90] Some legislative measures sought to articulate the legality of slavery in Maryland through positive law. In 1839, the year of Johnson's escape, one Maryland act declared affirmatively what had previously been presumed: an owner of slaves was entitled to the slave's services for life.[91]

Hence the pull of freedom in nearby northern states, the possibility of being sold south, and an ever-proliferating web of social and legal norms that diminished the lives of both enslaved and free blacks were all potent reasons that likely fueled the escape of Johnson and many other Maryland slaves. While many fleeing slaves were likely self-motivated, this did not mean that they acted without assistance. Most successful flights typically required assistance and planning, and some slaves were able to obtain aid from sympathetic persons. Some help came from small groups of persons who banded together and dedicated themselves to aiding slave escapes. Some of these groups adopted the metaphoric name "Underground Railroad" in reference to the literal railroads that began to cross the country during this period.[92]

Maryland slaves who used the Underground Railroad often escaped through a route that crossed into Delaware, Pennsylvania, New Jersey, and New York. Though Maryland's proximity to the North meant that there was a steady stream of fugitive slaves from the state, escape was by no means easy, and a number of obstacles had to be surmounted even after an individual reached a free state. Pennsylvania, for example, offered both attractions and dangers for Maryland fugitives. On the one hand, large groups of successful free blacks lived in Pennsylvania, especially in Philadelphia, and they often provided support and community

for newly arrived blacks. On the other hand, because of its nearby location, Pennsylvania was typically one of the first places that Maryland enslavers looked for escaped slaves. Maryland slave catchers frequently not
only sought actual fugitives in Pennsylvania but were also accused of
laying claim to free blacks.[93] Similarly, though New York offered a larger
population and thus a greater possibility of hiding among the masses, it
was also heavily patrolled by slave catchers and kidnappers.[94] To combat
this danger, in 1835 David Ruggles, a free-born black man, formed New
York City's Committee of Vigilance, a group comprising working- and
middle-class blacks and whites.[95] Members of the Committee of Vigilance helped thousands to escape, often by sending them farther north to
Canada. Members of the organization assisted by keeping a close watch
for pursuers, donating money to assist fugitives, and, at times, by physically
combating pursuers and kidnappers.[96] Hence, while Maryland fugitives
who reached Pennsylvania or New York could experience the benefits of
freedom in a large urban environment, they also faced heightened perils
of apprehension.

An alternate strategy for escaping to far northern locations called for
fugitives to blend into smaller communities along the route, as Johnson
did.[97] The Vigilant Committee of Philadelphia sometimes helped fugitives with this task. The Committee was the secret fund-raising and elec-
toral division of the Vigilant Association of Philadelphia, formed in 1837
by Robert Purvis, a wealthy mixed-race man from Charleston, Virginia.
Purvis was a dedicated abolitionist, and he and others helped make Philadelphia an important stop along the Underground Railroad. Purvis and
his organization aided fugitives who sought to travel to larger cities or
Canada, as well as those who sought to hide in smaller venues.

Did Johnson have help in effecting his escape to New Jersey? Did he
use the services of Purvis or another established operative on the Underground Railroad? It is difficult to know the answers to these questions.
The Vigilant Committee kept records of the cases the group handled
between June 4, 1839, and March 3, 1840, the period during which
Johnson would have been traveling from the site of his Maryland enslavement.[98] These records indicate that some of the slaves escaping did
so during the summer months, as did Johnson, probably due to better
weather and more daylight. Most of the slaves the documents refer to
are not named, a move likely undertaken to protect them from capture.
Hence it is difficult to know if Johnson sought their help. There is one
record of the committee from late July 1839 denoting "a man from the
Eastern shore of Maryland" sent to "P_____s, Willow Grove."[99] The

expenses for the man were fifty cents.[100] "P_____s" is apparently the partially redacted name of the person aiding the fugitive. The distance between Willow Grove and Princeton is about eighty miles. This might have been James Collins Johnson.

Perhaps one of the most significant sources of information about John-son's escape from Maryland to New Jersey is the account of his escape that Johnson gave in an 1895 interview with Andrew C. Imbrie, a student at Princeton from 1891 to 1895. Imbrie was the son of Charles Freder-ick Imbrie and Charlotte Martha Clerk Imbrie. He was a member of the third generation in his family to attend Princeton; his maternal uncle, father, and paternal grandfather had attended before him. Via these rela-tives, Andrew C. Imbrie knew the story of James Collins Johnson long before he actually met him.

Imbrie's maternal uncle, Andrew Harris Clerk, was a member of the College of New Jersey class of 1888. Clerk, the half-brother of Imbrie's mother, Charlotte Martha Clerk Imbrie, was an invalid for much his life. Because Clerk was only seven years older than Andrew C. Imbrie, and be-cause his infirmity likely caused him to lead a sedentary life at home, the two may have shared an intimacy and friendship greater than that typical for nephew and uncle. Although there is no evidence that Clerk had any special knowledge of Johnson, Johnson was a large presence on campus during Clerk's years, and Clerk also may have been the source of some of Imbrie's knowledge about and interest in attending Princeton and in the life of Johnson.

Andrew C. Imbrie's father, Charles Frederick Imbrie, was a mem-ber of the Princeton undergraduate class of 1870. Johnson was appar-ently acquainted with Charles Frederick Imbrie while he was a student at the college. Andrew C. Imbrie wrote in a letter to his mother dated March 10, 1895, that he was aware of the story of Johnson, whom he re-fers to as Jim _____, the blank signifying Stink, a familiar but then ob-scene name for Johnson.[101] On March 24, 1895, Imbrie wrote that he had begun his interview with Johnson.[102] On April 7, 1895, Imbrie wrote that he would finish his interview with Johnson on April 8, 1895. Imbrie's article on Johnson appeared in a campus publication in late April 1895.[103]

In an earlier letter to his mother, Andrew C. Imbrie wrote that John-son had told him that he knew Charles Frederick Imbrie during his years at the college.[104] Charles Frederick Imbrie's acquaintance with Johnson is perhaps not surprising given that the elder Imbrie evidenced sympa-thy for the plight of blacks in other matters. This is seen in some of his recollections as recorded in a volume of Imbrie family history. Charles

Frederick Imbrie's reminisces on the 1863 draft riots in New York and their spread to New Jersey are of particular consequence. Imbrie described "terrified people in New York" and "many colored people—against whom the anger of the mob was directed."[105] Charles Frederick Imbrie recalled that many New York blacks fled to Jersey City, where the Imbries then lived and where Charles Frederick's father, Charles Kisselman Imbrie, served as minister of the First Presbyterian Church. During the draft riots, the Imbries and other sympathetic whites helped hide fleeing blacks "until law and order should prevail."[106] Charles Kisselman Imbrie, a trustee of the College of New Jersey for thirty years, a member of the class of 1835, a graduate of the seminary in 1839, and a tutor of undergraduates at Princeton from 1838 until 1840, was another potential source of Andrew C. Imbrie's knowledge of and sympathy for Johnson.[107]

Imbrie had thus likely learned some details of Johnson's history through his father, his grandfather, and a maternal uncle before coming to Princeton. Imbrie, apparently intrigued by what he had heard of Johnson and by his own observations on campus, set out to interview Johnson and did so between March 24, 1895, and April 8, 1895.[108] Much of what is known about Johnson's life before arriving at Princeton comes from Andrew C. Imbrie's writings. Imbrie was a member of Whig Hall, one of the campus debating societies, and was also a member of the Philadelphia Society, a religious organization. Like his father before him, Andrew C. Imbrie was a prolific writer. He was a journalist for the college magazine the *Nassau Literary Magazine*.

According to the account Imbrie wrote, Johnson escaped Maryland when opportunity presented itself. This happened, Imbrie wrote, when Johnson's master gave him five dollars for an errand. Instead of completing the errand, Johnson fled on Thursday, August 8, 1839, walking from Maryland to Wilmington, Delaware, a journey of about eighty miles. From Wilmington, Johnson took a steamboat to Philadelphia, and from there he boarded a train to Trenton, New Jersey. From Trenton, Johnson took a train to Princeton, arriving there on Saturday, August 10, 1839.

Did Johnson provide Imbrie with the actual dates of his escape? Was Johnson in transit for only two days, and where did he take shelter during this period? Was Johnson's arrival in Princeton purely accidental? The latter question is especially intriguing. Despite Johnson's assertions that he arrived in Princeton almost by chance, it seems more likely that he must have had some plan. Though Johnson shared some details of his escape during his lifetime, he did not tell all. Johnson acknowledged his silence about some of the details of his escape; in an 1895 Maryland newspaper article, he seemed to indicate that he had help in escaping but refused to divulge more.[109] It seems improbable that so important and potentially perilous an undertaking as an escape from slavery could have been decided on haphazardly and without some significant degree of prior planning and knowledge of an escape route. There are many gaps in the story of Johnson's escape, beginning with Johnson's departure from Maryland.

Though there is some possibility that Johnson's departure from Maryland may have started at Baltimore, where his enslaver's family lived for much of Johnson's early life, in most accounts Johnson's escape is said to have begun from near Easton, Maryland. Philip Wallis owned a plantation in Queen Anne's County, and this may have been the site from which Johnson escaped. Johnson indicated that he walked from the farm to Church Hill, Maryland, where his wife of a few years lived. Johnson's wife, who was probably named Phillis, was a free woman who lived in her own cabin. Johnson visited Phyllis to bid her good-bye and tell her that he would send for her when he reached freedom.

Johnson said that he took the Wilmington road from Church Hill and reached Wilmington, Delaware, at 4 o'clock in the afternoon on August 9, 1839. The steamboat he took from Wilmington that afternoon arrived in Philadelphia in the early evening. He stayed the night in Philadelphia and from there took a train to Trenton, New Jersey, in the morning.[110] Johnson remained the rest of the day and the following night in Trenton, hoping to go as far north as possible. When he presented his remaining money for a train ticket, he received a ticket to Princeton, which was as far as the money would take him.

Reviewing the reported details of Johnson's trip suggests that much of it was possible. The parts of his journey that seem most difficult to envisage are his walks from Easton to Church Hill and from Church Hill to Wilmington. Assuming that the Church Hill mentioned in the Imbrie article is the same as the present-day community of Church Hill, Maryland, the distance from Easton to Church Hill is about thirty miles, not three, as the Imbrie article indicates. This would have meant a walk of nine hours or so. The distance from Church Hill to Wilmington was about sixty miles (though Johnson reports it as forty) and would have required about seventeen hours' walking time. Though somewhat improbable, the time Johnson reported that he arrived in Wilmington, Delaware (4 p.m. on August 9), does allow time for the lengthy journey on foot, assuming that he kept up a rapid pace and met no opposition.

The steamboat portion of Johnson's journey is more easily conceivable. In 1839 steamboats to Philadelphia ran frequently from Wilmington.

The steamboat *Newcastle*, for example, made regular round trips between Wilmington and Philadelphia beginning in 1835.[111] The steamboat *Telegraph* carried passengers between Wilmington and Philadelphia in connection with rail travel during this period as well. During the middle and late 1830s there was so much competition among steamboats on the Wilmington-Philadelphia route that the fares fluctuated from as high as five dollars to fifty cents or less.[112] Johnson may even have traded work for boat fare: at least one account of his steamboat journey says that Johnson was hired on as a cook on the steamboat, despite his apparently limited skill in this area.[113]

Johnson's use of a steamboat for part of his journey may have stemmed from either first- or close secondhand knowledge of such watercraft. Many blacks in Maryland were familiar with steamboats and other watercraft and their routes, as it was the practice for blacks to work as seamen in the region during the early to mid-1800s.[114] Blacks formed part of boat crews dating from the earliest days of transit in the Mid-Atlantic region.[115] Indeed, blacks made up a large part of the workforce on watercraft in many parts of the country.[116] Escape by boat thus proved to be especially attractive to enslaved persons even after the enactment of harsher laws in Maryland that made black boat travelers more subject to scrutiny. Escape by water was popular not only among fugitives from Maryland and other Mid-Atlantic states but also among enslaved people living along waterways in interior regions of the country. It was this reality that caused Maryland legislators to enact laws that required owners of watercraft sailing in Maryland waters to have on board at least one supervising white man over the age of eighteen.[117] Failure to abide by this rule resulted in mandatory forfeiture of the craft or the value of the craft; half of the funds went to the state and the other half to the informer.[118] Despite such laws, boats sometimes figured prominently in reports of escapes of enslaved blacks who lived and worked along waterways.[119]

Maryland, like other slaveholding areas close to waterways, saw its own tide of slave flight by watercraft. The flow of slaves out of Maryland through steamboat and train travel grew so large that in 1838 the legislature passed an act prohibiting any slave from traveling on a steamboat or train unless he or she was in the company of a master or had a signed pass.[120] Captains and railroads were subject to a fine of $500 for each violation. Owners of runaway slaves could recover full value from a railroad or boat line involved in an escape.[121]

The best-known Maryland escapee who traveled by boat and train in his bid for freedom was Frederick Douglass. Though in an early account of his flight from slavery Douglass intentionally withheld most of the details of his escape from Maryland, Douglass noted even in his early writings that he made his escape from a plantation in Easton in September 1838.[122] In later writings, Douglass offered more details of his escape.[123] Unlike Johnson, Douglass took a train from Maryland, his departure smoothed by the fact that he was wearing borrowed clothing and papers that identified him as a seaman.[124]

Like Johnson, Douglass boarded a ferry from Wilmington to Philadelphia. Douglass, however, continued by train from Philadelphia to New York, where he, like James Collins Johnson, also adopted the pseudonym Johnson before later changing his surname to Douglass. In New York Douglass married his first wife, Anna Murray, who had accompanied him. Murray, like Johnson's first wife, Phillis, was a free black Marylander.

The similarities in the lives of Douglass and Johnson may have been little more than coincidence, given that the general methods of escape, the choice of a free black spouse, and even the choice of the pseudonym Johnson were common for enslaved persons during this period. However, there is the possibility that Johnson may have had some interaction with Douglass that informed his actions leading up to his escape and afterward. In his later life Johnson claimed that his enslaver's plantation was near that of Douglass's enslavers and that he had been acquainted with Douglass during their youth. Perhaps most tantalizingly, Johnson claimed that Douglass had urged him to run away in 1838 but that Johnson had stayed back because of his wife. There is little to substantiate these claims, however.[125] Douglass spent much of his youth before his escape at locations in and around the Eastern Shore of Maryland. Johnson was based at times in Talbot County, but likely spent much of his youth in Baltimore, where Philip Wallis moved his family in 1816.

Johnson's description of the next-to-last leg of his journey, from Philadelphia to Trenton by train, is the least detailed portion of his story. Johnson indicates three travel days from Maryland to Princeton, from August 8 through August 10, but his claim that he stayed in Trenton does not fit with this timetable. Johnson reports spending the night in both Philadelphia and Trenton, but this would have placed him in Princeton on August 11 rather than August 10. This gap could be attributable to a simple error in memory; after all, over fifty years had passed from the time of Johnson's escape and his telling of the details. The gap could also have been part of an intentional effort to obscure the details. Although many decades had passed since Johnson's flight from Maryland, it was possible that if he received help, his benefactors or their immediate descendants were still alive. Even in the postbellum United States, abolitionism was sometimes popularly associated with radical social and religious groups and thus was to be eschewed in polite company.[126]

Even in and around Princeton during the 1830s, antislavery activists were sometimes met with disdain or threats of violence. In an 1835 letter to a friend in Beaufort, South Carolina, Thomas March Clark, then a student at the Princeton Theological Seminary, described the disturbance caused by a man soliciting for an abolitionist newsletter:

> The Abolition excitement seems to have burst out of late with great vigor. We hear but little said on the subject in Princeton. There are not a great many slaves in this state but I should think that in this region the blacks constitute about one half of the population. A man was found in a house in Princeton last week endeavoring to obtain subscribers to the Abolition periodicals. A mob of college students & town's people collected & paraded him through the streets of the edge of the village & then gave him his choice—either to run for it or receive a coat of tar & feathers. He wisely chose the former alternative & was heard of no more.[127]

As one scholar writes, abolitionism in New Jersey began slowly and fared poorly compared with other northern states.[128]

The last portion of Johnson's journey, from Trenton to Princeton by train, was more plausible because of the then-recent installation of the Trenton-New Brunswick segment of the Camden and Amboy Railroad. In 1839 the Princeton stop on the main line from Trenton was about three-quarters of a mile east of where the Princeton branch shuttle train (nicknamed the Dinky or the Princeton Junction and Back) currently stops. The Princeton train stop was originally at what is now called Alexander Road (then called Canal Road), adjacent to the Delaware and Raritan Canal. In 1839 train passengers who disembarked at the Princeton stop either traveled by horse and buggy into the town of Princeton or walked into town, as did Johnson. He arrived in Princeton on Saturday, August 10, 1839.

It is perhaps not accidental that Johnson's route to freedom took the shape that it did. Many slaves in the Mid-Atlantic region escaped through a route through Delaware, Pennsylvania, New Jersey, and New York. While many escaped slaves continued on to Canada, some stayed and blended into communities along the route.[129] One example of a Maryland slave who escaped, traveled north, and chose to remain in the northern United States instead of continuing of Canada is James F. Brown.

Brown fled Maryland in 1827 and lived first in New York City and later in upstate New York. Like Johnson, Brown was recognized as an escapee while working in the North and obtained his legal release through payment made to his Maryland owner.[130] The route through Princeton was a popular one for escaping slaves, likely because of the presence of "favorable conditions" in the form of "a continuous chain of Quaker families, many free negroes, swampy lands and pine forests."[131] Quakers were well-established members of the Princeton community in Johnson's time, as evidenced by the fact that one of the jurors at his fugitive slave trial, Josiah S. Worth, was a Quaker. Worth, a descendant of one of the first settlers of the town of Princeton, was a prominent Princeton citizen and served in many capacities, including as a member of local and state government.[132]

Unlike many other Maryland fugitives, Johnson did not continue on to New York or points north. This may have been because Princeton held additional allure for Johnson. The town was believed to have been a stop on the Underground Railroad; at least one account indicates that Princeton was part of a network of stops in southern and central New Jersey.[133] According to one account, before 1840 the towns of Trenton and Princeton worked together to secure freedom for runaway slaves.[134] One significant source of assistance for slaves fleeing north through New Jersey and other northern states was the African Methodist Episcopal (AME) Church, one of the best-known and most active institutional leaders in aiding slave escapees.[135] Princeton had an AME church from 1818. Finally, although Johnson apparently maintained throughout his life that his arrival in Princeton was happenstance, there were a large number of Maryland students at the school at the time Johnson arrived. At one point when Johnson was asked about his escape and his presence in Princeton, he suggested that there were some Maryland students who knew of his fugitive status but kept quiet.[136] Might one of them have encouraged Johnson, directly or indirectly, in choosing Princeton as his haven?

Princeton opened a world of opportunity for Johnson. Princeton also presented a whole new set of challenges for him.

2

Princeton Slavery, Princeton Freedom

> I started for New Jersey, where, I had
> been told, people were free, and nobody
> would disturb me.
>
> —*Alexander Helmsley (Nathan Mead); the*
> *alleged Maryland fugitive slave in the case of* State
> v. The Sheriff of Burlington County *(1836)*

> College was then in session, although it
> was the middle of August, and on the
> third day after his arrival at Princeton, Jim
> secured a position in Nassau Hall as janitor
> and bootblack—for, said he, as he glanced
> disapprovingly at my shoes, "in dose days, de
> gen'lemen all had dey boots clean."
>
> —*Andrew C. Imbrie, from his 1895 interview*
> *with James Collins Johnson*

When James Collins Johnson reached Princeton in the summer of 1839, he found a college that had grown beyond its origins as a small, religiously affiliated school to one that offered a more worldly outlook. Though New Jersey was still nominally a slave state when Johnson arrived in 1839, the population of enslaved New Jersey persons had diminished greatly over the first decades of the nineteenth century. This reduction was so great that many counted it as a free state by the middle of the century.[1] By 1840 there were fewer than seven hundred persons in all of New Jersey who were identified as slaves; they constituted less than .02 percent of the total population.[2] Only twelve of these enslaved persons were in the town of Princeton. This was in contrast to Maryland, where, in the 1830s, nearly three-quarters of the rural black population was enslaved.[3] Much of this reduction was due to an 1804 New Jersey

Lithograph of Nassau Hall, by John H. Buford, 1836. (Nassau Hall Iconography collection [AC 177] box 1.)

law calling for gradual abolition of slavery that left many people in term-limited servitude. However, as some New Jersey blacks complained, many of these persons were only nominally free.[4] Those enslaved for defined terms in New Jersey had no authority over themselves or their minor children and could be sold in much the same way as those who faced lifetime servitude.[5] On the surface, Johnson's 1839 escape to Princeton, New Jersey, from Maryland appears to be a familiar instance of exchanging South for North and thereby trading liberty for servitude. But while Princeton offered Johnson a refuge from Maryland slavery, the specter of slavery and its attendant practices loomed large in New Jersey. This was no less true at the college and in the town of Princeton.

Slavery in New Jersey

When James Collins Johnson reached New Jersey in 1839, slavery had been formally eliminated in many parts of the state. An 1804 law provided that children of slaves born after July 4, 1804, were nominally free.[6]

However, this did not herald an immediate end to slavery, as such children were required to serve their masters or the master's agent for several years. Because this provision required slaveholders to provide support for slave children during the children's unproductive early years and then release them just as they became valuable commodities, the law provided that slave children past early infancy could be abandoned to poorhouses and then bound out at state expense. Some formerly enslaved black children thus worked for white families who received state payments for children they had previously owned. Former slave owners were compensated under this provision until an 1811 law drew a halt to the practice.[7] That law noted that "in some instances the money drawn for their maintenance amounts to more than they would have brought if sold for life."[8]

Despite this process of gradual emancipation, the New Jersey Supreme Court held as late as 1827 that the 1804 law did not ban the sale of enslaved children, even those considered "apprentices." In *Ogden v. Price*, a thirteen-year-old girl was assigned to the defendants when her contract as an apprentice was sold. The court found that the 1804 law was not a bar to such sales.[9] Drawing on the language of the act that stated that an apprentice was subject to assignment, the supreme court upheld the contract, ruling that the child must continue as "a servant to the first owner or his assigns."[10] The court wrote: "The objection that her [the child's] services, if offered for sale by the assignees at public auction, will be an outrage upon humanity, if allowed its full weight, would do away *slavery itself* by an act of the *court*."[11] An 1846 law freed slave children born after its passage but deemed slaves born before that year to be "apprentices for life."[12] Although this applied to a relatively small group of people, they were effectively condemned to slavery by another name.

The plethora of acts that altered and amended conditions of servitude in New Jersey led to a flurry of litigation through which slaves contested their servitude. Despite the acts that were geared to the abolition of slavery, laws remained in place that were meant prevent slave escapes. One such law was at issue in the 1821 case of *Gibbons v. Morse*.[13] A slaveholder, Isaac Morse, complained that a boat owner, Thomas Gibbons, had conveyed Morse's slave Harry to New York, causing Morse to lose the value of Harry, some $400. Morse based his claim on a 1798 New Jersey law that provided that anyone who was found guilty of "harbouring, entertaining, or concealing any slave, or conveying or assisting to convey away such slave" under circumstances where the slave "should be lost, die, or be otherwise destroyed, or should be disabled or rendered unserviceable" was liable for the slave's value.[14] After losing at the trial level, Gibbons appealed. Although Gibbons argued that Morse had actually given permission for Harry to board the boat and was seeking to sell Harry in the more lucrative New Orleans market, the appeals court upheld the verdict that found Gibbons liable, noting that in New Jersey, all black men were presumed slaves until evidence to the contrary was presented. This presumption that blacks were slaves prevailed until 1836, when it was reversed in *Stoutenborough v. Haviland*.[15]

A number of New Jersey cases in the early and mid–nineteenth century were initiated not to claim ownership of slaves but to avoid being charged as the owner of a slave. As the use of slave labor diminished in the state, this meant that there was less of a market for slaves. The cost of slave owning increased because of revenue acts that placed assessments on certain slaves.[16] While some of the legislative provisions exempted owners from paying taxes for slaves who were unable to work or who were very young or old and in cases where the assessment caused the owner to have no profit, these exemptions were not always in place. Moreover, laws meant to discourage slavery made it more difficult to sell slaves outside the state and required those who sought to free slaves under the age of twenty-one or over the age of forty to offer two persons as sureties and to post a bond to avoid having slaves become public charges.[17] Thus owners faced increased financial responsibilities for the slaves they freed, especially for those who were aged and/or disabled. Because New Jersey enslavers typically owned relatively few slaves in small agricultural settings, there was little need for the labor of slaves who were unable to perform hard labor. Some owners sought to avoid liability for these infirm slaves by turning them out of their homes, moving out of state and leaving them behind, or, as in one case, refusing to sign the slave on again after a leasehold on the slave had expired.

For example, a Middlesex County slave owner named Henry Force sold the custody and services of his adult slave Minna to Elizabeth Haines from September 1822 until June 1826, when Minna was to be returned to Force.[18] At the expiration of that time, Haines attempted to return Minna to Force. Minna was said to be partially blind and ill-tempered. Force refused to receive Minna or to be responsible for her maintenance. Haines maintained Minna for about two years, then turned her out. After six months, Minna returned to Haines, who maintained her for about seven more years. Haines filed an action to recover the cost of maintaining Minna from Force. Though Haines won at the trial court level, the decision was reversed on appeal. The appeals court held that Haines could not recover costs because her actions had been done voluntarily and not at the owner's request.[19]

Several cases involved towns that sought to recover the costs of maintaining abandoned slaves from owners.[20] In an 1833 case, *Overseers of the Poor of Upper Freehold v. Overseers of the Poor of Hillsborough*, the court upheld an order of a justice of the peace that a black girl named Jenny who had been found begging in Hillsborough Township, Somerset County, should be sent to Upper Freehold Township for a determination of her residence on the basis of her statement that she lived in that township.[21] Jenny was about fifteen years old and had lived the last ten years (as far back as she could remember) in Upper Freehold in the family of David Hay. There was a possibility she owed service to him and was to have support from him. This possibility became a probability based on the deposition of a witness who indicated that Hay was under contract to keep Jenny until she reached the age of twenty-one in exchange for her services. Although Jenny first maintained that she had walked from Upper Freehold Township to Hillsborough (at least ten miles), evidence in the case suggested that her owner had carted her from Upper Freehold into Somerset County, set her down in the highway, and left her to beg. The court held that the girl should be sent to Upper Freehold Township, where Hay was liable for her support.

In an 1842 case, *Overseers of Poor of Perth Amboy v. Oversees of Poor of Piscataway*, two New Jersey towns disputed their liability for a black pauper named James Bruen.[22] Bruen was the former slave of Joseph Stille of Piscataway. Stille had sold him as a slave to Isaac Stille Jr., also of Piscataway, in April 1816. Sometime in 1825, Isaac Stille Jr. had sold Bruen either as a slave for life or for a term of years to M. Bruen of Perth Amboy. Whether this sale was for life or only for a term of years was a fact in dispute. The court held that there was no valid deed of manumission and that the owner of the slave, whoever that was determined to be, was liable to pay for Bruen's maintenance, not the towns where he had lived.

By many indications it appeared that for blacks in New Jersey in the nineteenth century, even near the time of James Collins Johnson's arrival, freedom was not entirely free. A group of free blacks in Patterson, New Jersey, in the north of the state asserted this in 1841 when they submitted an address to the New Jersey legislature. They decried the "disabilities, privations, and sufferings under which the colored population of our state labor."[23] In many parts of the state, including the northern part near New York City, abolitionism was frowned upon.[24] In Newark, New Jersey, just a few miles from New York City, newspapers often carried editorials expressing sympathy for slave owners.[25] Many Newark businesses in the antebellum period served a largely slaveholding southern clientele and helped provide food, clothing, and equipment for both master and slave.[26] Hence, despite legislative moves intended to gradually end slavery over several decades, slavery and slavery-related practices were rife in New Jersey until the Thirteenth Amendment was ratified in 1865.

Slavery at Princeton in the 1830s and 1840s

Much as was true in the rest of the state, slavery was part of the day-to-day experience at Princeton in the early years after its founding. Enslaved people served faculty, administrators, and trustees of the institution.[27] The explicit practice of campus slavery had, however, largely disappeared by Johnson's arrival at Princeton in 1839; at least fifteen years had passed since the last known enslaved person had lived there.[28]

But even before its disappearance from the campus, relatively little had been written about Princeton's role in slavery. There were few direct accounts of college figures and students owning slaves at Princeton. This silence on the topic of slaves and slavery may have been in keeping with the growth of an Enlightenment culture that began in the eighteenth century. This new educational vision moved beyond the bounds of the didactic moral treatises that formed the basis of much of the typical college education of the period. At the same time as the culture of colleges and universities broadened to embrace a life of the mind and belles lettres, it also grappled with the brutalities of slavery that made such a lifestyle possible.[29] Nowhere was this more evident than at Princeton, both on the campus and in the areas surrounding the campus.

But while slavery has largely been on the margins of recorded Princeton college history, its practice was never very far away from matters concerning faculty, administrators, and students. Part of the reason for how slavery was historically treated in and around the Princeton campus may lie in the school's religious origins. During the decades leading up to the Civil War, Princeton was the intellectual center of the American Presbyterian Church. As a result of its traditional affiliations, both the college and the theological seminary firmly but quietly aligned themselves on the conservative side of the growing religious, social, and political breach over abolitionism, slavery, and race relations.[30] This moderate view on slavery and emancipation was often expressed as support for the American Colonization Society.

The American Colonization Society (ACS), an organization whose principal mission was to transport free blacks from the United States and resettle them in Africa, is believed to have been formally founded in Washington, D.C., in 1817.[31] However, Archibald Alexander, one of the first professors at Princeton Theological Seminary and the father of William Cowper Alexander (later a lawyer for James Collins Johnson), asserted that the first public meeting of the ACS took place in Princeton, New Jersey, at the Presbyterian Church and that the meeting was attended by most of the professors of the college and the seminary.[32] The tenets of the ACS called for the gradual emancipation of slaves and their removal from the United States to African colonies that had been founded to support freed slaves. Some, like Archibald Alexander, believed that if the choice was between immediate abolition and allowing freed blacks to remain in the United States, the latter was preferable. Alexander wrote: "Painful as it is to express the opinion, I have no doubt that it would be unwise to emancipate them."[33] Views such as these, combined with the number of slave-owning southerners who supported the organization, caused many observers to view the ACS as an organization whose goals were less religiously inspired and more motivated by racial bias, support for the continuation of slavery in the United States, and ill feeling toward blacks.[34] Despite conflicting claims about its origins, Princeton faculty were at the center of the ACS from its founding. By the time of Johnson's arrival, the ACS shaped much campus thinking on slavery.

Princeton Administrators and Faculty in the 1830s and 1840s

By the 1840s Princeton boasted a world-class curriculum, thanks largely to skilled leaders and a renowned faculty.[35] Many of these figures had ties to the practice of slavery or were participants in public or private efforts to shape the practice of slavery. James Carnahan, who served as president of Princeton from 1823 until 1854, held office at the time of Johnson's arrival. Carnahan was born in Cumberland County, Pennsylvania, in 1775, and was a member of the Princeton class of 1800. He was ordained as a Presbyterian minister, and after ordination he accepted a post in Washington, D.C. During his almost dozen years in Washington, Carnahan owned at least two slaves.[36] In 1820 two enslaved children under fourteen were recorded as part of his household.[37] After moving to New Jersey, Carnahan listed no enslaved people in his household, but census reports in 1830 and 1840 show the presence of "free colored" adults, one or

Portrait of Betsey Stockton, circa 1865, who was enslaved by Princeton president Ashbel Green and lived on the Princeton campus during her enslavement. (Hawaiian Mission Children's Society, Portraits of American Protestant Missionaries to Hawaii [Honolulu: Hawaiian Gazette Company, 1901].)

more of whom may have been those same enslaved children. Like many of the faculty members he led, Carnahan was active in the ACS.[38] Several months before Johnson's arrival in Princeton, Carnahan made a pledge to the Princeton chapter of the ACS to help fund the transit of freed blacks to Liberia.[39]

Princeton professor Albert Baldwin Dod, an accomplished theologian and mathematician, was one of the few remaining faculty slaveholders in 1840.[40] Dod, though born in New Jersey in 1805, was from a family with Virginia roots.[41] A member of the class of 1822, Dod was ordained a Presbyterian minister and immediately thereafter spent four years as a tutor in Virginia. He joined the Princeton Theological Seminary in 1826 before being appointed a math professor at the college in 1830.[42] Dod held a conservative position on slavery and objected to abolitionist criticisms of slaveholders,[43] opinions likely influenced by his own role as an enslaver.

Other 1840s faculty luminaries included three professors appointed to serve in the then recently created, and ultimately short-lived, Princeton Law School: Richard Stockton Field, a former U.S. senator; Joseph Coerten Hornblower, who had been chief justice of New Jersey; and James Sproat Green, who served for several years as U.S. attorney for New Jersey.[44] As did many of their Princeton colleagues, Field, Hornblower, and Green often had significant involvements with the issue of slavery in New Jersey. And like many other faculty members, they supported African colonization for emancipated blacks. All were believers in gradual emancipation. Hornblower was also noteworthy for the abolitionist leanings he expressed in some judicial opinions.[45] Green, however, while in favor of black emancipation for purposes of African colonization, envisioned no place for free blacks in the United States.[46] A son of Princeton College president Ashbel Green, James S. Green had grown up and been educated with enslaved woman Betsey Stockton, who was often lauded as one of the most erudite women of her time, either black or white.[47] Stockton was enslaved by the Green family until her emancipation as a young woman; a few years thereafter she went abroad as a missionary. One wonders how this direct experience with an enslaved person might have shaped Ashbel Green's views.

Princeton administrators and professors were not alone in their engagements with slavery. Students, too, frequently found themselves enmeshed in the practice.

Princeton Students in the 1830s and 1840

There were 270 students on campus in 1839, including seven resident graduates of Princeton.[48] Students came from several states, and a few even came from outside the country. In the immediate antebellum decades the growing academic reputation of Princeton drew an increasing number of students from both the North and the South and even from abroad.[49] But even with this newly diverse student body, a substantial number of the students were wealthy, either slaveholding southerners or northerners whose families had slavery-related business concerns.

Much of the atmosphere on Princeton campus in the 1830s and 1840s was shaped by the growing presence of wealthy students. Though Princeton had long served the sons of the elite, it did not begin its history as a school exclusively for the rich. Before the American Revolution, wrote one scholar, Princeton provided the most economical college education in the colonies. However, during the war, the college lost its endowment of $10,000 and sustained damage caused by the fact that both American rebel troops and the British used the campus.[50] After the American Revolution, Princeton "became a college for the rich because it needed the resources that only they could provide. It served the affluent, not because it was wealthy, but because it was poor."[51] At the time Johnson arrived, in 1839, as was true for much of the period after the American Revolution, a number of sons of wealthy and prominent men were attending Princeton. Many of these young men came from slave-owning families or from families whose legacies of wealth grew from slavery. Despite its northern location, many families living in the antebellum southern United States found Princeton a congenial place for training their sons as future leaders and slave owners.[52]

Because of this historic role in educating southerners, Princeton has sometimes been referred to as the most southern of the Ivy League schools. So many students from the American South enrolled during the first several decades of the college that one observer wrote that one might take Princeton for a "Southern college slipped from its geographical moorings."[53]

Southern graduates of Princeton typically returned home to become political and business leaders, physicians, lawyers, and judges, positions they often held dually with their roles as slave-owning plantation heads.[58] But these prototypical southern students were not the only source of the slave-owning culture among students on campus. Many northern families that had business interests in the practice of slavery, or histories of wealth built on past slave ownership, also chose Princeton as a training ground for their sons. For example, Eli Whitney Jr. was a student at Princeton when James Collins Johnson arrived in 1839. Whitney Jr. was firmly rooted in the North; his father, cotton gin inventor Eli Whitney, had attended Yale, and the younger Whitney had enrolled there for a year before coming to Princeton.[59] Whitney Jr., moreover, was tied to the North by his strong Princeton roots: he was the great-grandson of theologian Jonathan Edwards, the third president of Princeton. But as the son of the man responsible for a device blamed for (or credited with) extending the practice of U.S. slavery by making cotton growing more profitable, Whitney Jr. enjoyed wealth and advantages that grew directly from slavery.

Another northern student with strong ties to slavery attending the college in Johnson's early years at Princeton was John Potter Stockton, class of 1844, the son of Robert Field Stockton and Harriet Maria Potter.[60] John P. Stockton was of old New Jersey stock, and members of his family had been instrumental in the founding of the college and of the town of Princeton. The Stocktons, like many other Princeton-area families, occupied positions on both sides of the slavery divide. Robert Field Stockton was seen as a moderate voice among those who opposed the emancipation of enslaved blacks, and he negotiated the purchase of a large swath of African coastland that became Liberia, an African colony created for U.S. freedmen.[61] But the Stocktons owned enslaved people from the early years of New Jersey slavery until the decades just before the Civil War.[62] And Robert Field Stockton's much-lauded involvement in founding Liberia was dimmed by a claim that he had used force to obtain the land from African natives.[63] James Potter Stockton's mother, Harriet Maria Potter Stockton, came from a large-scale slaveholding family in the South, with plantations in South Carolina and Georgia. Members of her family were involved in one of the most contentious fugitive slave cases of the antebellum period.[64]

While these northern students at Princeton in the 1830s and 1840s contributed to the culture of slavery on campus in sometimes unexpected ways, so, too, did some southern students participate in slavery in less conventional ways. One such student was Allan McFarlane, class of 1844, a native of Scotland. In an interesting parallel to James Collins Johnson, MacFarlane, too, ran away from his Scotland home in 1839, hoping to seek his fortune. There the similarity ends, however. Though MacFarlane grew up in an environment without enslaved labor, he moved to the home of a maternal uncle who owned vast South Carolina estates and hundreds of enslaved workers. MacFarlane's uncle, John Taylor Jr., paid for his education at Princeton. Later, the bulk of the uncle's estate, including plantations and enslaved people, fell to McFarlane.[65]

Other less typical students involved with slavery who were on campus during Johnson's early years were several sons of high-ranking members of the Cherokee tribe. While their Cherokee heritage set them apart from most of their classmates, Cherokee students at Princeton in the mid-1800s were largely the descendants of mixed-race Cherokee leaders whose intermarriages with Europeans dated back to early colonial times.[66] By the beginning of the nineteenth century, many Cherokee leaders were of substantial and in some cases majority white ancestry, and some practiced black enslavement. One such group was the Ross family. The patriarch of the Cherokee Rosses was John Ross (1790–1866), principal chief of the Cherokee from 1826 to 1866. A large-scale land and slave owner, he is often hailed as one of the most important Cherokee political leaders of the nineteenth century.[67]

Although Princeton did not have an explicit mission to educate Indians (as they were called in the early years of the college), several ab-

Portrait of William Potter Ross, class of 1842, one of several Cherokee students from slave-owning families who attended Princeton in Johnson's early years on campus. ([WA] WC064, M0365; Department of Rare Books and Special Collections, Princeton University Library. Original housed in the Archives & Manuscripts Division of the Oklahoma Historical Society.)

original people attended Princeton in the nineteenth century, including some Cherokee Rosses: John McDonald Ross (class of 1841); William Potter Ross (class of 1842), who later became the principal chief of the Cherokee nation; Robert Daniel Ross (class of 1843); Silas D. Ross (class of 1849); and George W. Ross (class of 1850). Two members of the Vann family, another prominent Cherokee family, attended Princeton in the 1850s—Cooey Vann and Clemm Vann. Though many members of the families of these Cherokee students completed a compulsory move to western U.S. territory in the 1830s during the Trail of Tears, these families took their slaves with them.[68] Like more typical enslavers, Cherokee also contended with the resistance and flight of enslaved people. One of the largest revolts of persons enslaved by the Cherokee took place in 1842 just months before Johnson was arrested on suspicion of being a fugitive slave.[69] If James Collins Johnson served any of the Cherokee students in the course of his early work at the college, he may have found little difference between them and other students regarding their opinions on enslaving blacks.

For many of the southern students, their enrollment at Princeton was the first (and sometimes their only) exposure to northern people and customs. Their proximity to northerners often went on for years without interruption; to avoid what was for some a long and expensive journey, southern students often remained in the North during holiday breaks.[70] These southerners, while not denying their families' roles as slave owners, often kept a low public profile on the matter of slavery. In response, northern students also typically avoided dwelling on the question of slavery. Both northerners and southerners on campus thus avoided obvious conflict on the question of slavery, even up to the period immediately before the Civil War.[71] This did not mean that slavery was never discussed on campus. A vibrant strain of slavery debate occurred at two student debating societies, the Cliosophic Society and the American Whig Society.[72] As early as 1793, the Cliosophic Society addressed the abolition of African slavery and concluded that it would not be "politic," and such discussion occurred up to the Civil War.[73] However, these campus rhetorical outings belied students' more muted and restrained practical engagements with slavery at Princeton during their time there. Many students at Princeton in 1830s and 1840s were the white sons of privilege, many of whose families owned slaves, had done so in earlier times, or had significant involvements in shaping the practice of slavery. There was little desire among students to disrupt the slavery status quo.

Given the pervasiveness of slave culture among those on campus, it is not surprising that some students disdained blacks and actively opposed emancipation. Such beliefs sometimes led to student violence against blacks on campus and in the town. One example that was well known in its time involved an 1836 incident in which Princeton Theological Seminary graduate Theodore Sedgwick Wright was assaulted by a Princeton undergraduate.[74] Wright maintained a close association with the college community. These ties brought Wright to campus for an alumni lecture at the Princeton chapel on September 20, 1836.[75] According to some accounts, when Wright attempted to take a seat in the chapel, the attacker seized and viciously kicked him and yelled, "Out with the nigger! Out

Theodore Sedgwick Wright, an 1828 graduate of Princeton Theological Seminary. A Princeton student beat Wright for attending chapel in 1836. (Folder 1249, box 50, Randolph Linsly Simpson African-American Collection, Beinecke Rare Book and Manuscript Library, Yale University.)

with the nigger!"[76] In describing the incident, Wright wrote, "I had not the least idea that I was the victim until seized by the collar by a young man *who kicked me two or three times in the most ruthless manner*—at the same time saying 'What do you do here? What do you do here? Don't let me see you again.'"[77] Wright noted that the attacker said that his name was Ancrum and did so "with an air of conscious self-importance, . . . as if he had effected some noble exploit."[78]

There were two Ancrums enrolled at Princeton in the 1830s, brothers William Alexander, class of 1836, and Thomas James, class of 1838, both of Camden, South Carolina.[79] It is unclear which Ancrum was Wright's assailant. It could have been William Alexander, since Thomas had apparently withdrawn from the college at the request of his guardian in June

1836 after being suspended in March 1836 for "going to tavern without permission."[80] But the assault on Wright occurred around the time of William Alexander's graduation, when the younger brother might have attended in September 1836. Moreover, in a letter to the press, Princeton president John Carnahan stated that Wright's assailant "was not a student," suggesting that it may well have been Thomas Ancrum.[81]

Just a year before Wright was assaulted, however, Thomas Ancrum was implicated in a September 1835 incident involving the invasion of a home in the black section of town to "lynch" a white abolitionist.[82] The incident was discussed in a letter sent by student John Witherspoon Woods, class of 1837.[83] Woods alluded to the matter in a letter to his mother, noting that about sixty students "went down to a negro man's house, where they heard this Abolitionist was holding a meeting."[84] Woods went on to indicate that the students had dragged the man out of the house and threatened to tar and feather him, but relented after the man begged them to stop. The students, said Woods, burned the man's papers but allowed the man to leave unharmed after a stern warning never to return.[85]

This incident was also recounted by Gilbert Rodman McCoy, a member of the class of 1837. McCoy recounted the incident in a letter to a friend in September 1835. McCoy's letter contained a good deal more violent detail, perhaps owing to the fact that he wrote to a contemporary and not to a parent, as Woods had:

> Last Friday evening as some of the fellows were walking out nigger lane [Witherspoon Street] they saw a white man in a nigger house and upon inquiring, found him to be an abolitionist. When they came back they mentioned it to the fellows at the gate, some of whom made a motion, which was seconded, put to the meeting, and carried magnanimously, that they should go down there and Lynch him. It was no sooner said than done, they immediately marched there in a body, called out the black owner of the house, and asked him if there was not a white man within; at first being almost frightened to death he answered no, but upon being more closely questioned said yes. He had scarcely said it before Tommy Ancrum and Judge rushed into the house seized the abolitionist by the throat and dragged him out taking away his papers they found that he was an agent for the Liberator, the Emancipator, and a parcel more of those infernal publications.[86]

Perhaps one of the most interesting aspects of McCoy's letter is the casual racism, cruelty, and hooliganism among students that is betrayed.

One of the students involved in attacking the abolitionist, Judge, was apparently Hilliard Means Judge of Winnsboro, South Carolina. Originally a member of the class of 1837, Judge was dismissed in April 1837 for pointing a pistol at a college officer, but he was later readmitted and graduated in 1840.[87] The letter also suggests that feelings of enmity for abolitionists were not limited to southern students. It seems clear that the writer McCoy opposed abolitionism and was sympathetic to the actions of the students he discusses, and he likely assumed the same sympathy on the part of the recipient of the letter. McCoy, unlike Ancrum and Judge, was from the North: his hometown was Martin's Creek, Pennsylvania.[88] The recipient of the letter, Gilbert Rodman Fox, class of 1835, was a relative of McCoy's and was also from Pennsylvania.[89] These were the students with whom James Collins Johnson and other blacks at the college and in the town of Princeton regularly interacted.

Incidents of student abuse of black residents in the town of Princeton were apparently not infrequent. One student, Westcott Wilkin, a member of the class of 1843, recounted in an 1841 letter to his mother that the college had nearly been closed in the wake of a riot in the dining hall to protest the possible disciplining of a student who went on a "spree" that involved breaking the doors and windows of the home of a black man in town.[90] According to Wilkin, students chiefly protested the fact that the case against the student was based on "negro testimony."[91] The protesting students even assaulted the college vice president, whom Wilkins referred to as "Old Johnny McLain" (John Maclean Jr., who later became college president) in the course of their melee. Wilkin's letter does not give the name of the black man whose home was attacked. While it may not have been Johnson's home that was attacked, mindful of incidents like this, he was undoubtedly well aware of the potential threat to his own safety.

Yet another incident involving student violence in the black community occurred in 1846 during what was then known as the Riot of 1846. The incident began when Grenville M. Peirce (or Pierce), class of 1846, and his friend Jerry Taylor were falsely (by their account) accused of taking "sundry manual familiarities" on a black Princeton woman on the street.[92] A black townsman came to her rescue, hitting Taylor.[93] Taylor, armed with a sword cane, attacked the black man, but failed to injure him. Taylor's efforts were in part thwarted by the presence of several other black residents who had gathered at the scene. The students retreated and, two days later, proceeded to the farm where the black man was employed, bringing with them several other Princeton students.[94] The students succeeded in taking the man from his home, but were interrupted by Professor John Maclean, who interceded and ensured, first, that the black man would be taken before a judge and not dealt the summary justice that the students desired, and second, that the judge discharged the man without charges.[95]

Some students, most of them southerners, grew angry, and refused to free the black man. Maclean and those students wishing for a peaceful ending to the matter entered into a free-for-all with the angry students, who eventually prevailed. The black man was seized and beaten almost to death.[96] For James Collins Johnson, the Princeton campus represented freedom, but that freedom was also bound up in norms of slavery, with the ever-present possibility of unprovoked or unjustified white violence on blacks, and the absence of redress for such incursions. This blurred nature of the slavery-freedom continuum was replicated in the town of Princeton for Johnson and other blacks, whose work on the campus placed them in a nether space between town and gown.

Princeton's Black Workers in the 1830s and 1840s: Between Town and Gown

When he arrived at Princeton from Maryland, James Collins Johnson went from an environment that was populated with large numbers of blacks to one where whites were the clear majority. Besides encountering far fewer blacks in Princeton than had been present in Maryland, Johnson also encountered a different social atmosphere than he knew in Maryland. The presence of the college as a centerpiece in the town created a special social dynamic.

Princeton society in the 1840s was described as having three tiers. There was first the "aristocratic" tier, dominated by wealthy families such as the Stocktons, the Potters, and the Thomsons, most of whom inter-married and were Episcopalians.[97] The second tier consisted of professors, doctors, ministers, lawyers, and other members of the learned professions.[98] Members of these two upper tiers sometimes intermarried. In the 1840s, Princeton's elite, who frequently bore the names of their Dutch and English forebears, were at the center of social, economic, and political life in the town. For example, near the time that Johnson arrived in Princeton, several prominent men of the town attended a meeting to form the New Jersey State Agricultural Society. The attendees read like a list of the town's who's who: Robert Field Stockton, Robert Stockton Olden, Abraham Cruser, Caleb Green Smith, William Gulick, John S. Van Dyke, George T. Olmstead, Emley Olden, Josiah S. Worth, and Isaac V.

Brown.[99] Some of these men would play key roles in Johnson's fugitive slave trial a few years later.[100]

The third tier of Princeton society was made up of storekeepers and master mechanics. While this third group sometimes interacted with the first two at church, in business, and in politics, there was little social intercourse between this last class and the upper two tiers.[101] It typically went without saying that the persons in all three tiers were white. While blacks such as Johnson did not figure in this social scheme, they interacted frequently with whites at all levels of society in the course of their work. Blacks in Princeton were everywhere yet nowhere, frequently crossing town and gown lines and without an acknowledged place in the social array. In the early and mid–nineteenth century, black workers performed much of the manual labor in and around the campus and town of Princeton. Some of these blacks were themselves freed slaves, or the descendants of enslaved persons. They formed communities and alliances with each other as a way to negotiate the liminal space between the college and the town.

When Johnson arrived in Princeton on August 10, 1839, he got off the train at the main terminal for Princeton in an area of town that came to be known as Princeton Basin, with the arrival of the railroad and the canal.[102] The neighborhood, a bustling hub of industrial works, offices, and retail shops, was the home of some members of Princeton's black community.[103] It was also a busy node on a rapidly growing transportation network along the East Coast. By early 1839 trains ran continuously along the route from Philadelphia to Jersey City, stopping in Trenton, Princeton, New Brunswick, and Newark along the way.[104] The first morning train left Philadelphia at 8:30 on weekdays and at 8:00 on Sundays.[105]

As he walked from the station after his arrival, Johnson encountered Peter Miller, a black man who worked as a sawyer at the college.[106] Miller offered lodgings at his house on Witherspoon Street and said that Johnson could pay once he found work. In 1840, according to the federal census, there were two black men named Peter Miller living in Princeton, both in the same household. Four free colored persons lived in the Miller household, two of whom were male and between the ages of ten and twenty-three, one who was female aged between thirty-six and fifty-four, and another who was a male aged between thirty-six and fifty-four. The elder Miller was apparently born around 1797.[107] James Collins Johnson may have been one of the younger men who was living in the Miller household. It is possible that Johnson fortuitously encountered Miller when he first arrived in Princeton. However, it is also possible that Johnson either knew or was put into contact with Miller before arriving in Princeton. Johnson's new address was in the heart of Princeton's free black community. Witherspoon Street had long been a part of Princeton's black community. Since the early nineteenth century (and possibly earlier), Witherspoon Street had been called African Lane, Guinea Lane, or, more pejoratively, Nigger Lane, because of the large number of blacks on the street. According to the U.S. Census, by 1840, blacks constituted almost 21 percent of the population of the town of Princeton.[108]

When Johnson began work at Princeton in 1839, he followed in the footsteps of many other members of Princeton's black community who were attached to the college. One black figure on campus in the nineteenth century was Sam Parker, who served as laboratory assistant to Professor Joseph Henry. Parker worked for Henry and his family from 1840 until Henry left Princeton for the Smithsonian Institution in 1846. Although Henry appreciated Parker's work to some extent, he also betrayed a casual disregard for him; he once referred to Parker as "an article" the college had provided for him.[109] Henry was well aware that he depended on Sam Parker; at one point he noted that his work had been disrupted because of Parker's illness.[110] Henry trained Parker to conduct some parts of his experiments, but a significant part of Parker's work consisted of relieving Henry "from all the dirty work of the laboratory."[111]

Parker also served as a general factotum to some of the students and provided food or other items (although apparently not liquor) to students in their rooms after hours.[112] According to student Edward Shippen, Parker, who was described as a "supple big yellow man" with light-colored eyes and a red beard (he was said to be mulatto), was both loved and hated by students.[113] Parker often played favorites with wealthier students while disregarding students of lesser means. He could be counted on to bring food such as a turkey and trimmings at late hours of the night. Students valued Sam "as an engine" who would and could supply their needs. However, they also hated Sam as a "ginger nigger who owned 100 suits of clothes, and put on airs." Parker apparently obtained his clothes by bartering his services, for example, by trading a prepared turkey for a suit of clothes.[114] Despite the uneasy relationship between Sam and the students, there was an underlying reciprocity: "We wanted Sam, and he wanted us," claimed Shippen.[115]

Another longtime black resident of Princeton with a long relationship to the college was the caterer Anthony Simmons. When he died in 1868, Simmons was said to be one of the wealthiest blacks in Princeton.[116] He was apparently a large-scale landholder who also did a brisk business in loans to many white residents of the town.[117] Simmons also provided wood to the college.[118] He was apparently born in New York State.[119] Yet another well-known black cook was "Aunt" Clara Voorhees. Voorhees, a twin, was born on May 10, 1793 (or 1795, according to some accounts). Born enslaved, both girls came into the ownership of John Joline of Princeton in 1806.[120] Clara Voorhees lived almost a century, and her presence, and that of many other "old time" blacks who had known both Princeton slavery and Princeton freedom, shaped Johnson's experience.

Shortly after his arrival Johnson found work at Princeton working in Old North, as Nassau Hall was known. Among his principal duties were cleaning rooms in the building, shining shoes, and emptying latrines. There Johnson worked in obscurity until events beyond his control brought him to broad public notice.

3
The Betrayal and Arrest
of James Collins Johnson

> He stood quaking before young Teakle
> Wallace, a picture of abject misery. Visions
> of the old days came back to him—careless
> and happy enough they were, for he had
> always been kindly treated; but he had tasted
> liberty since then, and his whole nature
> revolted at the idea of going back to once
> more become a slave.
>
> —*Andrew C. Imbrie, from his 1895 interview*
> *with James Collins Johnson*

The best-known written version of Johnson's story, the one told by
Andrew C. Imbrie in 1895, adheres to many of the conventions of
a slave narrative. It features an indulgent if not sympathetic and socially
well-placed white raconteur whose presence lends veracity to the tale;
provides assurances to the reader that the story is plain, unvarnished, and
true; offers an emancipatory plot; provides scarce details of the subject's
ancestry; queries the ethical implications of the subject's resistance and
rebellion; offers an engrossing escape adventure; and finally, focuses on
Johnson's happy ending.[1] But in one important aspect, the best-told
tale of Johnson's life, and others like it, departs from more conventional
slave narratives: it avoids a description of hardships he encountered either
during slavery or in the course of escape from slavery. Details of what
was one of the greatest crises of Johnson's young life, his betrayal and
arrest in Princeton, are two of the least-discussed aspects of Imbrie's
Johnson story and in all the versions that have been disseminated over the
years. This chapter expands, revises, and thereby seeks to reclaim Johnson's
tale of capture by bringing from the shadows details of his betrayal and
arrest.

In the telling of Johnson's tale, whether in the Imbrie account, in contemporaneous journalistic accounts of his arrest and trial, or in the versions repeated by Princeton alumni over the decades, the premise for recounting Johnson's story was not, as was the case in more typical slave narratives, to tell about the hardships of slavery and to thereby move the reader from spectatorship and sympathy for the enslaved to empathy and supportive action to dismantle slavery.[2] As some scholars have noted, a significant turn in the nature of mid-nineteenth-century moral philosophy was the notion that sympathy's proper role was an impulse to action, especially in the context of slavery. In the 1840s pro- and antislavery students at Princeton often debated over what actions sympathy for the enslaved ought to engender, with proslavery activists arguing that true philanthropy meant the reform of "local abuses" and individual benevolence instead of efforts to reform the entire system.[3] Accounts of Johnson's story supported this proslavery approach to local actions premised on sympathy. These accounts denied any pain that Johnson may have suffered and celebrated the virtue of Johnson's white folk, both his "kindly" enslavers and those he encountered at Princeton. How Johnson met trouble along the way, along with the precise nature of that trouble, is superseded by interest in the fact of his overcoming that trouble. The typical account of Johnson's story is a congratulatory paean to white goodness that fails to clearly assign responsibility for Johnson's enslavement, and especially for attempts to re-enslave him. Hence, the typical Johnson tale, with its eucatastrophic ending, is about maintaining slavery's status quo.[4]

Most accounts of Johnson's betrayal indicate that it was a Princeton student who betrayed Johnson's whereabouts to his owners. One name frequently mentioned was that of a student named Thomas.[5] A review of Princeton University alumni records suggests that this was most likely John Henry Thomas, a member of the class of 1844. A second person named was Simon Weeks, whom Johnson himself named as his betrayer. Other accounts identify student Joseph Augustus Wickes as the betrayer. The truth about who betrayed Johnson may never be known with any certainty. All three of these persons likely played some role, either alone or jointly, in Johnson's apprehension.

John Henry Thomas is most frequently named in conjunction with the betrayal of Johnson. Thomas was born on July 4, 1824, at the Cremona Plantation in Mechanicsville, Maryland, in the southern part of the state.[6] His parents were William Thomas and Eliza Tubman. John Henry's father, William, was a physician whose ownership of the De La Brooke and Cremona Plantations in St. Mary's County made him one of the largest landowners in his part of the state. Both De La Brooke and Cremona apparently relied upon slave labor.[7] John Henry Thomas did college preparatory work at Charlotte Hall Military Academy in St. Mary's County and at St. Mary's Seminary in Baltimore.[8] Thomas came early to slave ownership when, in 1839, at the age of fifteen, he became the owner of a large plantation in his own right, Trent Hall in St. Mary's County, Maryland. Thomas inherited the plantation from his maternal cousin, John Truman Hawkins.[9] Thomas was admitted to Princeton a few years later as a sophomore on May 20, 1842.[10]

There is much evidence to support the conclusion that John Henry Thomas is the Thomas of several accounts of Johnson's betrayal, including Thomas's own accounts of the events surrounding Johnson's arrest. Thomas apparently spoke of his involvement in the case throughout his life.[11] In addition, Thomas was employed as a lawyer with Johnson's owner Severn Teackle Wallis shortly after graduating from Princeton.[12] There is some possibility that the Wallis and Thomas families were closely acquainted or related and thus may have interacted before Johnson's fugitive slave trial in 1843. Thomas and Wallis had both attended St. Mary's Academy in Baltimore, albeit several years apart. A connection between the Thomas and Wallis families is also suggested by the fact that John Henry Thomas's sister, Anne M. Thomas Blackiston, named her eighth child, who was born in 1846, Teackle Wallis Blackiston.[13] This name may have been a means of honoring Severn Teackle Wallis or other Teackle and Wallis family members or acquaintances.[14] In 1850, seven years after Johnson's fugitive slave trial, Severn Teackle Wallis and John Henry Thomas apparently lived together at Wallis's Baltimore home, along with a black woman servant named Maria Anderson and a black male servant named Henry Williams.[15] Though the John H. Thomas shown in the 1850 census was described as a thirty-five-year-old lawyer, two years older than Severn Teackle Wallis, this was likely a recording error, as the John H. Thomas of Johnson's story would have just turned twenty-six a few weeks before the time of the 1850 census. Thomas's actual age is apparently correctly shown in the 1870 census.[16] The 1850 census does not list any slaves in the Wallis–Thomas household, despite the fact that the Maryland legislature had passed an act allowing Severn Teackle Wallis to bring into Maryland a "negro slave named Oliver" in 1845.[17] While it is possible that Wallis and Thomas, who were eight years apart in age, were acquainted before Johnson's apprehension and trial, it could also be the case that Thomas's assistance with the recovery of James Collins Johnson helped forge a new relationship with Johnson's enslaver Severn Teackle Wallis.

Though Thomas apparently spoke to others about the events surrounding Johnson's arrest and trial, his comments on his role in the Johnson matter do not provide many details. Thomas discussed his involvement in the case with young lawyers at his Baltimore, Maryland, law firm, including Richard Kelson Cross, a member of the Princeton class of 1863. Cross, born in 1842 to a prominent Baltimore family with substantial Princeton connections, came to Princeton two decades after Johnson's trial.[18] Cross wrote that he had spoken with John Thomas about the matter and that Thomas had indicated that he had recognized Johnson as the escaped slave who belonged to Wallis.[19] Another person acquainted with Thomas, Leroy Gresham, Princeton class of 1892, wrote that Thomas had told him much about Johnson's escape, and that this knowledge was based on the fact that Thomas "was a student in Princeton at the time and took a prominent part in the affair."[20] In all these accounts, Thomas seems to fall just short of acknowledging that he was the person who betrayed Johnson to the Wallises.

It is more likely that Johnson's betrayer was surnamed Wickes. Perhaps the best evidence of this is Johnson's own words. Johnson's interview with Andrew C. Imbrie reveals that the person who betrayed Johnson was Simon Weeks of Chestertown, Maryland.[21] Weeks is described in the Imbrie article as a student who was a friend of Johnson's co-owner, Severn Teackle Wallis. Student catalogs for the period, however, show no Simon Weeks among the students at Princeton. Similarly, present-day alumni indexes for the period show no Simon Weeks for the period 1746 through 1920.[22] According to Princeton records, only two students surnamed Weeks enrolled at the college before 1850: William Raymond Weeks, class of 1809, and Samuel Greeley Weeks, class of 1838.[23] Of these two, only Samuel was likely resident on campus at the time of Johnson's betrayal. One year after graduating in 1838 Samuel Weeks returned to the Princeton Theological Seminary, which he attended from 1839 to 1842.[24] During this time he also earned an A.M. from the college in 1841. Weeks, the son of Matthias and Mary Bennett Weeks, was from Gilmanton, New Hampshire.[25] He was one of the original twelve members of the class of 1838 who arrived on campus in the fall of 1834.[26]

Samuel Weeks, who was born on April 14, 1809, was something of an oddity among his peers; he was about ten years older than most of his undergraduate classmates. Those classmates described him as a grave, plain, and quiet student who frequently appeared in class in well-worn slippers. After graduating from the seminary, he was called to preach in Michigan and in Indiana. Weeks died in 1846, leaving a wife, Mary.[27] Besides the details of some of his pastoral assignments, his Princeton classmates knew little of him after his graduation. His class biographer lamented this paucity of information about Weeks, noting that neither his wife's maiden name nor whether Weeks had children were known.[28]

Samuel Weeks roomed with John J. Smith of Baltimore, during part of his undergraduate years.[29] It is possible that Smith and the Wallises were somehow connected, given the relatively small size of Baltimore's upper-class white community. If Smith and the Wallises were connected, perhaps Weeks learned something of Johnson from his roommate Smith. However, there is no known connection between Smith and the Wallises that might have given Smith access to knowledge about Johnson. Moreover, Weeks was studying at the seminary at the time of Johnson's betrayal and subsequent trial, putting him on the margins of undergraduate activities. In addition, Weeks's identity as a New Englander and his social outsider status make it unlikely that he would have reached out to betray Johnson to his master.

It is possible that when James Collins Johnson identified "Simon Weeks" as his betrayer, he meant Simon *Wickes* and not Weeks. Johnson was known to have a pronounced stutter, and Imbrie may have misunderstood Johnson during their interview. While there was no Simon Wickes attending school at Princeton during the time of Johnson's betrayal and trial (or, apparently, at any time before or after), students surnamed Wickes were on campus during this time. One was Joseph Augustus Wickes, a member of the class of 1845. His brother, Benjamin Chambers Wickes, class of 1843, was also at Princeton during this time. The Wickes brothers were from Chestertown, Maryland.[30]

J. Jefferson Looney, the editor of an annotated reprint of the 1853 book *College as It Is, or The Collegian's Manual,* by James Buchanan Henry and Christian Henry Scharff, identifies Joseph Augustus Wickes as Johnson's betrayer. *College as It Is* was a lighthearted 1853 account of the day-to-day lives of students at Princeton written while the authors were seniors at the college. In their book, Henry and Scharff discuss interactions with Johnson. Looney annotates the mention of Johnson, writing that Johnson, "escaped from bondage in 1839 and came to Princeton, where he was recognized and reported in 1843 by Joseph Augustus Wickes, AB 1845."[31] Looney's assertion thus provides some support for the notion that the surname of Johnson's accuser was Wickes, not Weeks. Even if

Joseph Augustus Wickes was not the betrayer, college records suggest that he and John Henry Thomas may have been acquainted and thus may each have played some part in Johnson's betrayal. John Henry Thomas, Joseph Wickes, James Buchanan Smith, Alfred H. Colquitt,[32] and Henry H. Welles,[33] all members of the Princeton classes of 1844 and 1845, took their meals together through a boarding arrangement at the home of Abraham J. Duvant in Princeton for at least part of their time in college.[34]

But Johnson said that Simon Weeks (or Wickes), not Joseph Wickes, betrayed him. Johnson may have had a sound basis for his claim. It appears that the Princeton-attending Wickes brothers had a young cousin named Simon Wickes.[35] The young Simon Wickes was born in October 1818 and thus was about the same age as the Wickes brothers, Severn Teackle Wallis, and James Collins Johnson. Young Simon Wickes's father, also named Simon Wickes, was born in 1781 and died in 1848. Did either the younger or the elder Simon Wickes betray Johnson? It is certainly possible. The younger Simon's sister, Anne Rebecca Wickes, married Benjamin Chambers Wickes in 1852. In 1865 Anne Rebecca Wickes married Benjamin's brother, Joseph Augustus Wickes. The Wickes brothers' marriages to their cousin Anne, the sister of their cousin Simon Wickes, might signal that there was an earlier close relationship between the younger Simon Wickes and his cousins at Princeton that gave him knowledge of Johnson's whereabouts. Given that Imbries's interview of Johnson occurred in the 1890s, some fifty years after Johnson's arrest and trial, it is, of course, possible that Johnson somehow confused one of the Princeton-attending Wickes brothers with their young cousin Simon Wickes, or that he intentionally misled his interlocutor.

The problems of reliability and accuracy are always endemic to oral recollections, especially those growing out of the trauma of slavery. But to dismiss Johnson as merely forgetful or as a fabricator risks promoting the racist trope of the foggy-brained or deceitful former slave.[36] Given how life-changing the arrest and trial were for Johnson, and given his reputation for remembering alumni decades after their student days at the college, it is perhaps all the more likely that Johnson neither forgot nor was confused about the identity of the betrayer whom he named as Simon Weeks.

Philip Wallis, Johnson's enslaver, wrote in his own account of the case that one of the witnesses who testified as to Johnson's identity at the trial was "Mr. Wickes" of Kent County.[37] This could have described several persons. An 1860 map of Maryland plantations showed several Wickes families living in Kent County.[38] It is most likely that the witness was one of two Wickes brothers, Joseph or Benjamin, who were already in Princeton attending school at the time of the trial, or their father, Joseph. It might also, however, have some other Kent County Wickes kinsman who had learned of Johnson's presence at the college. Johnson's arrest occurred on July 28, 1843, and his trial took place on August 1, 1843, both times when school was in session.[39] However, it is difficult to determine who was the most likely Wickes who revealed Johnson's whereabouts.

One possibility would be to look for clues to the personalities of the Wickes brothers who were on campus, assuming that someone who would expose Johnson would have a harsh, unyielding, or highly bureaucratic character. However, there is little published information about the personalities of the Wickes brothers. One observation made about Joseph Augustus Wickes near the end of his life noted that he had an "imperious temper" and was quite aloof after leaving the Maryland bench in 1897.[40] Even if this brief observation about Joseph Augustus Wickes were true, it does little to suggest whether he was the more likely of two Wickes brothers to expose Johnson.

Though many would have sympathized with how personally damaging the revelation was to Johnson and to his claim to freedom, others might have viewed such a revelation as merely following the law, as more a duty than a betrayal. From this perspective, exposing Johnson could have been viewed not as an act of malice but as an act of sober, heartfelt civic and social duty. Slavery was legal in the South and even to a limited extent in New Jersey during the time of Johnson's apprehension. The demands of honor for young men raised in the South may have made the compulsion to adhere to legal obligations even more intense. That a Wickes male would have felt it his duty to reveal the whereabouts of a slave belonging to the Wallis family is perhaps therefore understandable. Beyond the broader demands of law and honor, there may have been additional bonds of kinship, family, and business that may have made a young southerner feel honor bound to reveal Johnson's whereabouts. There appear to have been substantial familial and business ties between the Wallis and Wickes families in Maryland. One of the many properties that Johnson's enslaver, Philip Wallis, owned at one time was a house in Chesterton in Kent County now known as the Wallis–Wickes house.[41] Philip Wallis's father, Samuel Wallis, had this house built in 1769, and Philip later inherited it. The house, an impressive brick structure with a famed flower garden, later came into the ownership of members of the Wickes family.[42] Johnson was likely familiar with a number of the Wickeses, as the Wickes family sent some of its sons to Princeton during the years that Johnson worked there. The Wickeses, like the Wallises, had been in and around Kent County since the mid–seventeenth century and were large landowners and slave-holders for much of the time they lived there.[43]

Exploring the details of the betrayal and arrest of Johnson creates dissonance with many people's desire to believe that he was never a victim and always a victor. The identity of his betrayers, and the full nature of his arrest, though known in Johnson's time, appear to have been obscured in most subsequent accounts, thereby enabling the creation of a sunny slave rescue story that left the broader institution of slavery uninterrogated. But the story of Johnson's redemption makes sense only by recognizing the harms done to him as well as the benefits he gained.

The Arrest of James Collins Johnson

Johnson's apprehension began regularly enough. Philip Wallis apparently followed the established procedure for claiming a fugitive slave in New Jersey.[44] Slave owners who sought the help of New Jersey courts to recover escaped slaves were required to make application to a judge or justice for an arrest warrant using a very particular format. Procedural manuals offered detailed guidance and sample forms for attorneys acting on behalf of owners.[45] First, claimants were required to apply for an arrest warrant for the slave before one of the judges of the Court of Common Pleas in the county where the alleged slave was present. The application required that the claimant or his agent aver that the alleged slave was "held to labour or service: and that he had escaped said service."[46] The claimant then had to prepare an affidavit swearing that he was entitled to the service of the slave, indicating the age of the slave, and swearing that the person sought was in fact a slave under the laws of the state from which the person had fled.[47] The affidavit also had to include a physical description of the alleged slave, including unique markings such as scars.[48]

According to Wallis's account, once he received word that Johnson was in Princeton, he dispatched a Maryland man to represent him before the New Jersey authorities in compliance with established rules and, assuming success, to bring Johnson back to Maryland. Wallis entrusted these tasks to Madison Jeffers, who is identified in several accounts as a Baltimore policeman.[49] Before coming to Baltimore, Jeffers had been a constable in Washington, D.C. Jeffers was known as a slave catcher and slave trader in his off hours, and he engaged in much after-hours work, possibly to satisfy debts.[50] Jeffers, however, was no ordinary policeman or slave catcher. Along with his adult son, James Jeffers, he worked as a private slave catcher and political provocateur before and after Johnson's trial.[51]

Some have asserted that Jeffers was tied to several politically motivated proslavery prosecutions with Washington, D.C., district attorney Francis Scott Key, who wrote the lyrics to "The Star Spangled Banner."[52] Jeffers continued his work in full force well after his involvement with Johnson. He was involved with political intrigue and political street violence throughout his life. In the 1850s he was closely associated with Henry Gambrill, a member of Baltimore political gang the Plug Uglies.[53] Jeffers was also an influential member and operative for the American Party, an alternative name for the nativist Know-Nothing Party.[54] Jeffers was an active political operative even after suffering near-death in what was then one of worst railroad accidents in history.[55]

Born in Baltimore in 1810, Jeffers was likely of fairly modest social origins, judging from the fact that in 1826, when he was sixteen years old, he was apprenticed to Matthew French, a silver plater.[56] Most apprentices in the nineteenth-century United States had limited formal education and worked without wages for a fixed period of time in exchange for training, room and board, and a suit of clothes at the end of the apprenticeship.[57] The length of such apprenticeships varied, but seven years was typical. For much of the eighteenth century and for the early part of the nineteenth century, silver workers were among the elite of skilled workers and were seen as artists as much as tradesmen.[58] It is not clear when or how Jeffers moved from work as a silver plater or when he started his career as a policeman, but his career in silver work was not likely very long given that he was only about twenty-five years old when he came to wide public notice.

In 1835 Jeffers attained national notoriety for his involvement in the arrest of Reuben Crandall, a Washington, D.C., botanist, physician, and alleged abolitionist, on the charge of circulating "dangerous and insurrectionary writings and thereby attempting to incite an insurrection."[59] It was Jeffers who apparently incited a proslavery crowd against Crandall, helping ignite passions by showing abolitionist pamphlets that Crandall owned to several persons. A few days before seizing Crandall, Jeffers had been involved in arresting Arthur Bowen, a runaway slave accused of attempting to assault his mistress with an axe.[60] As he did in the Crandall case, Jeffers added to public indignation by spreading exaggerated accounts of Bowen's actions. The arrests of Crandall and Bowen and Jeffers's role as agitator were significant factors in inciting the Snow Riot in August 1835, which is believed to be the first race riot in Washington, D.C.[61]

Madison Jeffers achieved international notoriety after he was removed from public office in 1836 for having improperly seized an alleged fugitive slave from Alabama.[62] The alleged fugitive was employed in the house of Charles Bankhead, the secretary of the British delegation to the United States. The British delegation complained of Jeffers's actions to Secretary of State John Forsyth, who brought the matter before the federal court on an order to show cause as to why Jeffers should not be dismissed for violating diplomatic immunity. Although Jeffers submitted an affidavit indicating that he did not know that the removal of the servant was barred by diplomatic immunity, he was unable to show due cause and was dismissed as a Washington, D.C., constable on June 7, 1836.[63]

After he was removed from his job in Washington, Jeffers was hired as a constable in Baltimore, where he continued his sideline of slave catching and political machinations. In 1840 Jeffers was implicated in a plot to bring voters from Philadelphia to Baltimore to corrupt an election.[64] It was while serving in Baltimore that Jeffers was hired by the Wallises to recover James Collins Johnson. By engaging someone with Jeffers's reputation for inciting public violence and flouting the law, the Wallises sent a clear message about the lengths to which they would go to recapture Johnson.

There are varying accounts of Johnson's arrest. Some accounts suggest that when Severn Teackle Wallis confronted Johnson on Nassau Street, Johnson denied knowing him and fled.[65] According to these accounts, Johnson was almost immediately seized by southern students, among them Thomas Devereaux Hogg of Raleigh, North Carolina.[66] Johnson apparently bit Hogg's finger to the bone in the struggle.[67] Thomas Devereaux Hogg was born in North Carolina and descended from a Scottish father, Gavin Hogg, who was born to a poor Scottish family that had arrived in North Carolina in 1797. Hogg's mother, Mary Ann Bayard Johnson, was from Stratford, Connecticut, and descended directly from the Bayards, the Livingstons, and other well-established northern families. Hogg's father, the owner of at least seventeen enslaved peoples, lived between his Raleigh, North Carolina, home and his Bertie County plantation.[68] Hogg had attended preparatory school in Connecticut. Because of his northern mother and his early schooling among northern relatives, Hogg's sensibilities may have been as much northern as southern. Even though he was from a slave-owning family, he may have had some ambivalence about slavery and thus may have been of two minds about Johnson's emancipation.

Hogg's possible sympathy for the enslaved is perhaps evident in his handling of a matter concerning slaves given freedom under a will that he executed. In 1857 he became the executor of the estate of John L. Bryan, Hogg's partner in a Baltimore distillery and the uncle of his wife. In 1853, in a codicil to his will, Bryan wrote: "I give to my Slaves their Freedom."[69] Bryan's next of kin contested the proviso, which freed fifteen slaves. Hogg was unsure of how to proceed. He did not wish to disobey the command of the testator but feared that because "said negro slaves are all ignorant and uneducated," it was necessary that "their rights be guarded and protected."[70] Hogg asked the court to determine how the clause should be interpreted and asked that it instruct him on how to fulfill his duty as executor with regard to the slaves. Related documents reveal that the enslaved people were all willing to go to Liberia and were thus freed by a decree of the Supreme Court of North Carolina. Thomas Hogg later reported that "he has heard from them in their home in Liberia" and that he "is gratified that his duty in regard to them is fully and finally discharged."[71]

According to one account, when Hogg was approached for money to help purchase Johnson, he called the request impudent but donated nonetheless.[72] Other students from the South were also said to have donated to the cause of Johnson's freedom. Southern students constituted one of the largest geographic groupings of students at the Princeton in the period 1839–48.[73]

The betrayal and arrest of Johnson, while subject to differing accounts, were pivotal events in Johnson's story that brought his fugitive status to an end. The end of this status brought Johnson to trial: yet another beginning and another chance at freedom.

4

The Fugitive Slave Trial of James Collins Johnson

> A jury of good and reputable freeholders was
> summoned and sworn, and the case was tried
> at the city hotel, amidst great excitement,
> caused especially by the southern students,
> who feared that opposition to the Fugitive
> Slave law would be so great as to defeat the
> claim of the owner. They also apprehended
> that an effort would be made by the colored
> men of the town to rescue the slave if he
> should be remanded to the owner.
>
> —*John Frelinghuysen Hageman,*
> *attorney for the Wallis family*

James Collins Johnson's trial on the charge of being a fugitive slave from Maryland occurred after he was seized and taken into custody on July 28, 1843.[1] After four years working in the private obscurity of the campus, Johnson became a figure of public notoriety, as the details of his arrest and trial were disseminated locally and nationally via press accounts. The persons involved in Johnson's trial were a highly representative cross section of college and town figures, along with noteworthy persons from outside Princeton. The very public interactions of all these figures, along with the fact of the trial and its challenge to slavery, made it an unprecedented undertaking at the college and in the town of Princeton. Moreover, the substantive and procedural standards employed at the trial assailed prevailing legal norms and brought to the fore the college's, and the town's, mixed views on slavery.

The Record of the Trial

Johnson's trial was held on August 1, 1843, in the Inferior Court of Common Pleas of Mercer County, New Jersey.[2] It is important to note at the outset that there is no detailed account of the evidence presented in court, of the precise language of the parties, or the words of the court's ruling. As was the case in a number of legal proceedings conducted at the magistrate level in New Jersey during the early and middle nineteenth century, there was no official written opinion of the case. Contemporary readers of court proceedings may be struck by the absence of an official report in Johnson's matter given what was at stake. However, as some scholars have remarked, legal case reports in the early national period in the United States were often absent. This was especially true in matters conducted in lower courts as opposed to appellate tribunals. Modern courts also sometimes forgo rendering full opinions in cases, choosing to leave some cases "unpublished," that is, some decisions are intentionally framed as not constituting a part of legal precedent.[3] Most contemporary courts do, however, reduce opinions to writing in at least some cursory, unofficial form. The historic void in official written opinions in many U.S. lower courts created a vernacular legal culture where the oral transmission of legal norms was a central aspect of many local legal regimes. Even though such reports were present, they followed no particular paradigm and were sometimes imprecise renditions of the actual proceedings.[4]

In the absence of official reports, accounts of many cases were found in popular press and pamphlets or in private writings that sometimes betrayed bias and were laced with inflammatory remarks. Many post–Revolutionary era legal trial accounts were contemporaneously written by lawyers who were involved at various stages of proceedings. These accounts often featured flowery, literary, sensationalist, and, not surprisingly, decidedly one-sided accounts that sometimes switched from first to third person.[5] What this meant in practice is that the U.S. jurisprudential idea of stare decisis, basing cases on the precedent set by cases that came before it, was subject to the sometimes unstable foundation of prior legal proceedings. No less an authority than James Kent, one of the early shapers of U.S. law and legal education, opined that "the records of many of the courts in this country are replete with hasty and crude decisions." Kent understood and frequently stressed the interconnectedness of U.S. law with its English and European antecedents. Nonetheless, Kent hence urged jurists to examine previous cases with a critical eye and a willingness to correct error.[6]

It is not surprising, then, that much of what is known about Johnson's trial comes from an account published in newspapers by his enslaver, Philp Wallis, from a brief account in a regional history book written by the attorney for Johnson's enslaver, John Frelinghuysen Hageman, and from accounts of varying accuracy and limited facts written in newspapers throughout the United States. From these sources a picture may be drawn of the trial's participants, how it was conducted, and its outcome.

Participants in the Trial

The key participant in the trial was James Collins Johnson himself. In 1843, when Johnson was on trial, most enslaved persons in New Jersey were not permitted to testify in court proceedings.[7] Although Johnson's denial of his enslavement upon his arrest triggered the subsequent legal proceeding, that was the limit of his direct speech in the matter. Johnson's participation was barred by New Jersey law in effect at the time that, like many states, codified the frequently expressed opposition to "negro testimony."[8] Such laws were based on the ante- and post-bellum concern that blacks had tarnished character and little understanding of or regard for truth.[9] While the ability of blacks to testify in court was sometimes premised on slave or free status, concern about black testimony was not diminished by the free status of blacks.[10] Rather, the bar on black testimony was often premised on what was believed to be intrinsic racial inferiority and the resultant social exclusion.[11] As one legal scholar averred when writing a retrospective compilation of the law of U.S. enslavement of blacks: "That the negro, as a general rule, is mendacious, is a fact too well established to require the production of proof, either from history, travels, or craniology."[12]

Ironically, while blacks like Johnson were frequently treated as lacking civic agency and incapable of meeting the demands of citizenship, they were at the same time subject to the legal fiction of "double character," which attributed to them criminal agency all while denying their civic agency.[13] Antebellum legal and political discourses of slavery and resistance tended to ignore, disparage, or mischaracterize black voices. This was true even of abolitionist discourses that purported to "speak for the slave" when, as in Johnson's case, he could not speak for himself.[14] In the case of both enslaved and free blacks, antebellum law, even at times when it offered hope for emancipation, also suppressed the authority and authenticity of the enslaved. Hence law in such matters was often a tool of white oppression and a source of illegitimacy.[15]

Johnson was apparently a looming but silent presence at a proceeding that centered on him. In the story of the trial told by Hageman, it appears that arguments on Johnson's behalf were made by his counsel.[16] Although popular accounts of Johnson's life make no mention of how Johnson felt during the trial, it must have been excruciating for Johnson to sit mute and helpless as the greatest dilemma of his young life unfolded before him. Laws that prevented Johnson from testifying in his own behalf at his trial and the absence of an official record in his and many other such cases served to silence and manipulate the voices of enslaved persons like Johnson.[17] The construction of happy-go-lucky tales of Johnson's trial and his subsequent redemption are in part possible because of this gaping chasm of legal silence.

Johnson's trial was held at the Nassau Inn before Justice of the Peace John Lowrey. Lowrey was a popular figure who had extensive connections in the town and on the Princeton campus. Born in Philadelphia, and a tailor by trade, he came to Princeton as a young man, where he quickly became engaged in the civic life of the town.[18] Lowrey, according to one observer, "seems to have been a popular character, possessing the confidence of the entire community, and almost constantly holding official place."[19] He served at various times as a member of the New Jersey militia, a captain in the town militia, known as the "Princeton Blues," justice of the peace, mayor of the borough, Judge of the Common Pleas, as a member of the New Jersey Assembly, and in other local offices. Lowrey was also active in religious causes, and was especially involved in the Presbyterian Church in Princeton.[20] One of the acts for which Lowrey was known was his advocacy on behalf of black Princeton Presbyterians who sought to form their own church in 1840.[21] After being presented with evidence that supported the claim of Johnson's alleged owner Philip Wallis, Lowrey issued a warrant to Princeton constable Ralph Gulick, who supervised the arrest of Johnson and Johnson's presentation before the court.

Gulick was a Princeton merchant who became sheriff of Mercer County in 1836.[22] Like Lowrey, Gulick was prominent in local religious, social, and political affairs. Along with several other prominent men in Princeton, including Hageman, the lawyer for the Wallises, Gulick served as a trustee of the Mt. Lucas Orphan and Guardian Institute, which was founded in 1842 to care for destitute children and youth.[23] When the orphan asylum was closed and the property was sold to the town of

Princeton, the assets of the institution were transferred to the Ashmun Institute in Pennsylvania, now Lincoln University, a historically black educational institution.[24]

The lawyers who defended Johnson, William Cowper Alexander and Edward Armstrong, and those who prosecuted the case against him, Hageman and Severn Teackle Wallis, were some of the most socially prominent men of their times. Perhaps foremost among them was William Cowper Alexander. Thirty-seven years old at the time of the trial, Alexander was a well-known lawyer, a graduate of Princeton, and a member of a distinguished local family. Many members of the Alexander family had been students, faculty members, and trustees of Princeton.[25] Alexander was the second son of the Reverend Archibald Alexander, the first professor appointed to the Princeton Theological Seminary, and Janetta Waddell, the daughter of esteemed Presbyterian minister James Waddell. Born in 1806 in Prince Edward County, Virginia, William Cowper Alexander came to Princeton in 1812, when his father was appointed to the seminary, and graduated from Princeton in 1824. After reading law with James S. Green, a local attorney who later became a judge, U.S. Supreme Court reporter, and U.S. attorney, Alexander began a law practice after his admission to the New Jersey bar in 1828.[26] Alexander later served in the New Jersey State Assembly and in the New Jersey Senate and at one point was a candidate for governor of the state.[27]

It is not clear how or why Alexander undertook Johnson's representation. Both the college and the town of Princeton were relatively small in the early and middle nineteenth century, and it is possible that Johnson and Alexander knew each other, although no historical sources indicate this. It is perhaps curious that Alexander chose to defend Johnson in a battle against his enslaver. The Alexander family, like most upper-class southern families of the antebellum period, owned slaves in Virginia. When William Cowper Alexander's father, Archibald Alexander, left Virginia for the North in 1806, he went first to Philadelphia. The Alexanders brought with them at least one of the family's Virginia slaves, a woman called Daphne. In the words of Archibald Alexander's son, James Waddel Alexander, Daphne was "more friend than servant."[28] The descriptions of slaves as friends was not uncommon in settings involving relations between enslaved persons and their enslavers.[29] However, as one observer pointed out, even in relations where the enslaved might be momentarily treated as an equal, master-slave relations could never be separated from their social contexts in which enslaved people were subordinate.[30]

In their travel north the Alexander family also brought with them

Daphne's formerly enslaved husband, John Boatman, who had been owned by another family. Philadelphia Quakers and other sympathetic persons had purchased Boatman from his owner so he could accompany the Alexander family north.[31] Eventually Daphne fell ill and was unable to work. After the family's move to Princeton, she lived in poverty in alms-houses.[32] She was ultimately sent back to slavery in Virginia, where she resided with Alexander family relatives.[33] That Daphne was returned to slavery instead of being freed was perhaps not surprising. Archibald Alexander was one of the stalwart members of the American Colonization Society, and like many members of that group, he believed that it was not in the best interest of freed blacks to live among the general population of the United States. He described the "plan of colonizing the free people of colour in Africa" as "wise and benevolent."[34]

Just as the Alexander family's experience in the South as slave owners may have shaped their early political and legal views on abolition, the move to the North may equally as well have caused the family to question its position on slavery. While in the North, Archibald Alexander joined and became especially active in the ACS. Though the ACS as an organization took a moderate or even conservative position on the question of emancipation, and most if not all its early members owned slaves, later adherents were more progressive in their approaches to emancipation. Alexander, who was at the forefront of the national organization, ultimately came into contact with members whose views covered the spectrum from total and immediate emancipation to cautious and slow emancipation followed by removal to Africa.[35]

The younger members of the Alexander family may also have been strongly influenced by their move above the Mason-Dixon Line. William Cowper Alexander, along with his brothers James Waddel Alexander and Joseph Addison Alexander, received some of their early education from Princeton Theological Seminary student John Monteith from 1812 to 1816.[36] Monteith, who lived with Archibald Alexander and his family, was a community leader and institution builder. Over the course of his life, Monteith served as a professor at Hamilton College in Clinton, New York, organized the City Library of Detroit, and founded and served as first president of what is now the University of Michigan.[37] However, Monteith disdained many forms of civic, religious, and institutional authority. During his time at Hamilton College, he became embroiled in a bitter controversy with college president Henry Davis and some faculty members over their opposition to the emotional, evangelical styles of religious revivals that Monteith and some others favored. At one point,

Monteith rebuked the Hamilton faculty from the pulpit through a prayer: "Thou knowest, O Lord that the faculty of Hamilton College have sinned in high places: and we pray Thee, O Lord, if they are obstacles to Thy work, that Thou wouldst remove them out of the way."[38]

Part of Monteith's iconoclastic style was his fervent abolitionism. Monteith was a founding member of the American Anti-Slavery Society.[39] Thus, Monteith, who apparently maintained contact with the Alexander family later in his life, may have exerted a powerful influence on William Cowper Alexander, first in the latter's childhood and later in adulthood. For instance, when Monteith went to Detroit in 1816 as the first Protestant missionary to Michigan, he built up an impressive library partly from purchases and partly from books friends such as Archibald Alexander had given him.[40] Although William Cowper Alexander's father, Archibald Alexander, was opposed to the general and immediate emancipation of blacks, given the younger Alexander's early exposure to Monteith and his family's long interaction with him, William Cowper Alexander may have chosen to defend James Collins Johnson because of Monteith's abolitionist influence.

Alexander's co-counsel, Edward Armstrong, was a Philadelphia lawyer and amateur historian.[41] Armstrong was a member of the University of Pennsylvania class of 1832 and had been admitted to the Pennsylvania bar in 1838.[42] He was one of the founders of the Pennsylvania Historical Society and served as its recording secretary from 1843, the year of Johnson's fugitive slave trial, until 1853. It is not clear how Armstrong came to be associated with Johnson's case. One possibility was Armstrong's connections to people in and around the town of Princeton. For instance, a few years after Johnson's trial, in 1847, Princeton awarded Armstrong an honorary degree.[43] This could have been, at least in part, a grateful nod to Armstrong's involvement in Johnson's trial. Armstrong also had family connections in the area; he married Elizabeth Harrison Gulick of nearby Kingston, New Jersey, the daughter of William Gulick, a businessman with extensive interests in and near the town of Princeton.[44] Elizabeth's branch of the Gulick family, like many socially prominent New Jersey residents, apparently owned slaves at one point; in 1809 Elizabeth's father, William Gulick, purchased a slave named Tom from John Maclean Sr.[45] The Gulick family's position on slavery at the time of Johnson's arrest and trial is unclear. There was also at least one Gulick among the students at the college during the time of Johnson's arrest and trial, William Beekman Gulick, class of 1844, who was born in New Jersey and later relocated to North Carolina.[46] The constable who arrested Johnson, Ralph

Gulick, was also a member of this large and well-known Princeton-area family.[47]

One possible reason for Armstrong's participation in Johnson's case was the notoriety he had gained from his involvement in a nationally known case shortly before Johnson's trial: the prosecution in *United States v. Holmes* of one of the crewman of the ship *William Brown* after it sank in 1841.[48] Sixteen passengers were forced out of an overloaded lifeboat before the survivors were rescued. The ship, which was carrying seventeen crewmen and sixty-five passengers (mostly Scots and Irish emigrants), was en route to Philadelphia from Liverpool, England. On the night of April 19, 1841, while 250 miles from Newfoundland, the *William Brown* struck an iceberg and began to sink rapidly. There were two lifeboats, one small and one large. The captain and most of the crew took the small life-boat, and the passengers crowded aboard the large lifeboat. There was not enough space on the large lifeboat for all the passengers, and thirty-one died on board the *William Brown* when it sank. Alexander Holmes, who was the only crew member then in the city, was arrested and charged with the murder of Frank Askin, one of the men thrown overboard. Before trial, the charge was reduced to voluntary manslaughter after the grand jury refused to indict Holmes for murder.[49] Edward Armstrong was part of a team that also included David Paul Brown, a criminal defense attorney who was well known in abolitionist circles and litigated frequently on behalf of fugitive enslaved persons.[50] Historical records do not indicate whether Armstrong was also part of the Philadelphia abolitionist bar. However, his association with Brown, along with involvement in Johnson's case, suggests that he may have been. Throughout his legal and political career Armstrong was noted as a gifted orator. These gifts were apparently on display in Johnson's trial. Philip Wallis complained that Armstrong "forgot himself so far" as to resort to presenting in his comments "a picture of the horrors of slavery, and the blessings of freedom."[51]

Opposite Johnson's legal team was Hageman, a lawyer and historian whose wife was descended from one of the early presidents of the College of New Jersey.[52] Hageman argued the case alongside Johnson's co-owner, Severn Teackle Wallis. Hageman, who was twenty-seven at the time of the trial, belonged to a family that had lived in central New Jersey in and around Princeton for well over one hundred years by the time of the trial. He had studied at Rutgers University, graduated in 1836, and had been admitted to the bar in November 1839. Hageman received the designation counselor at law in February 1843, a few months before Johnson's trial.[53]

Hageman was involved in the professional and social life of the town and of the college throughout his adult life. Though neither Hageman nor any of his direct ancestors had attended the college, Hageman seemed deeply enamored of the college and its traditions and history. Hageman's sons John F. Frelinghuysen Jr. and Samuel Miller Frelinghuysen attended the College of New Jersey, graduating in the classes of 1868 and 1869, respectively.[54] Hageman's wife, Sarah Sergeant Miller Hageman, had numerous associations with Princeton. Her father was the Reverend Samuel Miller, a professor at Princeton Theological Seminary for over thirty years. Her brother, Samuel Miller Jr., was a member of the class of 1833. Sarah Hageman's maternal grandfather, Jonathan Dickinson Sergeant, was a member of the Princeton class of 1762 and a member of the Continental Congress. Her maternal great-great grandfather was Jonathan Dickinson, a cofounder and the first president of Princeton.

Hageman produced a number of writings during his life. Many were legal process manuals. Other works, however, were local histories. Like his opposing counsel, Edward Armstrong, Hageman was a historian and a member of his local historical society. The work for which he is perhaps best known is his multivolume work *The History of Princeton and Its Institutions*, in which he chronicles many of the events of the college and the town, and includes one of the only firsthand accounts of the trial of James Collins Johnson. Hageman's mention of Johnson's trial, besides its historical significance as part of the history of the town of Princeton, was also important as a form of case report. For many decades into the nineteenth century, the reporting of state and federal judicial decisions was not the responsibility of any public authority.[55] Although beginning in 1806, New Jersey legislatively mandated official law reports, not all opinions were subject to the requirement.[56] Often outcomes of cases in lower courts were unavailable in written form. Independent entrepreneurs who undertook the reporting of both state and federal decisions sometimes compensated for these gaps.[57] As a result, some cases were reported only in brief, were haphazardly reported, and were sometimes published years after a decision had been made.[58] Hageman, while endeavoring to maintain formal language, clearly evinces a bias for the Wallises, describing the evidence as "clear and irresistible" and extolling the verdict in favor of the enslavers, asserting that it was "homage to law—to the constitution of the United States, and not a want of sympathy for a poor slave seeking his liberty."[59]

Of all the lawyers involved in Johnson's trial, Severn Teackle Wallis stands out as the most famous and most accomplished. As an enslaver of James Collins Johnson and as a practicing lawyer, it is clear why he would have served as one of the lawyers in his effort to reenslave Johnson. Wallis attended St. Mary's College in Baltimore, graduating with a B.A. in 1832 and an M.A. in 1834.[60] He studied law with John Glenn and William Wirt. Glenn was a prominent attorney and large-scale plantation owner, and Wirt was a man of tremendous influence and legal renown, having served, among other roles, as the prosecutor in Aaron Burr Jr.'s treason trial in 1807.[61] Severn Teackle Wallis finished his legal studies in 1835 at the age of nineteen but was unable to begin practicing law until he reached his majority in 1837.

Wallis championed several political and social causes during his career. However, he was a political pragmatist, and thus, even after winning the case involving Johnson, he accepted the monetary settlement that freed Johnson after the trial. While his father, Philip Wallis, Johnson's co-enslaver, wrote and spoke widely about his anger about having to accept what he felt was a reduced value for Johnson, Severn Teackle Wallis, who was a prolific writer and public speaker, seems to have left no recorded references to Johnson's escape, recapture, and trial. This apparent forgetting of the matter may be a result of bitterness, but it may also have been an example of Severn Teackle Wallis's pragmatic approach to the questions of slavery and race. For instance, although he was aligned with Confederate interests in Maryland out of loyalty and sentiment, he opposed the Civil War and wanted to maintain the Union.[62]

Another example of Severn Teackle Wallis's pragmatism was seen decades later in his advocacy on behalf of two black men who sought to enter the University of Maryland Law School in 1887, Harry Sythe Cummings[63] and Charles W. Johnson.[64] Wallis, then provost of the University of Maryland, sided with a law faculty member in admitting the men to law school. Both Cummings and Johnson completed the three-year law course in two years. Some observers have suggested that Wallis, a former enslaver and an apologist for the Confederacy, backed the men chiefly to help bolster black loyalty to the Republican Party, which Wallis supported. Wallis's actions suggest that both later in his life and at the time of Johnson's trial, he was focused on reaching an achievable goal and not a dramatic win. As Wallis wrote decades after Johnson's trial: "Law undoubtedly has more of the stimulus which comes from personal collision and triumph. But the triumph dies almost with the struggle.[65]

The Conduct of Johnson's Trial

Before Johnson's trial began, Severn Teackle Wallis offered a preliminary motion that argued that the New Jersey law allowing for a jury trial was unconstitutional. He supported his motion by citing *Prigg v. Pennsylvania*. Ignoring *Prigg*, the magistrate ruled in favor of Alexander and allowed Johnson a jury trial.[66]

The trial, held under the Fugitive Slave Act of 1793, occurred just months after *Prigg v. Pennsylvania* was decided in March 1842.[67] In *Prigg*, the court held that most state-enacted protections for alleged fugitive slaves, such as the jury trials called for under New Jersey law, were violations of the 1793 act. Although Johnson's case should have been conducted under the standard enunciated in that case, the New Jersey judge declined to apply *Prigg*, as Johnson's owners wanted, and instead adopted the argument of Johnson's lawyers, applying a New Jersey law that afforded Johnson greater procedural protection.

Johnson's trial put into sharp relief what has been described as the moral-formalist dilemma: the conflict between the personal sentiments of judges and other legal actors and the need to adhere to existing legal norms.[68] Most of these conflicts in the context of slavery litigation were resolved in favor of legal rules.[69] Judges often avoided innovations in legal doctrine that might have resulted in alternative legal formulations in the slavery context.[70] For many slavery-era legal decision makers, following the law was the sine qua non of the legal enterprise and of the structure of justice itself. However, even where there was close fidelity to the rule of law, those who adhered sometimes did so not for the mere fact of avoiding change but for politically instrumental reasons.[71] Johnson's trial occurred at an especially volatile time when both federal and state rules about fugitive slaves were undergoing vast change. These changes coincided with a time of renewed focus on slavery as an economic institution in both the North and the South. In this dynamic environment, even long-established and well-defended legal norms sometimes gave way to or combined with social and political perspectives embraced by legal actors in the cases of fugitive slaves. This potent mix was at work in Johnson's trial.

Prigg concerned the case of Margaret Morgan, who was born in Maryland to parents who had been allowed to live as though they were free on the estate of their enslavers, John and Margaret Ashmore.[72] The Ashmores made no claim to Margaret, and during the life of her parents John Ashmore regularly declared that he had set them free.[73] She eventually married a man named Jerry Morgan and had children with him. After the death of Margaret's parents, the Morgans moved to Pennsylvania, where Margaret gave birth to other children.[74] In 1837 John Ashmore died, leaving a will that was silent on the matter of Margaret Morgan, her children, and her parents. Ashmore's widow, Margaret Ashmore, sent four resi-

dents of Hartford County, Maryland, to Pennsylvania to capture Margaret Morgan: her son-in-law, Nathan Bemis and neighboring slave owners
Edward Prigg, Jacob Forwood, and Stephen Lewis.[75] Prigg obtained an
arrest warrant in Pennsylvania and had Margaret and her children seized.
Prigg took them to Maryland, where a Maryland court declared Morgan
to be a fugitive slave. Morgan and her children, including the child who
was born in Pennsylvania and who should thus have been free under prevailing laws, were all sold south.[76]

In the aftermath of the case, the state of Pennsylvania charged Edward
Prigg and the other men with kidnapping under an 1826 Pennsylvania
statute that forbade the forcible removal of blacks in Pennsylvania to other
states with the object of enslaving them or selling them as slaves. After
first resisting extradition of the charged men, Maryland eventually allowed
the extradition of Edward Prigg. He was convicted by the special verdict
of a York County, Pennsylvania, court. He appealed his case to the U.S.
Supreme Court, which overturned his conviction in 1842. The Court
found that the Fugitive Slave Act of 1793 was constitutional and that no
state could impede its implementation by enacting state laws that added
additional requirements. It also found that no allegedly fugitive slave was
entitled to any due process or trial beyond a summary proceeding to determine his or her identity.

Justice Joseph Story, who wrote for the Court in *Prigg*, stated that
the Fugitive Slave Clause of the U.S. Constitution "manifestly contem-
plates the existence of a *positive unqualified right on the part of the owner* of
the fugitive slave, which no state law or regulation can in any way qual-
ify, regulate, control, or restrain."[77] This language and other unambiguous
statements of the powerlessness of the states to hinder federal norms of
slavery came as a surprise to some. Before *Prigg*, Justice Story had a reputation among some legal observers as being opposed to slavery.[78] This reputation was greatly enhanced by his decisions opposing slave trafficking in
cases involving the ships *La Jeune Eugenie* and *La Amistad*.[79]

Story had been the justice in *La Jeune Eugenie*, an 1822 case before the
U.S. Circuit Court for Massachusetts. The case involved a U.S. revenue
cutter that seized a French ship suspected of slave trafficking off the coast
of West Africa and transported the cutter to Boston.[80] The U.S. government confiscated the ship, asserting that slave trafficking from Africa to
a foreign port violated the law of nations and that seizure of the ship
was the appropriate remedy. The court upheld the argument of the government and refused to order return of the vessel to its owners. Story is
remembered for his impassioned rhetoric about the nature of slave traf-

ficking in the case. For example, he wrote: "It cannot admit of serious question that [such exploitation] is founded in a violation of some of the first principles which ought to govern nations. It is repugnant to the great principles of Christian duty, the dictates of natural religion, the obligations of good faith and morality, and the eternal maxims of social justice."[81] However, while Story turned to natural law in support of his decision, he was also mindful of the limits of his judicial role, which gave him only the authority to enforce the law of nations where it had not been "relaxed or waived by the consent of nations" as seen in their "general practice[s] and customs."[82]

In *La Amistad*, Story rendered a decision that freed African captives who had seized a ship at sea and entered the United States. While Justice Story's decision favored the captured Africans and while he may have condemned slavery, he also opposed abolitionism more broadly.[83] Story respected property rights and the rule of law. In finding for the allegedly enslaved Africans of the *Amistad*, Story concluded that when the ship entered U.S. waters, it was in the possession of blacks asserting their freedom.[84] These blacks did not intend "to import themselves here, as slaves, or for sale as slaves."[85] Since they had never been property, they could not, under existing legal norms, become property. In his later decision in *Prigg*, Story continued in this vein of close adherence to the letter of formal law.

In *Prigg*, Story may also have been motivated by a desire to respect the constitutional bargain the North and the South had made regarding slavery and to thus preserve the Union.[86] While this bargain forbade further imports of Africans after 1808, it also required that property rights in enslaved people be respected. One of the key features of *Prigg* is that it made slavery an issue of national import and was a vital step in the move toward the 1850 Fugitive Slave Law and the decision in *Dred Scott v. Sanford*.[87] In *Prigg*, both proslavery and antislavery forces looked to government intervention to protect their interests. *Prigg* is also an inversion of how many have come to characterize northern and southern approaches to slavery and race, as it involved the South's invocation of federal supremacy over the rights of northern states to enact state laws to impede slavery.

With *Prigg*, slavery became part of federal common law that made blacks subject to seizure anywhere in the country when a white person alleged that they were enslaved.[88] Some observers have suggested that although the *Prigg* decision authorized the interstate seizure of an enslaved woman and her children, the decision had wider implications for disrupting slavery because the decision removed the power to implement the Fugitive Slave Clause from states, thereby making it more difficult for slave owners to recover slaves.[89] However, this assertion likely attributes too much antislavery feeling to Justice Story. The decision in *Prigg v. Pennsylvania* was not simply the victory of a humane federalism framed in legal and judicial technicality; *Prigg* can also be seen as the height of politics and an example of statecraft used to tamp down a burgeoning regionalism. Even if Justice Story's opinion in *Prigg* should have been viewed, as he and his son claimed, as a "triumph of freedom" because of the limits *Prigg* placed on state legislatures in the arena of slavery, the case ended badly for Margaret Morgan and family.[90] Margaret Morgan and her children disappeared into the abyss of slavery, never to be heard of again, and her husband, Jerry Morgan, died while trying to free them.[91]

Given this chilling end for the Morgans, the judge in James Collins Johnson's case may have been especially sympathetic to the arguments of Johnson's lawyers that the norms of New Jersey state law should be applied in Johnson's case. The Wallises' employment of Madison Jeffers, a notorious slave catcher with a reputation for lawlessness and brutality, signaled a hardened and unbridled determination to retake Johnson. Moreover, Philip Wallis's Mississippi residency and his straitened circumstances compared with his earlier life in genteel Maryland surroundings did not bode well for Johnson's future if he were to be reenslaved. Hence, although *Prigg* essentially eliminated most state-enacted protections for allegedly fugitive slaves, Johnson was given full access to procedures under New Jersey's 1837 personal liberty laws. One of the most important of these rights was a jury trial. It can be inferred from accounts of Johnson's trial that his attorney-enslaver Severn Teackle Wallis and Wallis's co-counsel, Hageman, argued vigorously that jury trials were not legally permitted in fugitive slave trials after *Prigg*. Their defeat on this procedural issue was a significant legal achievement for Johnson.

Efforts to suppress the new federal procedural norm for slave recapture in *Prigg* was not limited to single fugitive slave cases such as Johnson's. This practice occurred often in New Jersey, so often that when the state revised its statutes in 1846 it kept the 1837 personal liberty law on its books. In New Jersey, as in other ostensibly free northern states, social, political, and legal norms worked together to govern conditions for blacks inside and outside the courtroom, and fugitive slave trials were no exception. While this sometimes meant that blacks such as Johnson enjoyed the benefit of positive outcomes in their legal matters, more often it did not. As one commentator wrote when describing Pennsylvania before the

Civil War, even if the courts did not "sustain the exclusion of the negro from legal rights, public opinion and individual rights were able to put beyond his reach many of the privileges in which he might have shared."[92]

An editor at the *National Anti-Slavery Standard*, the newspaper of the American Anti-Slavery Society, remarked that Johnson's case was the first time that a fugitive slave case had been put before a jury.[93] While the presence of a jury represented a victory for Johnson, it was a pyrrhic victory—the jury deliberated for thirty minutes before consigning him to slavery.[94] The chief juror in Johnson's case was Josiah S. Worth, a fifty-six-year-old farmer and miller from the Stony Brook section of Princeton.[95] Worth was involved in civic and political activities in and around the town of Princeton and was active in the local banking establishment.[96] From 1838 to 1839, he had served as the delegate to the New Jersey state legislature from Mercer County.[97] In 1837, he was a presidential elector from New Jersey.[98] Worth was descended from one of the original Quaker families to settle in Princeton in 1696, and some of his ancestors were instrumental in helping build the College of New Jersey. Though no record of their names survives, there were apparently several Quakers who served on Johnson's jury.[99]

Worth's identity as a Quaker caused some people to view the proceedings as more fair than they might otherwise have been.[100] Worth may also have had some sympathy for Johnson beyond that engendered by his religious practices. Worth, who had no children, had designated one of the nephews of his wife, Joseph H. Bruere, as his heir. Bruere was a member of the Princeton class of 1841.[101] Bruere lived at home until his senior year, when he lived at Old North, as Nassau Hall (then a dormitory and classroom building) was sometimes called.[102] Old North was Johnson's workplace for most of his early years at the college. Thus, via his nephew, Worth may have had a particular interest in, knowledge of, and even sympathy for James Collins Johnson.

Much of the reason for Johnson's courtroom loss appears to be the witnesses who testified against him. Key among these were Johnson's enslavers Philip Wallis and Severn Teackle Wallis.[103] A "Mr. Wickes" and his son also apparently also offered testimony about Johnson's identity, though which members of the Wickes family is unclear.[104] A majority of the argument turned on Johnson's identity and whether Johnson was in fact the slave James Collins who was owned by the Wallises.[105] Severn Teackle Wallis was said to have stated that he knew Johnson as well as he knew his own father.[106] The irony of this statement cannot be lost on contemporary readers, as it is a reminder of the almost perverse assertion by some enslavers that their enslaved workers were like members of the family.

The atmosphere at Johnson's trial was made even more contentious by the presence of persons outside the court proceeding. Local blacks apparently came to support Johnson, and southern students supported Wallis's claim.[107] Before, during, and after Johnson's trial local blacks and pro-slavery students of the college were in conflict, so much so that Wallis and his lawyer feared that Johnson would be released by an assault on the place where he was jailed. While southern students may have been chivalrous about addressing Johnson's plight after his conviction by supporting his purchase from slavery, some of them had also shown opposition to freeing Johnson and had helped Johnson's enslavers at the time of his arrest and after he was convicted.

According to a letter Philip Wallis wrote after Johnson was arrested as a fugitive slave in 1843, "strange negroes" appeared in Princeton to prevent Johnson's removal to Maryland.[108] The Wallises may have accepted payment to redeem Johnson largely to pacify this "gang of blacks" who made "every demonstration toward an immediate rescue."[109] When the mayor of Princeton was unable to control the rioters, Wallis wrote, "Southern students of Princeton" bearing arms helped hold off the black would-be rescuers."[110] Some reports noted that there was "some attempt to rescue" Johnson and that "Princeton college students from the South took part, and dirks and knives were drawn."[111]

The presence of antislavery protesters at the fugitive slave trials of alleged slaves was not unusual. Neither were more general antislavery protests. In the antebellum years, groups of antislavery protesters appeared frequently in parts of the North and were especially prevalent in New Jersey and Pennsylvania.[112] Blacks in northern states were especially active in staging public protests, such as at an 1837 demonstration in Newark, New Jersey, in response to a fugitive slave trial being held there.[113] Johnson apparently made an effort to escape after his conviction, and according to some accounts, southern students wielded weapons in the "fracas that ensued."[114] But it is unclear whether that "fracas" also involved would-be black rescuers threatening violence. If there was such a crowd of black supporters, the Wallises had every reason to fear that they might rescue Johnson, thereby depriving them of their slave and of the monetary value of that slave.

Help did come for Johnson, but not as he and others might have envisioned. Rather than redemption via the court system or by rescuing protesters, aid came in the form of what looked to be a lone woman.

5
The Rescue of James Collins Johnson

It was at this juncture that a kind-hearted
woman of Princeton came to his rescue,
bought him of his master for the sum of $550,
and set him free. But the students were not
to be outdone in generosity, and they made
up a purse of $100 (a great deal of money
in those days) and presented it to Jim. And
Jim—honest fellow that he is—assured me
that he eventually paid back every dollar
of the money with which his freedom
had been bought.

*—Andrew C. Imbrie, from his 1895 interview
with James Collins Johnson*

All accounts agree that James Collins Johnson was rescued from slavery via purchase. There is widespread accord in these stories that Johnson's enslaver agreed to accept a sum of money in exchange for not reclaiming him and conveying him back to slavery after he was deemed a fugitive slave in his Princeton trial. Where these accounts sometimes disagree is about who paid Johnson's slave price. Most accounts identify Theodosia Ann Mary Prevost as Johnson's redeemer. Even in the few accounts that suggest that others helped, Prevost is named as a key figure in Johnson's release. Though Theodosia Prevost figures as a heroine in most stories about Johnson, she is a heroine without apparent cause. Just as most renditions of Johnson's story obscure the details of his betrayal, arrest, and trial, those accounts frame Theodosia Prevost as a little-known gentlewoman whose actions in favor of Johnson neither had, nor needed, any clear or full explanation. This chapter first offers some sense of who Prevost was by considering her in the context of her family life and the places where she lived. It then explores the conditions under which Prevost redeemed Johnson. Finally, this chapter considers whether Theodosia Prevost's 1843 rescue of Johnson was the source of freedom and security for Johnson that it has been represented to be.

Although Theodosia Prevost was a white woman with family ties to some of the most prominent families in the United States, like many women of her times, she existed at the margins of history. Fortunately for posterity, her relationships to better-known male figures such as her father, John Bartow Prevost; her step-grandfather, Aaron Burr Jr., with whom she apparently had a close relationship; and her more distant ancestor, John Witherspoon, provide ways to gain insight into her life. Theodosia Prevost's connections to Princeton, her social and economic standing in the local community, and her gender likely all contributed to making her an ideal savior for James Collins Johnson. With her action to liberate Johnson, she played a major role in a slave rescue that in its time captured nationwide attention. Thus Theodosia Prevost stood out as a public figure at a time when women were typically relegated to home and hearth.

Some accounts suggest that Theodosia Prevost was a woman of modest means who lived a quiet, Spartan life and had a particular abhorrence of slavery that grew from her years of residence in Louisiana as a child and young woman. Other accounts suggest that Theodosia Prevost was a socially active woman who was known as a wealthy philanthropist.[1] It is clear, however, that Theodosia Prevost descended from a pedigreed family closely tied to Princeton, and with claims of distant royal ancestry.[2]

Theodosia Ann Mary Prevost was born on January 10, 1801, in New York City to Frances Anna Smith and John Bartow Prevost. At the time of her birth the family lived at 86 Greenwich Street in Lower Manhattan.[3] The street was part of a neighborhood that was popular among New York City's elite during the late colonial period and the early years of the republic.[4] Among the Prevost family's neighbors at the time of Theodosia's birth was Dewitt Clinton, who lived a few houses away at 82 Greenwich Street.[5] Clinton was soon to become a luminary in New York State politics; the year after Prevost's birth he became a U.S. senator, launching a career that culminated in his governorship of the state. Clinton was also a famous political rival of Prevost's step-grandfather, Aaron Burr Jr., who lived not far away on his Richmond Hill estate in Manhattan. Another of the Prevost family's neighbors was John Jacob Astor, the founder of the renowned Astor family in the United States.[6] John Bartow Prevost apparently had business dealings involving both Astor and Clinton.[7]

Two enslaved persons lived at the Prevosts' New York home.[8] The

Prevosts were not unusual in this regard. Though most enslavers held few enslaved people in New York City, slavery was relatively widespread during the late eighteenth and early nineteenth centuries.[9] Between 1790 and 1800, the number of slaves in New York City grew by 25 percent.[10] Many New York City enslavers at the beginning of the nineteenth century were owners who, like Theodosia Prevost's lawyer father, were professional men.[11] John Bartow Prevost appears to have sold his Greenwich Street house sometime around 1804 to Henry Kermit, a sea captain.[12] Kermit, like John Bartow Prevost and many other New Yorkers, also owned slaves.[13] Kermit is described as having worked in "the West Indies trade," a generalized term often describing commerce in slave-made or slave-harvested products and goods made or produced in the United States to supply the West Indies. It also frequently referred to the sale and transport of slaves.[14]

Theodosia Prevost was the eldest of four children; her younger siblings were James Marcus Prevost, Samuel Stanhope Prevost, and Frances Caroline Prevost.[15] Her mother, Frances Anna Smith, was the daughter of Samuel Stanhope Smith and Anne Witherspoon. Samuel Stanhope Smith was the founding president of Hampden-Sydney College in Virginia, which was, like Princeton, an all-male Presbyterian-affiliated college.[16] Smith was also the seventh president of Princeton (1795–1812); he was the first alumnus to fill the position of president. His wife, Anne Witherspoon, was the daughter of John Witherspoon, the sixth president of Princeton (1768–1794) and a signer of the Declaration of Independence. Theodosia Prevost's brothers, James Marcus Prevost and Samuel Stanhope Prevost, were both members of the Princeton class of 1818.[17] Theodosia Prevost's immediate and extended family, like many historic Princetonians, were linked by their ties to the college, their biological and marital kinships with each other, and their religious faith.[18]

Theodosia Prevost's early life in New York came to an end when in 1804, three years after her birth in New York City, President Thomas Jefferson appointed her father as one of the first judges in the Territory of Orleans; he took office shortly after the Louisiana Purchase was concluded in 1803.[19] John Bartow Prevost moved to Louisiana, taking with him his wife, his daughter Theodosia, and his two sons. The family's youngest child, Frances Caroline Prevost, was born on August 24, 1806, in New Orleans. Later that same year, John Bartow Prevost left the bench and began private law practice. Prevost, who was born in 1766 in Paramus, New Jersey, spent much of his career in public service, mostly as a civil servant; in 1794–1796, he was secretary to James Monroe while

Monroe was minister to France, and from 1801 to 1804, he served as recorder of NewYork City.[20] While serving as a judge in Louisiana, Prevost
was involved in the *Garcia* and *Bollman* cases, two noteworthy cases in
New Orleans, the latter of which had national implications.[21]

Prevost was highly learned and was one of the few attorneys in the
country who was fluent in English, French, and Spanish.[22] Though it is
not clear whether he took the enslaved persons he had owned in New
York with him to Louisiana, eight months after he arrived there, he
bought a plantation near New Orleans with thirty-five enslaved laborers
and a large sugar works.[23] In this respect Prevost was like the large number
of lawyers who took up residence in the lower South during the antebellum period. Many of these southern lawyers and judges either were
or aspired to be slave owners and planters.[24] However, Prevost's status as a
well-educated plantation owner descended from a prominent family was
belied by his financial standing; he had little money of his own.[25] Prevost
often struggled financially from his early adulthood.[26] He was said to have
left the Louisiana bench because the salary was low and he required more
money to support his family.[27] By some accounts, he was in debt to creditors at the time he left the bench.[28] Among his debts were mortgages on
his real property in New York[29] and a large mortgage on his plantation.[30]

Prevost practiced law in Louisiana for several years after he retired
from the bench in 1806. On October 31, 1807, just over a year after
the birth of her last child, Frances Anna Prevost died.[31] In 1817 President James Monroe appointed Prevost as a special agent to Peru, Buenos
Aires, and Chile.[32] Prevost sailed from NewYork on October 18, 1817.[33]
He likely won the position because of the political influence of his stepfather, Aaron Burr Jr.[34] Prevost moved to Peru and was apparently shortly
thereafter followed by his sons, Samuel Stanhope (often called Stanhope)
and James Marcus.[35] He left his daughters Theodosia and Frances behind
in the United States, perhaps deciding that the remote South American
posting offered little opportunity for regular visits to the United States
and was thus unsuited to two motherless, unmarried girls.

Prevost may have been correct in his assessment of the move. Although
his two sons traveled to the United States on some occasions, they lived
in Peru until their deaths decades later.[36] The Prevost men likely had
not intended to make their permanent residence in Peru. This is suggested in an August 1822 letter Stanhope Prevost wrote to John Maclean
Jr. of Princeton about five years after he moved to Peru. Stanhope Prevost described chaotic social conditions in Peru and detailed the preju-
dices against non-Catholics. Prevost also wrote that only Catholics could

receive a regular burial and that in order to marry, non-Catholics had to convert to Catholicism and renounce their original religions. Prevost wrote, "As I hope neither to marry or die in this country I don't care much about it."[37] Stanhope Prevost, contrary to the hopes he had expressed early in life, married a Peruvian woman, Maria Mauricia Moreyra Abella-Fuertes Querejazu, in 1841 and eventually had eight children with her.[38] He remained in Peru for the next several decades and served as U.S. consul to Peru from 1843 until 1851.[39] Stanhope Prevost, his father, John Bartow Prevost, and his brother, James Marcus Prevost, all died in Peru. Stanhope's father and brother died a few years after he wrote the 1822 letter.[40]

Judging from the importance that many members of her family gave to education, it is likely that Theodosia Prevost would have been as well educated as any of the women of her day. Her namesake and maternal grandmother, Theodosia Stillwell Bartow Prevost Burr, the wife of Aaron Burr Jr., was said to have been one of the most intelligent and well-educated women of her time; Burr was said to have been attracted to his wife chiefly because of her intelligence and erudition.[41] Aaron Burr Jr. closely guided the education of his stepsons, Augustine Frederick Prevost and John Bartow Prevost, Theodosia's father.[42] Burr also gave careful attention to the education of his own daughter Theodosia Burr and provided her with a classical education typically reserved for boys, along with an education in more feminine pursuits.[43] Like her father, brothers, and paternal aunt Theodosia Burr, Theodosia Prevost appears also to have had strong early education; her aunt Theodosia Burr remarked in a March 10, 1810, letter to John Bartow Prevost that she took pride in then-nine-year-old Theodosia Prevost's progress and that the child's letters "did her honor."[44]

It is not clear what became of Theodosia Prevost after the death of her mother in 1807 or after her father and brothers left for Peru a decade later. Theodosia Burr remarked in her March 10, 1810, letter that she had received several letters from young Theodosia Prevost, but there is no indication of where Theodosia Prevost resided when the letters were dispatched to her aunt.[45] It is possible that she was sent to the relatives closest at hand and that she joined the New Orleans household of her maternal uncle, John Witherspoon Smith, and his wife, Sarah Henrietta Livingston Duer Smith.[46] John Witherspoon Smith had served as a clerk of the Supreme Court in Louisiana. Smith, his wife, and their several children lived on Melpomene Street in New Orleans in gracious surroundings.[47]

Given this lifestyle of apparent luxury, Smith and his wife might easily have been able to afford to support their young niece Theodosia. Theodosia might also have been sent to live with her maternal aunt, Mary Clay Smith Breckinridge, and her aunt's husband, Joseph Cabell Breckinridge, in Kentucky.[48] Theodosia's sister, Frances, apparently went to live with these Kentucky relatives, and while still in her teens she married William Lewis Breckinridge, the brother of her aunt Mary's husband. However, though some records suggest that Theodosia's younger sister may have attended Lafayette Female Academy in Kentucky while in the care of her maternal aunt, there seems to be no evidence of Theodosia Prevost's presence in Kentucky or of her formal education.[49]

Certainly if Theodosia Prevost did spend time among the Breckinridges, this may have been one of the influences that helped shape her position on slavery and cause her to intercede to help James Collins Johnson gain freedom. There was a significant strain of antislavery activism among the Kentucky Breckinridges.[50] For instance, Prevost's uncle Joseph Cabell Breckinridge developed a reputation for abolitionist thought, a reputation that may have been first fostered by his close friendship with Princeton roommate James G. Birney, later an ardent abolitionist.[51] Prevost's brother-in-law, William Lewis Breckinridge, though he was himself a large-scale enslaver, became a prominent Presbyterian minister and antislavery activist.[52] Later in life when Theodosia Prevost lived in Princeton as a woman of independent means, she housed two of William and Frances's sons while they were students at Princeton. One of these nephews, John Bartow Breckinridge, was a member of the Princeton class of 1843 and thus was on campus during Johnson's trial.[53] The other nephew, Marcus Prevost Breckinridge, was a member of the class of 1848.[54]

One source suggests that Theodosia Prevost and her brothers were sent to Princeton shortly after the 1807 death of their mother, Frances Anna Smith.[55] However, the first clear indication of Theodosia's residence after the death of her mother is not seen until 1818.[56] There is evidence that Theodosia Prevost came to Princeton for at least a long-term visit around May 1818, several months after her father departed the United States for his appointment in Peru. A "Miss Prevost" arrived in nearby Philadelphia on a ship from New Orleans on May 15, 1818.[57] This could have been Theodosia Prevost. There is also what appears to be a reference to her presence in Princeton in a June 22, 1818, letter written by a relative, John Pintard, who also lived in Princeton.[58] In the letter Pintard noted seeing "Miss Prevost" and asked, "What has caused her return? Her father has not yet got back, nor will not probably."[59] In that letter Pintard disparages Theodosia Prevost's father, John Bartow Prevost, suggesting that although he was talented, he lacked industry and was "too proud" to work.[60]

It is likely that one of the younger adults among Theodosia Prevost's Princeton kin would have taken charge of the teenaged girl once she reached Princeton in 1818. Theodosia's grandmother Anne Witherspoon Smith had died on April 1, 1817, just over a year before Theodosia arrived in Princeton.[61] Her grandfather Samuel Stanhope Smith had resigned as president of the college in 1812 due to illness and pressure from the trustees; he died on August 21, 1819, just over a year after she arrived.[62] One of Theodosia's caretakers in Princeton may have been Susan French Smith Salomons, a maternal aunt.[63] However, Salomons apparently lived in somewhat narrow financial circumstances much of her adult life.[64] This might have limited Salomons's ability to care for Theodosia Prevost. Another of Theodosia Prevost's aunts, Elizabeth Smith Pintard, also lived in Princeton at that time, and she might equally as well have provided a home for young Theodosia.[65] There is some evidence that both Susan Salomons and Elizabeth Pintard had lived with Samuel Stanhope Smith at his home, which the college provided.[66] It is not clear where Salomons and Pintard lived after the housing provided by the college was no longer available.

While Theodosia Prevost was known as a wealthy woman throughout much of her adult life, the source of her money is not clear. One possible source may have been her father, John Bartow Prevost. Prevost's parents described him as industrious, hardworking, and bright, even in his youth and early career as a lawyer. In letters Aaron Burr Jr. exchanged with his wife, Theodosia, they often described Prevost's hard work.[67] However, views of Prevost's character and industry were sometimes less sanguine outside the gaze of his admiring parents. Prevost seems to have been short on funds for large parts of his career.[68] His fortunes may have changed during his residence in Peru; according to one source he was earning $4,500 per year by 1823, immediately before leaving his position in Peru and about a year before his death.[69] This was more than double what he had earned in Louisiana only a few years before when serving as a judge.[70]

Another possible source of Theodosia Prevost's money was her step-grandfather Aaron Burr Jr., who served as the third vice president of the United States under Thomas Jefferson. Burr was made infamous as the killer of Alexander Hamilton in a duel in 1804, and came into further disrepute as a result of his trial for treason in 1807.[71] According to some accounts, Burr was close to his step-granddaughter Theodosia Prevost, perhaps in part because she was named after Burr's beloved late wife and daughter, both of whom were also named Theodosia.[72] Burr was apparently a strong believer in women's independence and would likely have wanted to advance Theodosia Prevost's independent lifestyle were he able to do so.[73]

Though Aaron Burr Jr. was often magnanimous, he was likely not the source of Theodosia Prevost's money.[74] Perhaps in part because of his generosity, Burr was continuously embarrassed by debts. In one instance, for example, his stepson Augustine James Frederick Prevost pledged his farm as security for money that Burr owed. Upon Burr's failure to pay, the farm was advertised for sale to satisfy the debt, causing Burr's daughter Theodosia Burr to write to her brother John Bartow Prevost expressing fear that their brother might lose his property due to Burr's failure to pay.[75] Burr's debts extended beyond business dealings and even touched on charitable pledges. At one point, Burr was asked to pay an overdue gift subscription that he had pledged to Princeton while serving as vice president of the United States.[76] Burr owed large amounts to creditors, and he spent lavishly. There was always a shortage of money, and negotiations for loans and adjustments of debt consumed no small portion of his time. Burr was apparently in difficult financial circumstances even at the end of his life; one source suggests that Theodosia Prevost may have arranged and paid for Burr's funeral. Although Burr died leaving few assets, over twenty years after his death in 1836, real estate holdings valued at many thousands of dollars came into Burr's estate.[77] However, Theodosia Prevost appears not to have received any money from this windfall. Frances Ann Watson Tompkins, whom Burr left as a residuary legatee in his will and whom he identified as his daughter, inherited this property.[78] Burr also named another daughter, Elizabeth, as an heir in his will. Theodosia Prevost seems to have been left only a very small legacy in Burr's will: a cup bearing the likeness of Burr's daughter, Theodosia Burr Alston.[79]

Just as Theodosia Prevost's paternal grandparents appear not to have been the source of her wealth, neither is it likely that Prevost's money came from her maternal grandfather, Samuel Stanhope Smith. For one thing, several children and grandchildren survived Smith, and it seems most likely that he would have left any monetary legacy to his children rather than his grandchildren. In addition, Samuel Stanhope Smith may not have had much of a financial legacy to leave behind. In a letter discussing the death of Smith's wife, Anne Witherspoon Smith, John Pintard wrote that although the death was "a privation to the good man, still under existing circumstances it must be a consolation that his friend and partner is better provided for than by outliving him to have fallen a pensioner on the charity of Princeton College, or to have become burthensome on their children."[80] This quote suggests that Samuel Stanhope had little to leave his wife, much less to his grandchild Theodosia Prevost. A similar conclusion may be drawn from Pintard's reference to the generosity of the college in providing an additional quarter of salary to Smith's surviving family members and allowing use of the college-granted house until two of Smith's adult daughters could find other accommodations.[81]

Though looking at the movements and actions of her family members provides some sense of the early life of Theodosia Prevost from the time of her birth until her involvement in James Collins Johnson's case, very little is known directly of her. Theodosia Prevost apparently settled in her own household in Princeton sometime between 1830 and 1840.[82] One hint of the life that Theodosia Prevost may have led is seen in a letter written by Princeton professor Joseph Henry. On April 11, 1833, he wrote a letter to his wife, Harriet Henry, describing a trip to and from New York City. Theodosia Prevost accompanied him.[83] Henry described her as "very sociable" and referred to the large Greek revival house she owned in Princeton that was then known as the Parthenon.[84] Prevost had bought the house lot from a local builder, John Pattison, for $200 on September 24, 1832.[85] It is not clear whether Prevost herself or others named the house. It might have been Prevost; the name may have been her tribute to her status as an unmarried woman without immediate family encumbrances. "Parthenon" in Greek refers to either unmarried women's apartments or a place where virgin, unmarried women dwell.[86] This described Prevost, at least in that she was apparently never formally married. Prevost lived at one time with a companion. This may have been the Eleanor Prevost, whom, census records show, she lived with later in her life.[87] It might also have been Helen Hughes, whom Prevost described as a "trusty friend" and to whom she left some of her property after her death.

Prevost's Parthenon was located in the Jugtown section of Princeton at what is now 302 Nassau Street, Princeton.[88] The house was described as one of the grandest in town.[89] It originally featured an imposing six-pillared portico.[90] Prevost sold the Parthenon and its surrounding grounds to Alexander M. Cumming for $3,500 on July 27, 1836.[91] She also apparently built and lived in a house at what is now 7–8 Evelyn Place in Princeton. In Prevost's time and for several decades thereafter the house was known as the Red House. Prevost likely lived in the Red House in 1843 at the time of Johnson's trial.[92]

Contemporary photo of the Parthenon, home of Theodosia Ann Mary Prevost, 302 Nassau Street, Princeton, New Jersey. (Photo credit: Adrian Colarusso.)

It is not clear when or why Theodosia Prevost left Princeton. She was likely there as late as 1849; there is a house marked "Miss Prevost" in the area where her house was known to be on an 1849 map of Mercer County, New Jersey.[93] Prevost likely departed sometime in the early to middle 1850s, judging from letters she wrote to John Maclean Jr. while he served as president of the College of New Jersey.[94] The letters are among Maclean's correspondence for the period 1852–1855. These letters are the only examples, other than her last will and testament, of Prevost's voice in direct communications to others. In one letter Theodosia Prevost gave Maclean an introduction to a Mr. Dellenbusch, whom she described as a "friend" who was "much respected among her friends in Jersey City," and noted that she had become acquainted with Dellenbusch through these friends.[95] In the letter Prevost said that she relied on Maclean's "goodness and friendship" to give attention to Dellenbusch.[96] Dellenbusch was apparently the leader of a vocational training school.[97]

In a letter to Maclean dated November 24, 1855, Theodosia Prevost wrote that her brother had taken a Mr. McCord to "the city" (presumably New York) to retrieve her brother's eldest sons. Prevost added that she had been entrusted with her brother's two youngest sons, aged six and seven, for at least the upcoming winter.[98] Prevost was referring to her brother Samuel Stanhope Prevost, the only one of her two brothers to marry and have children, and the only one still alive in 1855.[99] Prevost asked Maclean if he knew of someone who could teach her brother's children for four hours per day, offering to pay an instructor on the basis of a salary of $200 per year.[100] Prevost also stated that she would not like to engage such a person beyond winter, as her brother might remove the children thereafter. She added that there was a possibility that her brother might leave the youngest child with her, and she asked Maclean to answer her letter quickly, since Prevost did not like "to take anyone into [her] house who is unknown to a friend."[101]

These letters suggest that Theodosia Prevost had an influential and close relationship with Maclean. The 1822 letter from Stanhope Prevost to Maclean supports this interpretation, as that earlier letter indicates a broader familial link between the Macleans and the Prevosts. Maclean was a contemporary of Theodosia and her siblings. The Prevost brothers had ample opportunity to form a relationship with Maclean in young adulthood; Maclean was just two years behind them during their studies at Princeton. This apparent closeness between Theodosia Prevost and Maclean may suggest that Prevost's involvement in Johnson's redemption was part of the college's involvement in Johnson's redemption.

Theodosia Prevost never married. She is shown in the 1860 census as a fifty-nine-year-old living in Hackensack (which was at that time known as New Barbadoes Township), New Jersey. It is not clear when Prevost bought the house in which she lived, but the 1860 census indicated that her real property was worth $15,000.[102] Prevost is shown in residence with someone named Eleanor Prevost, a fifty-five-year-old whose relationship to Prevost is not shown. The census taker listed the occupations of both Theodosia and Eleanor as "lady."[103] It is possible that Eleanor was a relative. There were a number of Prevost kinfolk in the region; Eleanor could have been a cousin.

In December 1861 Prevost made a will naming her "trusty friend" Helen Hughes as co-executor.[104] Prevost also named another friend as co-executor, James N. Platt.[105] While Prevost gave Hughes the use and occupancy of her house and farm or anyplace where she might live at the time of her death, Prevost willed the rest of her estate to her brother Stanhope Prevost of Lima, Peru.[106] Stanhope Prevost was likely chosen in light of the fact that her only other living sibling besides Stanhope at the time, Frances Caroline Prevost Breckinridge, had adult children and was apparently already well situated with her husband in Kentucky.[107] In contrast, Stanhope Prevost had married relatively late in life and had several young children in Peru for whom to provide.[108]

Why Did Prevost Act, and Did She Act Alone?

Perhaps one of the largest puzzles about Theodosia Prevost is why she was involved in the redemption of Johnson. It is, of course, possible that she simply wanted to help, and that though her family had owned enslaved people in her youth, she had also seen and may have been more strongly persuaded by examples of abolitionism. Prevost's reason for interceding may not have been tied to any antislavery fervor at all; she may simply have become acquainted with Johnson and, seeing him in need, decided to help. Both the college and the town of Princeton were relatively small in 1843; Prevost might easily have met Johnson in some prior dealing. Another clue may lie in the fact that one of Prevost's nephews, the son of Prevost's sister Frances Caroline Prevost Breckinridge, John Bartow Breckinridge, born in Kentucky in 1826, was a member of the undergraduate class of 1843.[109] Breckinridge was a senior at the college when Johnson was arrested and lived with Prevost in the academic year 1842–1843.[110] John Bartow Breckinridge likely knew Johnson from campus and may have told his aunt about Johnson's case, or even made her acquainted with him.

Even given these possible reasons for Prevost's involvement in Johnson's case, it is striking that at a male-only institution filled with sons of some of the most powerful men in nineteenth-century America, many of whom claimed sympathy for Johnson's plight, a woman was chiefly responsible for securing Johnson's release. Many scholars have suggested that white women were rarely engaged in the busisness of buying, selling, and hiring enslaved people.[111] The "nasty and unseemly business" of transacting for human beings was considered by some people behavior that was ill-suited to white women.[112] It is perhaps for this reason that while some of the accounts of Johnson's release give Prevost the entire credit for arranging the purchase, other accounts suggest that a man named Thomas Lavender "aided and facilitated" the purchase of Johnson's liberty.[113]

Thomas Lavender was a Quaker who lived at a plantation at the northeast of Princeton called Castle Howard.[114] Born in about 1789 in Hastings, England, into a Roman Catholic family, Lavender was orphaned at an early age and eventually taken into the care of a wealthy American sea captain, Joseph King.[115] King was a Quaker who had opposed slavery, although his farm in Queens, New York, had employed slave labor when his father-in-law, Charles Doughty, owned it. Doughty, also a Quaker, later became a leader in opposing slavery.[116] King was said to have employed some fugitive slaves at the farm during his ownership. With the help of King, Lavender eventually became captain of a ship, and through trade with China he became a wealthy merchant.

At age forty-five, Lavender retired from sailing and purchased a large farm in Princeton in 1839.[117] Lavender had a widespread reputation for philanthropy.[118] He was also closely associated with antislavery activism chiefly related to his association with Princeton-area Quakers. Though never formally admitted to Quaker membership, Lavender is said to have been among the last Quakers to worship at the Stony Brook Friends meeting place in Princeton.[119] Lavender served in many civic capacities in Princeton. He was, for instance, a New Jersey state commissioner for the development of a house of refuge.[120] Lavender also served as one of the first officers of the Princeton Mutual Fire Insurance in 1856.[121] Lavender was, in many instances, the proverbial and ever ready friend in need of many persons. Of him it was said: "The young, the destitute and the struggling, in whatever rank or profession, has strong claims on his sympathy; with his purse and voice he was ever ready to cheer and encourage them."[122] Lavender died on January 16, 1869.[123]

Theodosia Prevost's life in some ways paralleled that of Thomas Lavender. Though not engaged in some of the very public, official charitable pursuits that filled Lavender's time, Prevost apparently led a life of quiet yet equally focused philanthropy. Ironically, because Prevost was an unmarried, mature woman, she was freed from some of the constraints that might have faced a man who chose to act in Johnson's favor. Though a member of the community in high standing, she was not engaged in business or any other endeavor that depended on the goodwill of the community. She could, therefore, disregard any opposition by proslavery voices in the town or at the college. Prevost's act was popularly depicted as the kind act of a benevolent woman of independent wealth. However, Prevost's payment on Johnson's behalf, whether or not it had initially been intended as a gift, was not a gift. Many popular accounts indicate that Johnson painstakingly repaid the funds over several years. While these stories hail Johnson's thrift and virtue on this score, Theodosia Prevost's generosity in providing the money stand out as the crucial detail in Johnson's rescue.

Johnson's Repayment to Prevost

Many accounts of Johnson's story noted that he repaid his benefactor Prevost. According to some of these accounts, especially those most contemporaneous with the incident, Johnson was required to repay the funds and/or to serve Prevost as compensation for her payment on his behalf. It is not clear where the claim that Johnson was compelled to repay Prevost originated. The most likely source of the claim is Philip Wallis, Johnson's enslaver. Wallis asserted, in a bitter letter penned shortly after the trial, that Johnson was made to "serve" Prevost in order to pay her back. Wallis indicated that the term of service was for five years, and at the rate of $100 per year.[124] This would seem a direct contradiction to the most typical story told about Johnson, which is that he repaid Prevost only out of a sense of integrity and gratitude. This claim of compulsory repayment was repeated in other news accounts. One newspaper account noted: "The negro agreed to serve the lady five years, at the rate of $100 a year, in consideration of the five-hundred dollars she advanced him."[125] Other papers of the period carried similarly worded stories of the requirement of repayment.[126]

Because Philip Wallis was an enslaver bereft of his slave, he may have been particularly angry at Johnson's avoidance of slavery. Whether he had actual knowledge of such a forced repayment scheme, Wallis might easily have imagined that Prevost could only have helped Johnson under circumstances that involved Johnson's ongoing servitude or debt to his benefactor. However, the truth of Johnson's repayment may have been somewhere in between compulsory repayment and a gratitude-inspired, noncompulsory action. In describing Johnson's future repayment of the sum advanced by Prevost, the physicist Joseph Henry noted in a letter to his wife, Harriet Alexander Henry, that Prevost had given Johnson "a liberal *opportunity* offer of working out his time. Such is the rumor of the day."[127] It is not clear what Henry was trying to signal with this emphasis on the word *opportunity*. The fact that Henry mentioned the incident in his letter to his wife, Harriet, who was away with one of their children visiting relatives, suggests that the matter was of broad community interest. Henry indicated that his information has come from "rumor." The nature of the mention also suggests that the matter is one well within the knowledge of the Henrys and of ongoing interest to them: Joseph Henry says that "Miss Prevost has purchased 'the black slave'" in one communication to his wife without giving a lengthy description of either Prevost or Johnson.[128] The fact that Henry mentioned the outcome of Johnson's trial and Prevost's rescue in his letters to his wife most likely indicates how critical an event Johnson's trial and rescue was in the town and on the campus rather than any personal interest that Henry had in Johnson or black liberation. Though he was apparently not in favor of slavery, neither was Joseph Henry a supporter of black equality.[129] Henry decried the violence wrought by the Civil War but believed that servitude was the proper position of blacks.[130]

It is possible that Johnson was required to repay or felt obliged to repay the funds advanced because of the way Prevost obtained them. One article published in a Baltimore paper around the time of Johnson's redemption said this: "We learn that a female, that was much interested in [Johnson's] welfare, mortgaged some property and raised the sum of $550, which she paid to the claimant for his release."[131] Indeed, if Johnson was compelled to repay the funds, either by an actual threat of return to slavery or by immense social pressure, this could have been the genesis of a comment that was attributed to Johnson in his later life. In one of the most detailed interviews of Johnson, he evidenced bitterness when complaining about a white Civil War veteran who had been given a campus vending permit, hence invading into Johnson's fiefdom. When he was told that his anger was misplaced and that the white veteran had fought for Johnson's freedom, Johnson stated: "I never got no free papers. Princeton College bought me; Princeton College owns me; and Princeton College has got to give me my living."[132]

This moving quote points up a central but unacknowledged fact about Johnson's redemption from slavery: it was much less of a clear victory than most accounts suggest. In New Jersey, as in other ostensibly free northern states, both social and legal norms worked hand in hand to govern day-to-day conditions for blacks. As one commentator wrote when describing Pennsylvania before the Civil War, even if the courts did not "sustain the exclusion of the negro from legal rights, public opinion and individual rights were able to put beyond his reach many of the privileges in which he might have shared."[133] This was nowhere more true than in New Jersey in the 1830s and 1840s. While Johnson's arrival in New Jersey offered the promise of freedom, it was a promise that was circumscribed by a social and legal history of enslavement that in many ways belied New Jersey's label as a free state.

Both the town of Princeton and the college were particular strongholds of pro-slavery feeling in a state that was greatly divided on the issue. Johnson's arrest and fugitive slave trial are reminders of this fracture. Al-

though Johnson's life in New Jersey in the two decades after his redemption and before the Emancipation Proclamation offered much greater
possibilities than his enslavement in Maryland would have, his life following redemption from slavery remained riddled with uncertainty and
limitations as he lived among a community of whites who had mixed
opinions on slavery and on the rights of blacks. In this fraught and tense
political and social environment, Johnson's unclear legal status left him
vulnerable and circumscribed the choices he could make. Although Johnson remained in Princeton in the decades after his fugitive slave trial and
made a life that was likely better than what he would have faced as an
enslaved person in Maryland, the seemingly happy portrait of his abiding
presence may have had somber undertones. It is unlikely that he could
have left Princeton, for example, because he had no papers documenting
his status as a free man. Still, an ambiguous and circumscribed rescue was
better than no rescue at all.

6

Johnson's Princeton Life after the Trial

The business of janitor and boot-black
had not proved particularly lucrative, and
now that his second wife (whom he had
married in 1852) demanded more luxurious
apartments than he was able to furnish, Jim
established his famous second-hand clothing
store on the spot since desecrated by the
erection of University Hall.

—*Andrew C. Imbrie, from his 1895 interview*
with James Collins Johnson

Once James Collins Johnson was released after his fugitive slave trial
in 1843, his life resumed a more steady pace. Johnson continued his
work as a college servant during this period; at least one source shows him
listed among persons paid for doing student laundry.[1] The next decades
of his life, however, were not without challenges. These difficulties were
due in part to a persistent racial gulf between blacks and whites on the
Princeton campus and in the town community. Johnson, however, often
bridged this gap by carrying on a dynamic, seemingly carefree public life
that hid a quieter and more purposive private life.

It is not surprising that there were strained racial relations between
town and gown in the years after Johnson's trial. While life in the antebellum North was often markedly better for blacks than life in the southern states, many racial problems persisted for blacks even in the North.
It was true that blacks who migrated to the North often enjoyed greater
economic freedom than they had experienced in the antebellum South.
The crucial fact of being a wage-earning campus worker rather than an
enslaved person made manifest the amelioration in Johnson's position.
However, this clearly improved economic status did not necessarily herald
substantially better social conditions for Johnson.

While there had been much popular support on campus and beyond for freeing Johnson during his trial, this did not mean that Johnson and other blacks in Princeton enjoyed a life free of all the limitations of bondage. Many of those who rallied to free Johnson were themselves slaveholding Princeton students or town residents who opposed the full and equal participation of blacks in civic and social life. For a large number of northern whites, including many of those on the Princeton campus and in the town of Princeton, blacks were barely tolerated, often disdained, and largely invisible outside their roles as servants. For the most part, in the antebellum period free blacks in rural and suburban New Jersey served whites as common laborers or in domestic capacities, though many blacks managed to supplement their jobs with some amount of private enterprise. In the years immediately after his fugitive slave trial in 1843, Johnson followed this path of merging domestic service with entrepreneurial endeavors, continuing to work as a servant at Princeton while working on his own account. But Johnson's work at the college was for many years all-consuming and demeaning.

Given his narrow escape from slavery, Johnson was likely grateful for his job as a campus servant. It was not an easy job, however. During most of the years of Johnson's employment at Princeton, students were not allowed to keep personal servants (the word *slave* was never employed in campus rule compilations) on campus.[2] This proscription ostensibly included slaves.[3] Many students therefore relied on Johnson and other servants the college employed for their personal needs. Each college building typically had only one servant to attend to all the rooms and to the students in those rooms.[4] Johnson and the other servants cleaned rooms and outer hallways, helped maintain and organize students' belongings, delivered and retrieved clothing from town laundry services (or cleaned laundry themselves for an additional fee), obtained fuel for lamps,[5] and fetched wood for fireplaces and woodstoves. Servicing woodstoves was an onerous task for servants such as Johnson, as the pipe connecting the stove to the chimney often filled with smoke or became disconnected, leaving the floors covered in soot.[6] Soot was an especially chronic problem in the rooms in Nassau Hall, where Johnson worked.[7]

Students sometimes complained that servants did shoddy or abbreviated work. Some students even claimed that in order to ensure that their beds were made or their floors swept, they needed to muss their covers or dirty their floors.[8] However, if servants were inattentive to some of their assigned tasks, it may have been due to the sheer volume of the work. Each servant's workday typically lasted well into the evening, as students often kept late hours, and their rooms required heating for much of the day. And servants' days began very early, since in the morning each building servant was required fill the water pitchers students had placed outside their doors.[9] Students also left their shoes outside their doors for cleaning.[10] Once water pitchers had been filled and shoes cleaned, each servant would walk into the entry of the dormitory for which he was responsible, blowing a horn to wake students for morning prayers by 7 a.m.

Although white and black servants often shared some of the same duties, cleaning and polishing shoes was left to black servants such as James Collins Johnson. As one student noted, referring to Johnson and other black servants at the college, "The blacking department is entrusted to darkies, who black every morning the boots and shoes which are put in the entries at the risk of the owner."[11] One of the most disagreeable duties that befell servants was the emptying of chamber pots. The Princeton campus featured no indoor plumbing in the 1840s and for many decades thereafter. Thus servants such as Johnson had to empty chamber pots into nearby wooden outhouses, or "back campus buildings," as they were euphemistically called.[12]

These wooden outhouses were frequently burned down, blown up, vandalized, and otherwise ravaged by the students, making heavy work for the servants in addition to their regular daily tasks.[13] Servants on the Princeton campus carried night soil buckets to outhouses long after a large, multistalled latrine, nicknamed "cloaca maximus" (after a Roman sewer system), was installed between the Whig and Clio buildings on campus in 1861. From this unpleasant work Johnson is said to have obtained the nickname "Jim Stink" or "James Odoriferous" not long after his arrival.[14] Some stories say that Johnson was so named because of an 1879 incident in which he was paid to retrieve a gold watch from a Nassau Hall privy.[15] However, references to Johnson diving into privies or other waste water to retrieve student belongings were made as early as the 1850s.[16] There is some suggestion that Johnson chose work in the latrines rather than being compelled to undertake the work and that Johnson's willingness to do any task accounted for some of his popularity.[17] If this was Johnson's attitude, it was an attitude also demonstrated by scores of blacks even decades after Johnson reached the North. As W. E. B. Du Bois explored in his 1899 book *The Philadelphia Negro*, even near the end of the nineteenth century, many northern white employers believed that black workers were "more willing and obliging" than white servants.[18] However, Johnson's options were likely constrained by his hesitancy to offend patrons. His willingness to do unpleasant work may have been shaped by a context where frequently the only jobs available were those that white workmen disdained.[19] Northern blacks like Johnson were often able to make a living only by performing these disagreeable tasks.[20]

Johnson's derisive nickname, while cruel, was emblematic of Princeton students' treatment of those in their midst whom they deemed social inferiors, and this included both blacks and whites. However, cruelty to subordinate whites was considered bad form for gentlemen.[21] As one student in the class of 1852 noted about white servants, "Some of the boys cuff them [Irish servants] about a little, but this is entirely beneath gentlemen, and argues too little of self-respect and good breeding to be prevalent even to a limited extent."[22] Judging from some of the types of abuse recorded against blacks on and near the Princeton campus in the antebellum period, there seem to have been fewer social prohibitions against causing them harm.

Incidents of abuse of black residents in the town of Princeton were apparently not infrequent. Indeed, in the late antebellum period of the 1840s and 1850s and in the period shortly before the Civil War, Johnson faced almost as much adversity as he had when he was a fugitive slave. Although Johnson and other formerly enslaved persons who had escaped to the North were ostensibly free people, they still faced the challenge of claiming economic, legal, and political rights, not to mention social rights. During the period leading up to the Civil War and shortly afterward, whites in both the North and the South became increasingly uneasy about the social changes that freedom for former slaves would bring.[23] Blacks and whites remained separated both before and after the Civil War. In the years before the war, blacks and whites in many communities lived in relative proximity.[24] After the war, residential segregation became the norm.[25] When workplaces such as Princeton chose to hire both blacks and whites, they carefully separated the races in ways that maintained existing racial hierarchies. Although blacks and whites sometimes performed the same duties at Princeton and at other workplaces, employers were careful to preserve racial distinctions that placed blacks at the bottom. Even so, blacks in northern communities sometimes suffered threats of violence in connection with their work, especially as growing numbers of white immigrant workers competed with them for jobs on canals and railroads and in other industries.[26] Violence also sometimes erupted when whites confronted blacks who worked on shared job sites or who were otherwise perceived as threats to white immigrant success.[27]

In addition to threatened and actual white violence related to work, blacks in New Jersey often suffered near penury as a result of almost slave-like systems of employment in the period immediately before the Civil War. Some of Johnson's black New Jersey contemporaries did not have access to wage-paying labor. In some cases, they were paid in food, shelter, or clothing instead of cash. An 1853 *New York Daily Times* article described the conditions of blacks in the Ramapo Valley of northwestern New Jersey, noting that they were paid in food and clothing so they could not use cash to purchase alcohol.[28] "They are free; can come and go when they please, but they do not often receive wages," stated the article.[29] The writer, seemingly a slavery sympathizer, added gratuitously that the blacks of the Ramapo Valley were ignorant, licentious, and neglectful of their children.[30] Even decades after the Civil War and the passage of the Thirteenth Amendment, there were sporadic complaints of slavery-like conditions for black workers in New Jersey.[31]

Amid these harsh economic conditions and disquieting social relations between blacks and whites, Johnson and other members of the Princeton black community struggled to survive in Princeton. Johnson, not unlike many other blacks in town, addressed these difficulties with efforts launched from two distinct strands of his life, one private and the other public.

Johnson's Private Life

Documents suggest that it was not until sometime after his arrival in Princeton that James Collins began calling himself James Collins Johnson. In the 1850 census, there is no James Johnson in Princeton, only a James Collins, a black man from Maryland born around 1819 who lived with a woman named Phillis and a child, Thomas Collins, born around 1843, both of whom were also born in Maryland.[32] This is likely the entry for James Collins Johnson, his wife, and his son. It indicates that Johnson may have traveled back to Maryland between 1839 and the date of his fugitive slave trial in order for Phillis to become pregnant and give birth to the couple's child in Maryland. Or Phillis may have joined Johnson in Princeton before the trial and traveled back to Maryland for the birth. It is also possible that Thomas was not Johnson's biological child and that he claimed the child as his own. Although Johnson made a brief reference to his first wife in his 1895 interview with Andrew C. Imbrie, noting his marriage to her and her death, Johnson does not give precise dates for either of those events, and he never mentioned how or when Phillis traveled to join him in New Jersey. It is not surprising that in the limited published materials about Johnson, little is presented about Phillis and other women in his life. Patriarchal norms of the era tended to keep women and minor children outside public accounts; this was true for black women as well as white.[33] Hence, much of what is known about Phillis and other Johnson family members must be gleaned from other sources.

If the 1850 entry for James Collins is for James Collins Johnson, it is not clear why he would have given his name as Collins. On the one hand, in 1850, his fugitive trial was well over, and ostensibly he would have been safe using the name Collins once again. On the other hand, he had come to be known as James Collins Johnson in the town of Princeton and at the college. Perhaps he gave the Collins name because of the official nature of the census. Perhaps he did so to obscure or forget his former status as a slave.

Thomas Collins seems to disappear from official records after the 1850 census. One possibility is that he died young. Although precise data on child mortality in the United States are not available until around 1900, it is likely that children died in the middle 1800s at much the same rate, if not at a higher rate, than children in 1900 and thereafter.[34] In 1900 almost one out of five children died before the age of five; rates were likely the same or higher in earlier decades because of the absence of widespread sanitary practices and inadequate nutrition.[35] The rate of child mortality was substantially higher for blacks in the late nineteenth century, especially for urban blacks.[36] Thomas Collins might also have been sent to live with relatives in Maryland, especially given the early death of his mother. The name Thomas Collins appears in several instances in the Maryland census; for instance, an entry for a black Thomas Collins of the same approximate age appears in the 1870 Maryland census. This Thomas was living in Dorchester County, Maryland, a short distance from Easton, Maryland, which James Collins Johnson claimed as his birthplace.[37] Although it would seem unlikely that Johnson would send his son back to Maryland, a slave state from which he had fled, his need to find a caretaker for his son might have outweighed this concern, especially given that Thomas's mother, Phillis, was apparently free, thus likely giving Thomas free status under then-extant laws.

Johnson's first wife, Phillis, likely died on July 17, 1852, and was buried in Princeton.[38] Johnson married his second wife, Catherine McCrea, on December 23, 1852.[39] Johnson and his bride, listed as widower and widow, were married by a Reverend Duffield.[40] This was probably John Thomas

Duffield, a member of the Princeton faculty during this time.[41] Duffield graduated Princeton in 1841, so it is likely that he was acquainted with Johnson during Johnson's earliest years on campus.

The census of 1860 recorded that a woman named Catherine and a child named Emily were living with Johnson, and all were designated by the surname Johnson. Emily was born around 1853.[42] Emily is listed as attending school in the 1860 census. It is possible that she was educated in the town of Princeton, as there had been some education for blacks there since the 1830s.[43] Ten years later, the 1870 census records that James Collins Johnson was living with Catherine Johnson and a seventeen-year-old named Emily Sorter.[44] Sorter is presumably the Emily Johnson seen in the Johnsons' household in 1860, drawing inferences from the common first name and the residence of the Emilies. If Emily Sorter is Emily Johnson, she may have married between the 1860 and 1870 census; teenage marriage was quite common in this period.[45] Emily's last name, Sorter, or Sortor, as it was spelled by many area blacks, was one that was prominent in the Princeton black community.[46] A review of census records shows that there was one young man, Malon Sorter, a mulatto born in 1849, living in the area when both Emily and Malon were small children.[47] He might later have been Emily's husband. However, Malon does not appear in the 1870 census.

Although Emily was still living in the household with James Collins Johnson and Catherine Johnson in 1870, she was no longer attending school. This is not surprising. At seventeen years old, Emily was of an age when some students would have been in high school or undergoing vocational training during the nineteenth and early twentieth centuries. However, high school attendance in the late nineteenth century was not common.[48] Adding to the difficulties, there was no high school training for blacks in Princeton through the late 1800s. Even near the beginning of the twentieth century, Princeton blacks seeking formal education beyond common (lower) school were largely limited to three choices: they could attend a normal school, they could go to Trenton to attend the public high school in that town, or they could seek private tutoring.[49] Moreover, if Emily had married as a teenager, this likely would have triggered the end of her school career, as early marriage was for decades viewed as an alternative to additional schooling for many young women.[50]

Emily Johnson Sorter, like Thomas Collins and Malon Sorter, seems to disappear from census records after 1880. She may have died young. A substantial alternative possibility is that Emily Johnson Sorter remarried, again changing her surname. Census records leave a trail suggesting that this was the case. In the 1880 census, a Princeton resident black woman named Emily Gordon is age twenty-seven and thus was born around 1853, the year Emily Johnson was likely born. The birthplace of the mother of Emily Gordon is noted as New Jersey; the birthplace of her father is indicated as Maryland. Emily Gordon was living with a husband named William S. Gordon and a boarder named Alexander Sorter. Sorter was likely the surname of Emily Johnson's first husband, suggesting that Alexander Sorter may have been a relative of her former spouse. Emily and William had two children in 1880: Walter, born in 1878, and Sarah, born in 1879.[51] Emily and William also appear to have had one other child. An Emily W. Sortor Gordon born in New Jersey is shown as the mother of a son born in Washington, D.C., on June 4, 1887.[52] The father of the child was William S. Gordon, also born in New Jersey.[53]

William S. Gordon, who was born around 1843 in Princeton, was a sailor during the Civil War.[54] William's first wife was likely a woman named Annie, also born around 1843.[55] William appears to have been a man of some standing in the Princeton black community; he may have been a member of a family of Gordons who were described by one writer as "a large and influential family."[56] Upon his return from the Civil War, he was apparently one of a group of black men who sought greater political power for blacks in Princeton.[57] William's heightened social standing may have been part of what allowed William and Emily to relocate to Washington, D.C., where William worked as a clerk. Records show that William S. Gordon, a married Washington, D.C., clerk born in New Jersey, died on August 16, 1891, and was buried in Princeton, New Jersey.[58] On September 7, 1891, a widow's claim was filed under William S. Gordon's Civil War pension.[59] A widowed woman named Emily W. Gordon died August 9, 1895, in Princeton, New Jersey.[60] It appears that one or more of William Gordon's children filed a claim under William's pension after the death of Emily.[61] The U.S. government awarded pensions to Union veterans of the Civil War, and to their widows, minor children, and dependent fathers and mothers.[62] These details all tend to suggest that Emily Johnson became Emily Sorter and then Emily Gordon.

Emily's mother, Catherine McCrea Johnson, died on June 22, 1880, in Princeton.[63] Her death certificate, signed by Dr. A. K. Macdonald, indicates that she died of cardiac dropsy.[64] A. K. Macdonald was likely Arthur Kendrick Macdonald, a prominent Princeton physician.[65] Macdonald had begun private practice in Princeton in December 1877, just a few years before Catherine Johnson died.[66] He apparently had close ties to prominent figures during his career. For example, he was the personal physician

of former president Grover Cleveland during Cleveland's residence in
Princeton, and he served as medical supervisor for athletics at the College of New Jersey.[67] Given Johnson's unofficial role as college mascot,
Macdonald almost certainly knew him through his role as physician to
Princeton's athletic teams. It is not clear whether Macdonald served as
a regular physician for Catherine Johnson or her husband. He was likely
one of few physicians in Princeton during this period.[68] Catherine Johnson was ill for at least a few weeks before her death, as the 1880 census
record, which was made on June 6, 1880, noted that she was suffering
from dropsy, a nineteenth-century term for edema.[69]

Another major change in Johnson's post-trial life was his purchase of
a home in 1851. Johnson bought the house at what is now 32 Witherspoon Street at auction from the estate of Joseph Scott for $187.[70] It is not
clear how Johnson raised the funds for the purchase. According to several
accounts, Johnson spent the years immediately after his fugitive slave trial
repaying the money that Theodosia Prevost had advanced to pay Johnson's owner. How difficult this schedule of payment might have been is
related to Johnson's wages and to other expenses he might have faced.

Johnson is described as a laborer, as are most of the black male residents of Princeton who appear in the 1850 census.[71] In the early 1850s
Johnson apparently still worked as a campus servant. Although a number
of enrollment brochures for the period from 1840 to 1850 indicate that
students generally paid the college from two to three dollars per academic
year for servants, it is not clear what the college paid the servants. It is
possible to speculate based on wages of the day: in 1840 a general laborer
in a large brewery in New York received 62 cents per day, while skilled
workers such as carpenters earned over one dollar per day.[72] However,
blacks often earned lower than average wages for whites. Another factor
that complicates estimates of Johnson's income is the fact that workers in
service industries may have earned tips. Johnson was the frequent recipient of gratuities, some of which were perhaps given because of his role
as campus mascot and good fellow. In one account, for example, Johnson
is described as currying favor with graduates to induce them to "come
down" with a quarter.[73] The price of student largesse at times involved
subjecting himself to mockery.

Johnson provided meals for students, such as the oyster suppers recalled
fondly by one former student. He sometimes accepted not only cash but
also used clothes to be sold in his shop, and as one former student wrote,
"Many a good pair of trousers has passed into his shop to square an
account for a feast already eaten."[74] Johnson also purchased furniture from

departing students and resold it to new students.[75] One account from the 1850s describes a student bargaining with Johnson for the purchase of a table.[76] Campus servants apparently sold the furniture students left behind as a way of supplementing their incomes. Johnson also extended credit for the purchase of some of his wares and made loans to students.[77] Some of Johnson's loans to students were at what one student described as "enormous interest rates."[78]

Still, even assuming that Johnson sold used items, received a wage of as much as one dollar per day (which was on the high side), and obtained gratuities and proceeds from loans to students, it might have been difficult for him to amass the capital needed to repay Theodosia Prevost for the money she had advanced to his slave owner, pay his day-to-day expenses, and at the same time save the money needed to buy a house outright. It is possible that Johnson might have received bonus work pay or extra assignments from the college in order to save some of the money he needed to buy a house. There are, for instance, receipts from James Collins Johnson for funds the college paid to him for laundry services in the 1840s where he is among the highest payees.[79] In other cases the receipts from the college do not specify what the money was for or what period of time they covered. These sums ranged from five dollars to fifty dollars. In one case, for example, five dollars was paid to Johnson "on account."[80] Some of Johnson's financial footing may have been because Johnson may have been a particular favorite of college officials. In one instance, on December 19, 1852, Johnson received fifty dollars from Princeton "for services rendered."[81] This was just a few days before his marriage to Catherine McCrea on December 23, 1852.[82] It is conceivable that this money, a relatively large sum that would seem to be well beyond wages of that period, was provided to help pay for the nuptials.

Given Johnson's financial relationship to the college, it is also possible to surmise that the college was involved in Johnson's land purchase. One clue may be the fact that Johnson's lot was immediately adjacent to the home of James Carnahan, then the president of the college. Moreover, the original recorded deed to Johnson's lot is contained in the files of Princeton University in a folder labeled "College Lands."[83] Accompanying the deed with a recording date of December 25, 1851, is a pencil sketch of the property showing Johnson's land relative to Carnahan's and another neighbor.[84] The date of December 23, 1851, is written on the sketch along with several calculations of dollar amounts. There is no indication of who made the pencil sketch; perhaps it was Johnson, who then gave the deed and the sketch to the college for safekeeping. Or perhaps a college official was the creator of the sketch and Johnson's home was considered, in some respect, college land.

Johnson was not the only black person in the town of Princeton to own his own home, to be immersed in the community, or to have a satisfying family life. There were several others, as entries indicate in an 1855 diary belonging to Ann Maria Davison, a white antislavery advocate.[85] Some Princeton blacks, she noted, owned their own homes or were in process of buying them. Others rented their homes but had a decent standard of living. Davison was a New Jersey native who had lived in Louisiana for several years.[86] Her abolitionist leanings, and her insistence on teaching black children to read, raised the ire of her white Louisiana neighbors.[87] Besides teaching blacks, Davison also closely studied the living conditions of blacks in Louisiana and in places she visited. When she traveled to Princeton, her curiosity was piqued by the dignified bearing of the blacks she encountered at her hotel:

> I had observed my washerwoman at the Hotel to be respectable in her deportment, neat and clean in her appearance—also the waiter at the Hotel where I was staying, was polite and civil, and altogether a very decent man. I saw a seamstress of much intelligence and propriety of behavior, and in the street one day a group of some five or six colored children, as if just out of school dressed well, deporting themselves as well as white children, with their school bags on their arms, seeming to contain a goodly number of books.[88]

Davison visited the black community in Princeton and interviewed several people, but before doing so, she was discouraged by students at the college and others, as she noted in this entry:

> I have been frequently in Princeton and always remarked the black people that seem'd to cluster around the College; wait in public houses &c—I inquired about the manner of their living—in what way they supported themselves, and what were their character generally? The answers were from Students and such persons as chance through in the way of passing travelers; that they were a poor miserable degraded set of beings, improvident, living from hand to mouth, all congregated together in what they called Negro Town.[89]

Davison persisted nonetheless. On May 26, 1855, before departing for Philadelphia, Davison visited the homes of fourteen black families. What she found apparently surprised her. She first stopped at the home of William Simpson, who sold confections.[90] When she asked him how he made a living selling items with such little value, Simpson told her that he not only owned his home and confectionery but also owned another, better house that he rented out for income.[91]

Davison noted that when she asked for pencil and paper with which to write down Simpson's name and the names of other interviewees, "a very well looking woman," likely Simpson's wife, told her: "I guess Madam you will not go into any of the houses of the colored people that you will not find pen, and ink, or paper and pencil."[92] Although the families she visited exhibited varying degrees of comfort and wealth, all, Davison observed, had pen, pencil, ink, and paper.[93] At the conclusion of her visits, Davison wondered "how it could, truthfully be said, that they were so wretched and destitute."[94] She concluded by writing: "The only satisfactory explanation I could make to myself, was, the comparison I supposed to the white population must be constantly making, between their own spacious Mansions, and the humble homes of the poor black man."[95] It is not clear whether Davison met James Collins Johnson during her time in Princeton, as he is not mentioned by name in her writings. However, she may well have encountered him, as Johnson and William Simpson were neighbors in what Davison called "Negro town," and their 1860 census listings appear in proximity to each other on the same census reporting sheet.[96]

Johnson's own entrepreneurial enterprises expanded greatly when Nassau Hall burned down in 1855. After this event, Johnson obtained a license to work almost full time in a business that he had only previously dabbled in—selling food and used clothing to students.[97] The used clothing business grew out of informal loans that Johnson sometimes made to students. To help encourage repayment, Johnson often requested security in the form of pieces of clothing. In the 1860 census Johnson is listed as working in a clothing store, and this was shown as his main occupation until 1880.[98]

Johnson's move from being a servant to being a vendor represented a substantial life change. He went from being a little-remarked figure in student writings and other publications to being regularly called out in print as a noteworthy part of life in town and on campus. His entrepreneurship placed him among a small but vibrant group of business-minded Princeton blacks that had captured Davison's attention.

Besides changes in his work life, the years after Johnson's trial also yielded changes in his personal life. One source notes that Johnson married four times.[99] However, after the 1880 death of Catherine, records are silent about his marital status until 1895. Johnson married again in 1895,

James Collins Johnson and a young man believed by some to be Archibald Camp-
bell "Spader" Seruby circa 1895. Others suggest that this photo may have been of
Johnson's nephew, Alexander "Ting" Taylor. (Princeton University Mudd Archives,
Historical Photograph Collection, Individuals Series [AC67], Box MP4.)

when he was almost seventy-nine, and his new wife, Anetta Webb War-
den, was apparently in her fifties.[100] The 1900 census record for Anetta
Johnson shows her as having been born about 1851.[101] But tracing Anetta
Johnson back through census records shows that she was likely born
Anetta Webb in Maryland on April 8, 1844.[102] Her parents were Harrison
Holmes Webb Sr. and Ann Webb, who were living in Columbia, Pennsylvania, in 1850. Some sources indicate that Harrison Holmes Webb Sr. was
born in Pennsylvania in 1805, but the 1850 manuscript census lists Maryland as the birthplace of both Harrison and Ann Webb.[103] Ann Webb was
born in 1815.[104] It is not clear whether they were born enslaved or free or
whether they had attained the status of free blacks in Pennsylvania. While

Pennsylvania began gradual emancipation of slavery in 1780, some blacks remained enslaved there until as late as 1847.[105]

The Webbs lived in an independent household in Maryland, a slave state, in 1860, a fact that suggests that the family was free by that time.[106] Harrison H. Webb was granted a license as a reader in the Episcopal Church in 1841 and was ordained as an Episcopal minister in 1854. He became the rector of St. James Church in Baltimore in that year.[107] Webb was lauded as a self-made man who was a "fine scholar" and eminent theologian.[108] By 1860 the Webb family was living in Baltimore.[109] The Reverend Harrison Webb was listed in an 1872 Baltimore city directory as an assistant cashier at the National Freedmen's Savings Bank.[110] Harrison Webb apparently had some wealth at the end of his life; at his death in 1878 he left each of his three children $400 and each of his two grandchildren $100.[111]

The Webbs, or at least some of them, were apparently light-skinned mulattos. Although Harrison H. Webb Sr. and his wife and children were designated mulattos in the 1850 census, Anetta Johnson's brother Harrison H. Webb Jr. and his wife and children are listed as white in the 1880 Baltimore census. Webb Jr. is listed as a music teacher or professor of music in the various census reports.

In the 1870s Anetta was married to Jordan Warden.[112] He likely died sometime between 1880 and 1885. Anetta may have had no children with Jordan, as none are listed in her household in either 1870 or 1880. Although the 1900 census indicates that James Collins Johnson married Anetta in 1881, this is likely an error (or possibly Johnson's mistaken reference to his marriage to an unidentified and unverified third wife). According to an 1885 Baltimore city directory, Anetta was living at 812 Low Street, listed as the widow of Jordan Warden.[113] A dressmaker named Annette Warden was shown living at 812 Low Street in Baltimore as late as 1894.[114] James Waddel Alexander, a brother of Johnson's fugitive trial attorney, William Cowper Alexander, noted that Johnson "was married for the fourth [sic] time in 1895, at the age of seventy-eight, the bride being a resident of Baltimore."[115] A Baltimore Sun article indicates that Johnson was present in Baltimore in August 1895 for the first time since his escape from Maryland in 1839; he may have traveled there for his wedding to Anetta.[116] In marrying so often, and in marrying at all, Johnson was like many other late nineteenth-century blacks who showed a high propensity for formal wedlock, despite having lived under the shadow of slavery and its often brutal aftermath.[117] While Johnson's last marriage likely signaled a high point in his private life, this was also a time of loss: his daughter Emily Johnson Sorter Gordon died on August 9, 1895, possibly while her father was away for his wedding.[118]

Johnson's Public and Campus Life

Much of what was known about the public and campus life of James Collins Johnson and his interactions on campus in the years after his fugitive slave trial comes from students. Many of them saw him as a source of humor and frequently mocked him and framed him as the butt of jokes. Many student and alumni of Princeton spoke of "Jimmy" or "Jim _____" (leaving out the word *stink*) in their school scrapbooks, their letters home, and in recollections offered years after they graduated. Ridicule of Johnson even appeared in campus publications, such as in fictitious dialogues and cartoons published by an off-color student humor journal, the *Nassau Rake*. The *Nassau Rake* made fun of students, faculty, and staff alike, but found particular humor in mocking black staffers and envisioning them in embarrassing associations with students. For instance, in a June 1854 issue, a dialogue imagines Johnson being asked to dive into a latrine for the belongings of a student, with the accompanying cartoon showing a shirtless black man kneeling to well-dressed white men and tendering something, while the white men hold their noses.[119] The cartoon is captioned: "Returns from fishing and presents Gans. with what he has caught."[120] An 1859 *Nassau Rake* article imagines that James Collins Johnson (called "Mr. Stink" in the article) is the partner of a Mr. Dimon, likely a student named David Foster Dimon, class of 1860.[121] The pair are said to be engaged in a used clothing business, which was Johnson's real life work, and they seek to "call the attention of the public generally, and the niggers especially" to their secondhand goods.[122] Another student, Charles William Petrie, class of 1862, is referred to as the mulatto errand boy of Johnson.[123]

It was the practice of some Princeton students to prepare elaborate scrapbooks and essay collections memorializing their time at the college that included mementos of academic life such as exam notices, clippings from campus newspapers, personal notes, signatures, and drawings. Although such recollections were sometimes warm, other times they were derisive, especially when it came to Johnson and his habit of stuttering.[124] There were also joking recollections of cheating Johnson, such as a jest titled "Stahl's Speculation" aimed at Nicholas Frederick Stahl and A. A. Speer, members of the class of 1869:

James Collins Johnson with student Babcock, circa 1892–1893. (Historical Photograph Collection: Individuals series, box AC067.SP001, folder 050.001; Princeton University Archives, Department of Rare Books and Special Collections, Princeton University Library.)

The immaculate Stahl, who always sports a white necktie in the coldest season, achieved the greatest triumph in economy this last winter that Nassau Hall has ever witnessed. Being in Speer's room one day he picked up an old stove-pipe hat and asked Speer why he didn't wear it. O, says he, I've just sold it to Jim Stink, for ten cents. "Thunder!" says he. "I'd have given you fifteen for it." Speer, with his usual avarice, immediately closed with him, having no more manliness than to cheat a negro, and Stahl became the happy possessor of a fifteen cent hat.[125]

Another jest that featured parodies of want ads took aim at David John Ross Milligan of Philadelphia, a member of the class of 1871: Wanted—by Milligan—a chance to cheat a poor negro out of $25."[126] An asterisk

Returns from fishing and presents Gans. with what he has caught.

Cartoon from a student journal, *Nassau Rake*, depicting James Collins Johnson as
having dived into a latrine to retrieve a student's belonging.

next to the pretend advertisement noted: "Inquire of Jim Stink about
that coat."[127]

Through it all, Johnson seemed to have maintained an outward ap-
pearance of general affability. This may simply have been examples of his
guileless, open demeanor. However, his sunny good humor may also have
been an ironic subterfuge that Johnson used for pragmatic reasons such as
gaining favor with or pacifying members of the heavily southern student
body. Or he may have sought to obscure his underlying anger or sadness
at the trying circumstances of his day-to-day life. Like countless blacks
before and after him, he may have played the buffoon with steely-eyed
intentionality. Although such behavior has long been described as playful
mimicry carried on by blacks at leisure, closer examination suggests that
such behavior frequently was part of an intentionally deployed ritual. The
seemingly carefree merrymaking of blacks such as Johnson was sometimes part of a broadly shared but hidden process of transgression. Such
transgressive, oppositional black public behavior functioned to obscure
and hence protect the individuality of blacks who were constrained by

dominant white power structures.[128] The need for blacks like Johnson to dissemble regarding their true feelings was especially necessary as sectional tensions grew with the start of the Civil War.

Certainly the key national event in Johnson's lifetime that affected his public standing was the Civil War and the subsequent emancipation of blacks throughout the country. The start of the Civil War brought substantial changes to the college. Because a large number of students were from the South, Princeton forbade public displays of sympathy among the students. Faculty were guarded about sharing their opinions about the war, and the college remained silent on its position on the war at the start of the conflict.[129] This silence did little to quell student tension. Students fought, for example, over the display of the U.S. flag at the start of the Civil War.[130] Most southern students supported the Confederate cause and withdrew from the college as the conflict progressed. And there was a good deal of sympathy regarding secession among the northern students.[131]

One northern student who held publicly pro-Confederate sympathies was seized from his bed by several pro-Union students and doused with water at the college water pump.[132] This led to the suspension of the offending students.[133] John Maclean, who by 1861 was president of the college, articulated the position of the college in a letter to the *Newark Advertiser* that the *New York Times* reprinted. Maclean wrote: "On the one hand, the Faculty will allow of no mobs among the students; and, on the other hand, they will not permit the utterance of sentiments denunciatory of those who are engaged in efforts to maintain the integrity of the National Government; nor will they allow of any public expression of sympathy with those who are endeavoring to destroy that Government."[134] Maclean's letter aroused the ire of some students and townspeople who were concerned about the college's failure to clearly state a pro-Union position.

Although the town of Princeton was largely pro-Union in its sympathies, some of its citizens were Confederate sympathizers. In some cases, citizens who were not expressly pro-Confederate became less supportive of Union goals when draft laws made some whites subject to Union military service. Blacks, who were not deemed citizens, were exempt from the draft. In March 1863 a federal draft law subjected all male U.S. citizens between the ages of twenty and thirty-five and all unmarried men between the ages of thirty-five and forty-five to military duty. Draftees could purchase their way out of the federal army by paying $300 for a substitute. One of the first large-scale drafts in the North began in New

York City on July 11, 1863. It was conducted by a lottery drawing of the names of white working-class men whom local officials had gathered.[135]

This first New York City drawing took place without incident. However, on July 13, 1863, white working-class men gathered at the New York City office of the draft and began what was four days of white-on-black violence. Scores of black men, women, and children died as a result of mob and individual violence.[136] Antiblack rioting spilled over to other towns and cities, including Staten Island and Jersey City, New Jersey.[137] By mid-July 1863 it seemed possible that the draft riots would spread to Princeton. According to one account, some of the Irish workers on a section of the railroad at Penn's Neck, New Jersey, left their work, gathered in Princeton, and threatened violence against Princeton blacks and local white families whom they believed were in favor of the draft.[138] Fearing an assault, town leaders collected muskets stored in a town building and secured them at the College of New Jersey. An observer at the time suggested that large-scale violence was avoided in Princeton for two reasons. First, heavy rain made outdoor gatherings difficult to sustain. Second, and perhaps foremost, a "well-known and courageous colored man" stated that if the Irish began an assault on Princeton blacks, the blacks would in turn set fire to every Irish house in the town.[139] Although is not clear who this "courageous colored man" was, it was likely not James Collins Johnson, given the nature of his work and his need to remain in good stead with the white community. But even if Johnson did not actively lead the black community in such matters, his quieter presence likely helped to steady the volatile climate.

Just as Johnson apparently took a more reserved role in town and gown issues between blacks and whites during the Civil War, he similarly held no active role in the war itself. Although even free blacks were not subject to the draft, about fifty Princeton blacks joined the Union Army. At least four of these men died during their service, including one man, Joe Oncque, who died while bearing the flag in battle.[140] James Collins Johnson was not a member of the military. He was forty-seven years old when other black men from Princeton began joining the Union army in 1863. This would have made him two years older than the maximum age of forty-five for entering the military.[141] It may still have been possible for Johnson to enlist, as recruiters routinely accepted volunteers who were over age or who did not strictly meet other qualifications.[142] However, Johnson may have been reluctant to go to war. By the early 1860s he had come into his own in many ways. He and his second wife, Catherine, were the parents of a daughter, and they owned their own home. He no longer did the onerous work of a campus building servant and instead worked selling used clothes and furniture and foodstuffs. While his work was still no doubt rigorous, he had more independence and control over his working conditions than he likely did at any other time in his life.

In addition to the Civil War, there were other events of note in the 1860s in Princeton that may have affected Johnson. One incident involved one of the most sensational murders in the history of the town. On November 13, 1862, Charles Lewis, an itinerant white confidence man, killed James Rowland, a watchmaker and jeweler who kept a shop on Nassau Street near Witherspoon Street, not far from Johnson's home. On that day, as Rowland headed to his own residence on Witherspoon Street after closing up his shop, Lewis waylaid him and apparently beat him to death, leaving his body in the Princeton Cemetery very near Johnson's Witherspoon Street home. The inquest featured several "colored" witnesses, all residents of the town of Princeton: Peter Lane, Anna Johnson (apparently no relation to James Collins Johnson), Samuel Little, Charles Wycoff, and Moses Cudjo.[143] This incident caused whites and blacks in the town to close ranks against an outside assailant without immediate regard to race. Though it did not eliminate the town's racial barriers, it was a reminder that all members of the small town depended heavily on each other for safety and well-being.

Even a decade after the Civil War, there remained stark social divides between blacks and whites at the college and in the town of Princeton. For one thing, although Harvard graduated a black student in 1870, and Yale did so in 1857, Princeton was among the last of elite colleges to have blacks as undergraduate students.[144] The first known black students to receive an undergraduate degree at Princeton, John Howard and Arthur Jewell Wilson, graduated in 1947.[145] Students at the college during the 1860s and 1870s were at times vociferous about their unwillingness to welcome blacks as fellow students even well after the Civil War. In one incident in 1876, a black student from the Princeton Theological Seminary entered the undergraduate philosophy class of college president James McCosh and took a seat.[146] The incident, described as "a serious crisis," caused the students in the class to stand and leave the room.[147] The incident gave rise to a poem that was published in the *Princetonian* newspaper a short time thereafter:

We repeat the remark,
And our language is squ-ah
That a man which is dark

And has kinks in his hai-ah
Isn't coming to college with "we" "uns"
And "we" "uns" consent to be there.[148]

The attitude of Princeton on the admission of blacks remained fixed even at the dawn of the twentieth century, near the end of Johnson's life, and in the years immediately thereafter. As the sociologist W. E. B. Du Bois noted in a study on the education of blacks, Princeton was one of several eastern colleges that had no black undergraduates.[149] Du Bois quoted a letter written to him by a Princeton administrator:

> *We have never had any colored students here, though there is nothing in the university statutes to prevent their admission.* It is possible, however, in view of our proximity to the South, and the large number of Southern students here, that negro students would find Princeton less comfortable than some other institutions; but I may be wrong in this, as the trial has never been made. There is, as I say, nothing in the laws of the college to prevent their admission.[150]

One interesting exception to Princeton's intolerance of blacks in the classroom at the college was Alexander Dumas Watkins, a black man who served as an instructor in several courses at the college from 1895 until his death in 1903. Watkins's background is somewhat unclear; according to some sources, he was first employed at the college as an assistant to William Libbey, a professor of physical geography.[151] Watkins proved so adept at the work that he was allowed to tutor what one news source described as "the less intelligent students in histology."[152] He eventually became a classroom instructor and served in that capacity for eight years.[153] Before arriving in Princeton, it appears that Watkins worked at Bellevue Hospital in New York, where he was described as a "colored servant" whom Libbey took to Princeton.[154] Watkins apparently showed himself to be highly capable at Bellevue also. One description of Watkins stated that "the colored servant at Bellevue, *Alexander Dumas Watkins*, watched Welch inject so many cadavers that, until officially restrained, he sent off notices to undertakers offering instruction in embalming in the manner of Dr. Welch."[155] Watkins was described by one person as "the brightest negro in Princeton."[156] He remained, nonetheless, a rare exception to what was a policy of racial division on campus.

Black-white relations in and near the town of Princeton remained just as polarized as those on campus, even near the end of Johnson's life. This was seen in April 1887, when twenty-five-year-old Cornelius Van Tilbergh, the white son of a prosperous farmer in nearby Rocky Hill, New Jersey, eloped to Princeton with his twenty-year-old black bride, Lizzie Simmons.[157] Interracial marriage was not illegal in New Jersey at the time; New Jersey is one of three of the thirteen original colonies to never have had an antimiscegenation law.[158] In the years before interracial marriage was sanctioned in the United States, whites sometimes passed as black or allowed inquirers to assume that they were black in order to avoid the legal and social difficulties involved with marrying blacks. Similarly, some light-skinned people of African ancestry passed as white in some towns or at various times in their lives (as some members of the family of Johnson's wife, Anetta Webb, had) in order to live in better neighborhoods or obtain better jobs. Although in Princeton and other New Jersey towns black-white intermarriage was not illegal, interracial couples involved in such marriages often faced severe social sanction.

William Drew Robeson, the father of Paul Robeson, apparently performed the marriage ceremony of Tilbergh and Simmons, though he is referred to as a "colored" minister named "Robinson" in some reports. Robeson was the minister of the Witherspoon Presbyterian Church from 1880 until 1901. The church was located near Johnson's Witherspoon Street house. Some residents of their Rocky Hill community were especially incensed and had threatened to tar and feather Van Tilbergh, but ultimately calm prevailed. In the 1900 federal census, Van Tilbergh, his wife, and all their children are described as black.[159] By 1910 Lizzie had died and Van Tilbergh was once again described as white, although his only child then at home was described as mulatto.[160]

Despite social disapprobation, blacks and whites married and/or produced children together with some frequency in and near Princeton. A substantial number of the persons listed in federal census reports in Princeton in the mid–nineteenth century are described as mulattos. One area near Princeton, Sourland Mountain, much of which is part of what is now Somerset County, New Jersey, was especially noteworthy for the amount of black-white mixing that occurred there.[161] Although contemporary histories of Sourland Mountain and surrounding areas often note the presence of early Native Americans, few describe the mixed-race black-white communities in the region that began in the 1700s. Many of these mixed-race persons owned land and conducted businesses that were handed down for decades.

Some observers decried this racial intermingling and alleged that it began when "promiscuous" black women from the Sourland Mountain area who operated as vendors or as domestic workers in Princeton had sexual relations with white men in the town.[162] Many Sourland Mountain women lived and worked in Princeton.[163] A black resident of Sourland Mountain who was interviewed in the 1880s explained the large number of mixed-race people in the area by stating that Sourland Mountain black women were often impregnated by white men while they worked in Princeton. He suggested that the interactions were not always consensual and that the women's assailants were "white trash." Some of them were Princeton students, he asserted.[164]

Black women were sometimes the butt of Princeton students' salacious jokes and comments. Some sources suggest that Princeton students sometimes went even further and engaged in sexual relationships with area black women. A cartoon published in an 1853 issue of the *Nassau Rake* alludes to such interest among the students. In the cartoon, two white male figures compare the looks of (apparently white) women in Alabama with those in New Jersey, and find New Jersey women lacking. One figure comments, as they look at a dark-skinned woman passing: "But I'll be darned if there ain't some right good looking niggar [*sic*] gals here, ain't they?"[165] Members of Johnson's family were not exempt from such ribaldry. In an 1858 issue of the *Nassau Rake*, an extended joke article envisions the writer as a white man named James McDougal who is "the brother-in-law of Jim Stink," meaning that the man is married to a black woman.[166] The article goes on to end: "Give my love to my wife, and also to that dear child—Who is a father's pet and a mother's joy, a darling little nigger boy."[167]

Another incident that cast a pall over the Princeton campus and town, and fractured relations between blacks and whites near the end of Johnson's life, was the 1895 killing of a Princeton student. In June 1895 John Collins, a young black man from the town of Princeton, killed Frederick Ohl, then a Princeton freshman. Collins was apparently no relation to James Collins Johnson; he was said to have appeared in Princeton in late 1894, and did odd jobs around the town.[168] A black man named Stephen Downes, who was not indicted for the killing of Ohl, apparently accompanied Collins during the incident.[169]

The trial itself and the period leading up to it were a national spectacle, as young, wealthy white women with no connection to the trial made the trip from New York City and Philadelphia to Trenton to attend the proceedings.[170] John Collins, who faced threats of lynching in the aftermath of Ohl's killing, was ultimately convicted of second-degree murder and sentenced to twenty years' hard labor. The death of Ohl and the subsequent trial of Collins quieted relations between whites and blacks

Scene from Real Life.—The Street.

P. and *A.,* (looking about as green as ever.)

P.—I say, A., these gals here ain't a darned bit pretty, are they ?

A.—No, that they ain't; why down in Alabama, the gals are right down handsome.
But they ain't so here.

P.—But I'll be darned if there ain't some right good looking niggar gals here, ain't
they ?

A.—Darned if they ain't.

Cartoon from a student journal, *Nassau Rake,* depicting two white men comment-
ing on the attractiveness of black women in Princeton.

for more than a decade. Students acted to form a boycott of Princeton
blacks, with a goal of employing only blacks who had lived in Princeton
at least three years. This, it was hoped, would drive many black newcom-
ers from the town.[171] Though James Collins Johnson was by this time in
no danger of being taken for a newcomer in Princeton, he likely felt the
pressure of heightened white enmity against blacks in the town. This ill
will stemming from the death of Ohl persisted for decades. Collins was
freed in 1909 after serving fourteen years as a model prisoner. Though a
news article noted that Collins had been an exemplary prisoner and had
learned the shoemaking trade in prison, both of which contributed to his
early release, it was also observed that the killing of Ohl was still fresh in
the minds of area residents.[172]

Johnson Near the End of His Life

Johnson had settled into what appeared to be a steady pattern of entrepreneurial endeavors at the start of the last decade of his life. He and his wife, Anetta, were proprietors of a boarding house on Witherspoon Street in 1892.[173] In a letter dated September 16, 1892, Frank Howard Braislin, a member of the Princeton class of 1894, wrote to an unidentified person encouraging him to try Johnson's establishment at 32 Witherspoon Street.[174] Noting that it was his preferred lodging in Princeton, Braislin wrote: "It is a place well known to me, and has a fair man, in desire and principle I think, if not in color, for a landlord and proprietor—and is a good one. His name, on the campus, is 'Aromatic James': but his house is a good one, to my knowledge and testatorship."[175] Though Braislin clearly thinks well of Johnson and his wife as business people, he nonetheless manages to include insulting references to Johnson's race and his old nickname, "Jim Stink." But while Johnson and his wife were conducting a well-regarded business in 1892, by 1896 Johnson had apparently fallen on hard times. A May 16, 1896, article from the *Princeton Press* included a plea for charitable contributions that would go to pay Johnson's rent.[176] Three citizens of Princeton, two of whom were graduates of the college, spearheaded the collections: Augustus Macdonald, class of 1862; John Wesley Fielder Jr., class of 1887; and Joseph S. Schank.[177] A few years later, the Johnsons were apparently no longer boarding house proprietors; the 1900 census shows that Johnson and Anetta and several members of Anetta's family were living at 77 Witherspoon Street in Princeton in a rented house.[178] It is not clear what became of the property at 32 Witherspoon Street. It is possible that the property was sold or, worse, taken for taxes, a fate that befell at least one other elderly black Princeton resident in the early twentieth century, Richard "Uncle" Dicky Redding.[179]

With Johnson's advancing age came infirmity, and this may have meant that money was in short supply. Anetta may have worked to support the family as a dressmaker during this period.[180] Still, even in his later years, Johnson remained a vital part of the black community. During the last few years of his life Johnson lived across the street from the young Paul Robeson on Witherspoon Street. Johnson was approaching eighty-two years old at the time of Robeson's birth in April 1898. The great age difference between the two suggests that Johnson may have had few interactions with Paul Robeson, who became a famed intellectual, activist, actor, and singer. There is, however, documentation showing interactions between members of the Johnson household and members of the

Robeson household. Alexander "Ting" Taylor, one of Anetta Johnson's nephews, who lived in the house at 77 Witherspoon in 1900, indicated that his family was closely acquainted with and knowledgeable about the Robeson household, according to interviews Taylor gave to a Robeson biographer.[181] The interactions between the Robeson household and the Johnson household were in keeping with what has been described as the strong cohesiveness of the Princeton black community during the late nineteenth and early twentieth centuries. The proximity of the households and the fact that William Drew Robeson was the minister of Witherspoon Presbyterian Church, the oldest and largest black church in town, made it likely that there would have been a sustained relationship between the families.[182]

The boldness and flamboyance that characterized Johnson in his earlier decades in Princeton gave way to a quieter, more humble demeanor. As one student from the class of 1886 recalled, Johnson was by the late 1800s "small, shabby, insignificant, but not deserving of his malodorous sobriquet, Jim Stink."[183] And though Johnson was "always there and in his day a pattern of industry and humility," by the 1880s some students on campus did not know his real name or where he lived.[184] Johnson's financial struggles and lower profile may have been the result of broader economic woes felt throughout the country and across racial groups. A depression in the 1870s, and a subsequent economic crisis during the 1890s, affected millions of workers.[185] While this general environment of financial instability may have contributed to Johnson's plight near the end of his life, a larger contributing factor was likely that he had grown old and feeble and could no longer work with the same vigor that had characterized his younger days. Although Johnson was ever present on campus until close to the end of his life, he was much reduced in strength in his last years. As one observer wrote, Johnson could be seen:

> down at the Varsity grounds when the big games are on, you may see his stooping figure moving slowly through the crowd; and when the game is over, he returns to the campus, his wheelbarrow shamefully despoiled of its wares; and now and then he stops in the dusty road in his characteristic way until he can regain his breath and pluck up the courage to go on.[186]

Moreover, while Johnson had a younger wife whose labor might have helped support the couple, near the eve of his death he apparently had no living or nearby children, and no grandchildren, who could have assisted him. Formerly enslaved people like Johnson often depended heavily on kinship frameworks for support in their least productive years.[187] Exacerbating the problems of a poor economy, old age, and an absence of younger supporting family members were the effects of ongoing racial discrimination on Johnson and other blacks in Princeton.

Life for Princeton blacks near the end of the nineteenth century and at the beginning of the twentieth century differed little from some of the antebellum conditions. As Paul Robeson noted in a speech he made in the 1940s that recalled his early life in Princeton: "Almost every Negro in Princeton lived off the college and accepted the social status that went with it. We lived for all intents and purposes on a Southern plantation. And with no more dignity than that suggests—all the bowing and scraping to the drunken rich, all the vile names, all the Uncle Tomming to earn enough to lead miserable lives."[188] Although public officials boasted that at the beginning of the twentieth century there were no publicly supported paupers in Princeton, the black community often suffered particular economic and social ills.[189] James Collins Johnson saw many changes over the sixty years he lived and worked in the town of Princeton. But two things changed little from the 1830s to the early 1900s: blacks and whites rarely worked in conditions of equality, and while they sometimes lived in proximity to one another, they remained separate in virtually every social setting.

An interesting exception to the persistent separation between whites and blacks in town and campus life was the case of Belle Da Costa Greene, a light-skinned black woman who came to Princeton around 1901. Greene, who passed as white, worked at the university library until 1905, when she became librarian to J. P. Morgan. In addition to adopting a white identity at work, Greene lived with white (or apparently white) housemates and socialized extensively with undergraduates and with white town society.[190] Later in her life she boasted that had she remained in Princeton, she might have married a Princeton man.[191] Born Belle Marion Greener in Washington, D.C., on November 26, 1879, Greene spent much of her childhood there before moving to New York City. She was the child of two mixed-raced parents of social prominence: her mother, Genevieve Ida Fleet, was a member of a well-known family in Washington, while her father, Richard Theodore Greener, was a lawyer. Greener served as dean of the Howard University School of Law and was the first black student at and the first black to graduate from Harvard in 1870.[192] After her parents separated, Belle, her mother, and her siblings passed as white, starting with changing their surname to obscure their background. In an effort to feign Dutch ancestry, Genevieve Ida Fleet often claimed that her middle name was Van Vliet.[193] Genevieve Fleet also used the maiden name Da Costa; Belle Greener used this as her middle name, claiming Portuguese ancestry.[194] This was a common ploy passing blacks used to explain their dark coloring.[195] Belle Da Costa Greene, like Johnson, had substantial interaction with white Princeton. But Greene, unlike Johnson, was able to cross the bridge between the two races and dwell permanently on the white side of the breach.

Johnson died on July 22, 1902, leaving a Princeton that, while much different from the town he had encountered in 1839, remained much the same in terms of how the college operated and how social life was conducted in town. Johnson's death was covered by journals well outside Princeton, in much the same way that his 1843 fugitive slave trial had been covered by publications beyond the small town of Princeton.[196] Some alumni offered recollections immediately after Johnson's death and even for decades thereafter.[197] As Anna Bustill Smith wrote, Johnson was "ever affectionately regarded by the students."[198] Some of the students and alumni memorialized that fond feeling with a granite tombstone mounted on his grave in the Princeton Cemetery.[199] On the tombstone, Johnson is called "the students' friend."[200] But however dear Johnson may have been to town and gown, at the time of his death, he and the town's black community remained outside the mainstream of white life.

Johnson's wife, Anetta, survived him. She is shown in the 1910 census as a widowed dressmaker living with her sister Clara Webb.[201] Anetta retained her social status in Princeton's black community. Bustill, in her chronicle of some of Princeton's notable blacks, observed that Johnson's widow "was a woman of fine presence, cultured and refined."[202] Anetta, apparently the last surviving member of Johnson's immediate family (neither Bustill nor any other accounts written later in Johnson's life or after his death reference any direct descendants), died in 1913, bringing to a close Johnson's private life.[203]

Conclusion

His [James Collins Johnson's] history is part
of the history of our country.

—*James Waddel Alexander,* Princeton—Old and
New: Recollections of Undergraduate Life

A key objective of this book is to look at the story of James Collins
Johnson in a way that attempts to explore, expose, and ultimately
to give a clearer picture of Johnson on his own terms. Johnson lived long,
and at times, he lived well. And though Johnson spent more of his life as
a free (or ostensibly free) man than he did as an enslaved man, the memory of slavery, with its "pain, loss, silence, denial, and endurance," likely
hung over him for all of his long life.[1] There is a tendency to historicize
African-ancestored slavery as an institution frozen in time and of limited
reach, instead of framing it as a remembrance of a series of ongoing events
with very real, harsh consequences for enslaved black people and for their
descendants. The treatment of African-ancestored people during slavery
and in its aftermath is more than a part of a somber past. African women,
children, and men were removed from their homes and introduced into a
system of bondage that was violent and capricious and deprived them of
the essence of their humanity: freedom in the present and hope for and
opportunity in the future. And this deprivation is part of history, memory,
presence, and future.

Johnson lived to become a revered figure in his waning years. I have
seen photos of a hale and hearty James Collins Johnson (or Jimmy, as I
came to think of him fondly) at age forty-five and photos of him in his
seventies, looking a bit less hearty but still strong, bemused, and even de-
fiant. I feel as if I am communicating with him through the photos. It is a
bit frightening, as many of the old photos seem to capture parts of his very
soul—it is no wonder that some "primitive" peoples don't like photos or
like to control how they are taken. (I feel the same way, perhaps for much

129

the same reason—I have to be ready and willing to "give" something of myself to a photo and I don't like most depictions of myself; I never have.)

Creating a bridge between the history and the memory of slavery poses a number of problems. Perhaps most prominent among those problems is to avoid judging a slave past that in some measures defies critique by its very historicity: the nineteenth century is not the twenty-first century. It is at best facile and misguided to employ the norms that guide us today when assessing the period of slavery. Nonetheless, African-ancestored slavery and its aftermath remain a searing memory that scorches the fabric of modernity, thereby meriting ongoing attention. The notion of people as property makes manifest Pierre Nora's notion of *lieux de mémoires*, disparate sites where "memory crystallizes and secretes itself."[2] While Nora envisions such sites as places, concepts, or objects that symbolize the past of a community, in the case of slavery, the bodies of enslaved black men, women, and children are themselves sites of memory. James Collins Johnson is one such compelling site of memory.

This book looks outside the center of what is known about slavery in the town of Princeton and at Princeton University during the antebellum period in much the same way that a viewer of a painting or photograph looks outside the center of the intended visual frame to gain a new perspective on the entire image. James Collins Johnson is a historical figure whose role in making history and shaping memory is perhaps just as large as that of the renowned people he served.

While this book tells a great deal about Johnson, it does so not just by coloring in the faint outline of Johnson that has been left by history and public memory but also by sketching in the background in which Johnson appears: the Maryland enslavement into which he was born and spent his early life; the antebellum New Jersey setting to which he escaped, including the town of Princeton and Princeton University as it neared the end of its centennial; the betrayal of Johnson and the people who played a role in both his capture and redemption; and the many decades of Johnson's life in Princeton after his trial.

Johnson's fuller biography offers insight into slavery and social relations between blacks and whites in the United States, in the Mid-Atlantic states and New Jersey, in the town of Princeton, and at the College of New Jersey. Besides offering a social history, an examination of Johnson's life offers a look at how the laws of slavery sometimes functioned. As some scholars have noted, slavery was a regime of formal and informal governance. Slavery functioned through a dynamic and potent rule regime that was created and maintained through informal social rules that worked in tandem with narrowly prescribed formal legal frames. James Collins Johnson's early life of allegedly easygoing, casual relations with his enslavers and the stark and harrowing formality of Johnson's fugitive slave trial exemplify slavery's dual nature of informality and formality.

James Collins Johnson, like Princeton University, is also a site of memory.[3] This book shows Johnson as a vital figure of wider import by exposing many previously unknown details of his life. Johnson carried memories of slavery in the Mid-Atlantic and in the northern United States and memories of justice and law more broadly. Perhaps the most striking memories Johnson carried were the memories of antebellum Princeton, both the town and the university. Johnson is in many respects a symbol of the glorious patrimony of Princeton and of the alumni, some illustrious, some little-known, who interacted with Johnson as students, eagerly sought him out when they returned as alumni, and fondly recalled him even long after his death. In the body of James Collins Johnson, in life and in death, founding myths of the university reside. As one former Princeton student wrote of Johnson: "His history is part of the history of our country."[4]

As noted at the beginning of this book, the contemporary Princeton University has made efforts to address historic inequities in the form of efforts at recognition and reconciliation. Nonetheless, a crucial r-word is missing from such efforts: reparations. While a number of colleges and universities, Princeton included, have joined the movement to interrogate their institutions' engagement with slavery, the move to consider whether and what reparations are due, and to whom, is likely for many a bridge too far. There has been some discussion of apologies and even of forms of reparations at some universities. In October 2018 the University of North Carolina made news when, during an event celebrating its 225th birthday, Chancellor Carol L. Folt offered a formal apology for the university's involvement in slavery.[5] While the chancellor indicated that the University of North Carolina is committed to "facing squarely and working to right the wrongs of history so they are never again inflicted," there was no indication of what concrete steps would be taken in the future, or if reparations would be included. Alfred Brophy notes that one school, Brown University, discussed reparations in a report on its involvement with slavery, but as yet there has been no concrete action in this regard.[6] Perhaps the clearest movement toward actual reparations that any U.S. educational institution has undertaken is seen in Georgetown University's offer of free tuition for the narrow class descendants of persons enslaved by Georgetown in the nineteenth century.[7] Georgetown students also weighed in on the issue. In a nonbinding referendum, undergraduates at Georgetown voted to raise their tuition by $27.20 per student per semester in order to benefit descendants of the 272 enslaved Africans that the Jesuits who ran the school sold in 1838.[8] One university outside the United States, the University of Glasgow, has committed to reparatory payments. Glasgow has agreed to pay the University of the West Indies 200 million pounds in view of the wealth that was extracted from Jamaica by Jamaican enslavers and others who made the University of Glasgow their university of choice.[9] This type of explicit reparational payment may be, however, difficult for some U.S. administrators, faculty, alumni and students to embrace.

Princeton, like many other colleges and universities, has started a conversation on slavery that in many cases serves as an acknowledgment of culpability for harms to people like James Collins Johnson and others who labored on campuses in slavery or slavery-like conditions. But as Alfred Brophy notes, there has almost grown to be a fashion in admitting involvement with slavery, since schools examining their own engagements with slavery are often those venerable enough to have existed during the period of antebellum enslavement in the United States.[10] It is one thing to say mea culpa, I am guilty, to the classes of individuals harmed by Princeton's and other universities' involvement with slavery and its aftermath. It is quite another to say *debitor sum*—I am indebted. For this we must wait.

Acknowledgments

> The closer a book comes to being a genuine
> work of art, a true creation fully alive with
> a life of its own, the less likely it is that
> the author had a full control and a clear
> understanding of what he wrote.
>
> — *Simon Leys, "The Imitation of Our Lord
> Don Quixote"*

Although the quote above refers to works of fiction, I believe, like the scholar Simon Leys, that the same may be said of nonfiction writing. This book, though perhaps not a work of art, is, at the same time that it is a systematic, organized creation that is the culmination of work over several years, also a project that offers its own autonomous "tale." The first job of my principal critics, many of whom I name and thank below, was to ensure that while following the road that I set for myself, I did not disregard the secondary paths that sometimes presented themselves as alternate routes in a shifting journey. It is such critics, as well as the larger body of readers, who also make this book, in the words of Michel de Certeau, "habitable": that is, through their readings they act upon my text and make it a space that is well suited to the scholarly endeavor.[1]

I am indebted to the many people and institutions that made this work possible. Not all of them are named here, as they are legion. There are some, though, who stand out, and so shall be named. I begin with my late mother, Claretta Estelle "Marie" Asbery. My beloved Marie served as an inspiration to me in completing this project. I thank my husband, Daryl Inniss, and my children, Christopher, Charles, and Marie Claire, for their tremendous love and support throughout this project. Special thanks go to my daughter, Marie Claire, who spent several school breaks in and around Princeton during my research on this book. In undertaking this book, I was by necessity forced to forgo many hours of family together-ness. Moreover, through my many hours of research, James Collins John-son has become like a member of our family. His exploits, his successes and challenges, were often the stuff of our day-to-day family conversa-tions. I am grateful that my family has extended James Collins Johnson so warm a welcome.

Next I give tremendous thanks to the people who helped this project to come together in its final form. I first thank Fordham University Press editors Fredric Nachbur and Will Cerbone, who believed in me and this project and made it a reality. I also thank copyeditor Paula Dragosh for her close reading and editing of my manuscript in its final stages. I am in addition deeply grateful to copyeditor Kate Babbit, who aided me when I despaired of ever tying together the loose ends of this work. Her gentle yet firm insistence that I fine-tune various sections or go out and find just the right reference have helped me to see this project to completion. Besides thanking those who assisted me through to the end, I give thanks to those who inspired and aided me near the beginning of this research. Key among these was the "Slavery and the University" conference orga-nized by Professor Leslie Harris and other scholars at Emory University in February 2011. This conference was instrumental in inspiring me to plunge into this work. At that conference more than thirty colleges and universities from throughout the country met to discuss the history and legacy of slavery's role in higher education. As many scholars in this area have shown, colleges were often intimately involved in slavery, and some even owned slaves. Some antebellum faculty and students in both the North and the South opposed slavery privately. Their reasons for opposi-tion varied from the moral to the practical. Because of the social tensions around slavery, relatively few of these persons were willing to publicly or to loudly voice their opposition. This same reticence was also sometimes seen among those who favored slavery, especially in northern college set-tings. Thus, many stories of enslavement and colleges and university are often hidden from view. The February 2011 Emory conference was the place where I first came into contact with many of the researchers in the area of slavery and the university, and I am deeply indebted for the op-portunity to present my work there.

I next want to thank the many persons who were kind enough to serve as referees as I sought to gain funding for this work. I especially thank Professor Alfred Brophy for serving as a referee time and time again. I thank also Professors Imani Perry, Craig Steven Wilder, and Melynda Price for their support, advice, and comments on early drafts of this work.

I thank Professor Martha Sandweiss of Princeton University for inviting me to give a public lecture on my work in progress at the Department of History at Princeton University and for hosting me in her slavery seminar. The comments of Professor Sandweiss and her students were wonderfully thought-provoking, and they helped me to explore some new perspectives. I am also very deeply grateful to Professor Taja-Nia Henderson for her close reading of portions of this book and her detailed, insightful comments.

I also thank the New Jersey Historical Society and the Friends of the Princeton University Library for helping to fund some of the archival research required for this project. I am especially grateful to Princeton University archivist Daniel Linke and his staff for their patience and kind assistance over the years of this project. Often I was the first to arrive at the Princeton University Mudd archives and the last to leave, and invariably some of my requests focused on materials that were little known and little used. I also want to particularly thank Wanda Gunning for her very useful references on the family of Samuel Stanhope Smith and on historic homes in the town of Princeton. Ms. Gunning provided valuable pieces of data about the existence of the Underground Railroad in the town of Princeton. Thanks also to my Princeton classmate Sev Onyskevich, who very generously allowed me to review parts of his private collection of Princeton historical material, and whose donations helped enrich the collection of the Princeton University archives. I am additionally grateful to the Historical Society of Princeton and especially to Eileen K. Morales for her help in locating news items about James Collins Johnson. I am also very grateful to Hamilton College for financial support for researching and writing this book. I also thank the faculty, staff, and students of Hamilton College who were so welcoming during my visit from 2012 to 2014. The atmosphere of collegiality and engaged intellectuality made Hamilton College a wonderful place in which to develop and share some of the ideas expressed in this book. I am also deeply grateful to the NYU–Centre National de la Recherche Scientifique Memory program for providing me with the resources and support to share my ideas among a vibrant set of scholars in Paris, France, in Spring 2012. In addition, I thank Cleveland State University and Cleveland-Marshall College of Law for providing me with some of the funding for this project. I particularly thank Dean Lee Fisher of Cleveland-Marshall College of Law who, even though he was then new to the school and did not know much about me or my project, approved funding to help me to complete the first full draft. I am also greatly indebted to Dean Jennifer Collins of the SMU Dedman

School of Law for approving the generous funding that allowed me to complete this project, especially via the Glenn Portman Faculty Research Fund. I send a special word of thanks to Professor Adelle Blackett and her students and colleagues for hosting me at McGill Law School in November 2018. I received enthusiastic and astute attention when I lectured on this topic at McGill, and the insightful questions of the audience allowed me to make some important finishing touches on the work.

I am, moreover, grateful to the following persons: the librarians at Cleveland–Marshall College of Law, especially Amy Burchfield, Neeri Rao, and their student assistants; the librarians at SMU Dedman School of Law, with particular thanks to Cassie DuBay; and my SMU Dedman School of Law administrative assistant TaLibra Ferguson. I also thank Michael Schuster, a Wallis family researcher, as well as James Floyd Jr. and James Floyd Sr., members of an old and esteemed Princeton, New Jersey, family; all of these persons provided valuable genealogical help. In this regard I also thank George H. Taylor Jr., a great-grand-nephew of James Collins Johnson's last wife, Anetta Webb Warden Johnson, for helping me to confirm information about Johnson's last days. I was thrilled to locate a family member of James Collins Johnson. I again thank Professor Taja-Nia Henderson of Rutgers University Law School, who was kind enough to provide me with copies of documents concerning student life at Princeton in the 1830s from the John Wesley Hart Papers of the Filson Historical Society in Louisville, Kentucky. I thank Adrian Colarusso for his photographs of 302 Nassau Street, one of the Princeton homes of Theodosia Ann Mary Prevost. I also again thank my sons, Charles Inniss and Christopher Inniss, who, along with Susan Natacha Gonzalez, hosted me in their home during my research in New York City. I am also grateful to Charles Inniss for providing me with photographs of the Manhattan neighborhood where Theodosia Prevost lived at the time of her birth in 1801. I also warmly thank Linda Gilmore of Nassau Presbyterian Church in Princeton for providing me with some useful information about the burial of James Collins Johnson at Princeton Cemetery. It was especially gratifying to receive help from Nassau Presbyterian, as it was my church home for many of the years that I lived in and near Princeton.

Last and far from least, I offer fervid regards and sincere thanks to the members of the Lutie A. Lytle Black Women Law Faculty Writing Workshop. The insightful scholarly critiques coupled with the warm emotional support of this group over the last several years have nourished me as I have worked toward the end of this project, and have given me the zeal to undertake new projects.

Notes

Preface

Epigraph: Philip Severn Wallis, telephone interview with author, April 28, 2018.

1. James D. Faubion, *The Ethics of Kinship: Ethnographic Inquiries* (Lanham, Md.: Rowman and Littlefield, 2001), 248. Faubion notes that studies on kinship and belonging have been largely silent on the history of how stories are told, especially oral transmissions of stories. Such stories shape nostalgia, modes of belonging, and help determine who really counts as kinfolk.

2. Marion Mills Miller, "Jimmy Johnson, D.C.L.: Reminiscenses of an Alumnus on [a] Famous Character of the Nineties," *Princeton Alumni Weekly*, April 23, 1948, 10.

3. Lea VanderVelde, *Mrs. Dred Scott: A Life on Slavery's Frontier* (New York: Oxford University Press, 2009), 229.

4. During the early and middle nineteenth century at the University of Virginia, for example, enslaved people were routinely leased from their owners in order to construct campus buildings and provide domestic services. See Kelley Fanto Deetz, "Finding Dignity in a Landscape of Fear: Enslaved Women and Girls at the University of Virginia," *Slavery and Abolition* 39, no. 2 (2018): 251–66.

5. Jody L. Allen, "Thomas Dew and the Rise of Proslavery Ideology at William & Mary," *Slavery and Abolition* 39, no. 2 (2018): 267–79. Allen leads the Lemon Project, a multifaceted effort to address wrongs perpetrated against African Americans by William and Mary. The program focuses on contributing to and encouraging scholarship on the decades-old relationship between

African Americans and William and Mary. For more information on the
Lemon Project, see https://www.wm.edu/sites/lemonproject/.

6. Craig Steven Wilder, *Ebony and Ivy: Race, Slavery, and the Troubled History of America's Universities* (New York: Bloomsbury, 2013).

7. Kendra Boyd, Miya Carey, and Christopher Blakley, "Old Money: Rutgers University and the Political Economy of Slavery in New Jersey," in *Scarlet and Black: Slavery and Dispossession in Rutgers History*, vol. 1, ed. Marisa J. Fuentes and Deborah Gray White (New Brunswick, N.J.: Rutgers University Press, 2016).

8. See *Slavery and Abolition* 39, no. 2 (2018) for several articles on slavery at universities, including my article on Princeton: Lolita Buckner Inniss, "'A Southern College Slipped from Its Geographical Moorings': Slavery at Princeton," *Slavery and Abolition* 39, no. 2 (2018): 236–50.

9. Edward Baptist, *The Half Has Never Been Told: Slavery and the Making of American Capitalism* (New York: Basic Books, 2012).

10. James C. Scott, *Domination and the Arts of Resistance: Hidden Transcripts* (New Haven, Conn.: Yale University Press, 1990), 2.

11. Cheryl D. Hicks, *Talk with You like a Woman: African American Women, Justice, and Reform in New York* (Chapel Hill: University of North Carolina Press, 2010).

12. The "Happy Negro" archetype refers to the notion that African-ancestored people are perennially smiling and happy, chiefly because of a childlike grasp of life and extreme religiosity. The trope was seen frequently in both fiction and nonfiction writings beginning in the early nineteenth century in both England and the United States, where accounts of enslaved blacks who were contented were offered as evidence of the essential humble, pious, and "happy" nature of well-cared-for enslaved blacks. This trope thus served to justify race-based slavery and oppression. See, e.g., American Tract Society, *The Happy Negro*, in *Tracts Published by the New England Tract Society*, vol. 1 (Andover, Mass.: Flagg and Gould, 1814), 49–52. A related trope was that of the "grateful Negro," enslaved blacks who were "grateful" for the civilizing influence of their white masters. This is captured in a fictional tale of the early 1800s in which a black slave is rendered grateful when his white master disabuses him of his belief in black folk superstitions. See George Boulukos, *The Grateful Slave: The Emergence of Race in Eighteenth-Century British and American Culture* (Cambridge: Cambridge University Press, 2008). See also Maria Edgeworth, "The Grateful Negro," in *Popular Tales*, vol. 3 (London: J. Johnson, 1811), 171.

13. In slaveholding areas, it was often viewed as a legal, moral, and even religious duty to report runaway slaves. Failing to do so, or worse, helping runaways escape, rendered such helpers subject to prosecution for aiding slaves and to calumny and scorn. See John Hope Franklin and Loren Schweninger, *Runaway Slaves: Rebels on the Plantation* (New York: Oxford University Press, 2000), 278. Beyond any legal or moral duty, some persons used knowledge of an escaped slave's status as a means of profit or revenge. For instance, in the mid-nineteenth century in Pennsylvania, some groups of working-class whites profited from

kidnapping and revealing escaped slaves to their owners. See Thomas P. Slaughter, *Bloody Dawn: The Christiana Riot and Racial Violence in the Antebellum North* (New York: Oxford University Press, 1994), 44–45. In the context of contemporary undocumented aliens, some employers have also used the threat of revealing undocumented status as a weapon to control undocumented workers. Courts have consistently found it impermissible under state and federal antiretaliation laws for employers to use immigration status as a weapon for defeating labor organizing campaigns or an employee's individual exercise of labor rights. See, e.g., *Contreras v. Corinthian Vigor Ins. Co.*, 25 F.Supp.2d 1053 (N.D. Cal. 1998) (I); and *Singh v. Jutla & C. D. & R's Oil, Inc.*, 214 F.Supp.2d 1056 (N.D. Cal. 2002), Nonetheless, some employers continue to use immigration laws against some employees.

14. Henry Clow, a campus administrator and food purveyor, said of Trent: "On the Fourth of July he [Trent] was often decorated with an old cocked hat and a continental coat, and after assisting them [the students] in firing the cannon, he was in the habit of using it as a temporary stage, on which he would deliver an Anglo-African speech, much to the amusement of his audience." See Henry Clow, "Princeton Forty-Six Years Ago," *Monmouth Democrat* (1850), reproduced in John Frelinghuysen Hageman, *History of Princeton and Its Institutions* (Philadelphia: J. B. Lippincott, 1879), 1:212.

15. "Stop the Runaway!," *New Jersey State Gazette*, January 23, 1793; "To Be Sold," *New Jersey State Gazette*, January 12, 1795.

16. Receipt from Peter Scudder to John Maclean, box 2, folder 2, Treasurer's Records, AC 128, Princeton University Archives.

17. Jack Washington, *The Quest for Equality: Trenton's Black Community, 1890–1965* (Trenton, N.J.: Africa World, 1993), 3.

18. "The Waldorf Peanut Man," *Trenton Evening Times*, published as *Trenton Sunday Advertiser* (Trenton, N.J.), December 27, 1909, 9.

19. *Princeton Pictorial Review*, February 20, 1915, 161. While Princeton University archival markings on the photograph suggest that the child may be Archibald Campbell "Spader" Seruby, Johnson's last wife's nephew, Alexander Ting Taylor, indicated that he often accompanied Johnson to work in the period around 1900 when this photo was taken. See Richard D. Smith, *Legendary Locals of Princeton* (Charleston, S.C.: Arcadia, 2014), 75.

20. *Princeton Alumni Weekly*, February 14, 1903, 307.

21. Lorraine Seabrook and Jack Seabrook, *Hopewell Valley* (Charleston, S.C.: Arcadia, 2000), 76.

22. *Princeton Alumni Weekly*, February 14, 1903, 307; "Spader at White City," *Trenton Evening Times*, July 14, 1907, 1; "Spader the Peanut Man, Still Offers His Wares," *Daily Princetonian*, June 15, 1929, 3.

23. Lolita Buckner Inniss, "Archibald Campbell 'Spader' Seruby, the Peanut King," in *African American National Biography Online*, edited by Henry Louis Gates and Evelyn Higginbotham (Oxford: Oxford University Press, 2012).

24. "Death Terminates Career of 'Ole Nassau' Vendor of 'Winnin' Peanuts'

at Princeton," *Daily Princetonian*, September 25, 1935, 1; "Princeton Vendor of Peanuts Dies Trenton," *Asbury Park Press*, September 24, 1935, 11.

25. T. A. C. Crimmins, "Jimmy Stink of Princeton," *Nassau Literary Review* 100, no. 1 (November 1, 1941): 1; "Jigger," *Nassau Sovereign*, March 1948, 18.

26. William Barksdale Maynard, *Woodrow Wilson: Princeton to the Presidency* (New Haven, Conn.: Yale University Press, 2014), 45–46.

27. "The Bulletin of the Committee of Fifty," *Princeton Alumni Weekly*, January 12, 1907, 232, 239.

28. Arthur Evans Wood, *Some Unsolved Social Problems of a University Town* (Ann Arbor, Mich.: C. W. Graham, 1920), 6. According to Wood, after blacks were fired en masse, Greek workers were brought in to replace them. The university built "a commodious and clean building for its Greek employees" (ibid.). See also Katheryn Watterson, *I Hear My People Singing: Voices of African American Princeton* (Princeton, N.J.: Princeton University Press, 2017), 173.

29. Wood, *Some Unsolved Social Problems of a University Town*. Wood had experience in several university towns. After graduating from Harvard, Wood taught social science for four years at Reed College in Portland, Oregon, and then returned to take graduate work at the University of Pennsylvania. He conducted a social survey of Princeton's "lower classes" for his doctoral dissertation at the University of Pennsylvania. Wood was appointed to an instructorship at the University of Michigan with the understanding that he was to develop social work courses and to cooperate in every way practicable with the social workers of the state. See Charles Horton Cooley, "The Development of Sociology at Michigan," in *Sociological Theory and Social Research: Being Selected Papers of Charles Horton Cooley* (New York: Henry Holt, 1930), 3–14.

30. Wood, *Some Unsolved Social Problems of a University Town*, 5. Wood reported that the three previous studies were bound together in one volume but had very limited circulation. Lucy F. Friday, a graduate of Wellesley College, was a white social worker who lived and worked in various locations in New England and the Mid-Atlantic states. See *Wellesley Magazine* 5 (1892), 47, manuscript census of 1870, Erie, Pennsylvania; federal manuscript census of 1910, Baltimore, Maryland; and *Charities*, June 25, 1904, 663–64, 825. Interestingly, Princeton University employment records and archives do not show a Lucy F. Friday as an employee in the late nineteenth or early twentieth centuries.

31. Wood, *Some Unsolved Social Problems of a University Town*, 5.

32. Ann Maria Davison, "Chap 19th, A Visit to the Colored People of Princeton," May 1855, Ann Maria Davison Papers, 1814–1866, MC 234, Schlesinger Library, Radcliffe Institute, Harvard University, https://iiif.lib .harvard.edu/manifests/view/drs:49311486$1i.

33. "Begin Work This Week on Princeton Centre," *New York Times*, July 28, 1929, S28.

34. "Witherspoon Street," *Nassau Sovereign*, January 1950, 8–9, 23.

35. Lee A. Daniels, "Princeton's Blacks Fighting to Keep Their Area Intact," *New York Times*, July 16, 1981, B1.

36. Iver Peterson, "Amid Boom, Black Enclave Shrinks," *New York Times*, October 28, 1986, B1.

37. Iver Peterson, "As Princeton Changes, a Black Community Fears for Future," *New York Times*, September 3, 2001, B2.

38. Ibid.

39. James Reese, James Albert, and Amy Lincoln, "Report on the Witherspoon Street Presbyterian Church," February 4, 2016, http://oga.pcusa.org /site_media/media/uploads/oga/pdf/mid_council_ministries/tr-15-01 _robeson_report_final_draft.pdf.

40. Ann Levin, "Formal Apology and a $175,000 Gift Mark Witherspoon Church Milestone," *Town Topics*, November 15, 2015, http://www.towntopics .com/wordpress/2015/11/18/formal-apology-and-a-175000-gift-mark -witherspoon-church-milestone/.

41. Ibid. The report on the church called Rev. Robeson's removal an "ecclesiastical lynching." See Reese, Albert, and Lincoln, "Report on the Witherspoon Street Presbyterian Church," 3.

42. Anna Merriman, "Princeton's Witherspoon-Jackson Neighborhood to Become Historic District," *NJ.com*, April 14, 2016, http://www.nj.com/mercer /index.ssf/2016/04/princetons_witherspoon-jackson_neighborhood_to_bec .html.

43. 016-38 An Ordinance by the Municipality of Princeton Establishing a Civil Rights Commission and Amending the "Code of the Borough of Princeton, New Jersey, 1974"; and "Code of the Township of Princeton, New Jersey, 1968."

44. Dr. Robert Joseph Rivers grew up in Princeton as a member of a family with generations of service to Princeton. In April 2019 a campus street was named in his honor. See Emily Aronson, Office of Communications, "Campus Roadway Will Be Named for Pioneering African American Alumnus and Princeton Resident Robert Rivers," https://www.princeton.edu/news/2019 /04/09/campus-roadway-will-be-named-pioneering-african-american -alumnus-and-princeton.

45. William A. McWhirter, "On the Campus," *Princeton Alumni Weekly*, January 26, 1962, 14.

46. Ibid.; Marcia Graham Synnott, *Student Diversity at the Big Three: Changes at Harvard, Yale, and Princeton since the 1920s* (New Brunswick, N.J.: Transaction Publishers, 2013), 180. In 1995 blacks constituted 6.75 percent of matriculating students at Princeton (ibid., 202).

47. "Honorary Princeton Degree Is 'Apology' for Past Injustice," *Crisis* 108 (September–October 2001): 12; Jerome Karabel, *The Chosen: The Hidden History of Admission and Exclusion at Harvard, Yale, and Princeton* (Boston: Houghton Mifflin Harcourt, 2006), 232–33.

48. Andy Newman, "At Princeton, Woodrow Wilson, a Heralded Alum, Is Recast as an Intolerant One," *New York Times*, November 23, 2015, A1.

49. Students aligned with a group called the Black Justice League submitted

a list of antiracist demands to the university. Though most were not granted, the university agreed to instate a general-education requirement on the history of a marginalized people and to create a cultural space on campus dedicated to black students. See Alexandra Markovich, "Despite Outcry, Princeton Board Says Wilson's Name Will Stay on Campus," *New York Times*, April 5, 2016, A23.

50. Sanford Levinson, *Written in Stone: Public Monuments in Changing Societies* (Durham, N.C.: Duke University Press, 2018). Levinson suggests that the report was "relatively lacking in systemic argument" and established a presumption that names adopted by the university should remain.

51. *Report of the Trustee Committee on Woodrow Wilson's Legacy* (Princeton, N.J.: Princeton University, 2016), https://www.princeton.edu/sites/default/files/documents/2017/08/Wilson-Committee-Report-Final.pdf.

52. Stefan M. Bradley, "The Southern-Most Ivy: Princeton University from Jim Crow Admissions to Anti-Apartheid Protests, 1794–1969," *American Studies* 51, nos. 3–4 (2010): 109–30.

53. Professor Valerie Smith became dean of the College at Princeton and later was appointed president of Swarthmore College. Ruth Simmons served as vice provost of Princeton and later served as provost of Spellman College and as president of Smith College, Brown University, and Prairie View A & M University. See Synnott, *Student Diversity at the Big Three*, 153, 154.

54. Although black studies courses were taught at Princeton since the 1960s, most such courses were cross-listed in other departments or billed as special courses, and students concentrating in such topics were limited to certificates in African American studies. In 2009 the Center for African American Studies was created, with then English professor, later vice provost, Valerie Smith as director. In 2015 African American studies attained departmental status.

55. "Class Begins to Paint Picture of Princeton's Ties to Slavery," *Princeton Alumni Weekly*, May 15, 2013, https://paw.princeton.edu/article/class-begins-paint-picture-princeton%E2%80%99s-ties-slavery.

56. A brief overview of this book is available as part of the Princeton and Slavery Project. See https://slavery.princeton.edu/; https://slavery.princeton.edu/stories/james-collins-johnson.

57. Jennifer Schuessler, "Princeton to Name Two Campus Spaces in Honor of Slaves," *New York Times*, April 18, 2018, C3.

58. Philip Wallis (1899–1960), graduated Princeton in 1921. See Princeton University Alumni Profile, Philip Wallis '21. The son of Philip Wallis '21, George Roberts Wallis, was a member of the Princeton class of 1953. See Princeton University Alumni Profile, George R. Wallis.

59. The son of George Roberts Wallis; see Philip S. Wallis, Princeton University Alumni Profile, Philip S. Wallis '81.

Introduction

Epigraph: William H. Hudnut, quoted in "Class Notes," *Princeton Alumni Weekly*, October 9, 1959, 52. Hudnut contributed the class notes for 1886. In 1962 Hudnut was recorded as the oldest Princeton alumnus then living, and thus his perspective on the history of Princeton was shaped by decades of observation. See "Hudnut Oldest Alumnus," *Daily Princetonian*, September 25, 1962, 4.

1. Annette Gordon-Reed, *The Hemingses of Monticello: An American Family* (New York: W. W. Norton, 2008), 23.

2. Henry J. Van Dyke Jr., "Princeton College," *Manhattan*, July 20, 1883, 16. Johnson and other black male vendors were not the only black figures who served as mascots at university sporting events in the immediate antebellum years. In one instance, Princeton students, hoping to outdo the bulldog mascot display of Yale students at the Princeton–Yale football game of 1891, dressed a "comely young colored girl" in all orange and had her parade about the field while eating an orange. See "Victory Rests with Yale," *New York Times*, November 27, 1891, 1.

3. In the 1860 census Johnson reported that no one over the age of twenty in his house was illiterate. Other evidence of Johnson's literacy is seen in what appears to be some of Johnson's signed college pay receipts from the 1840s and 1850s; see Office of the Treasurer Records, ACS 128, box 2, folder 1, Princeton University Archives, Department of Rare Books and Special Collections, Princeton University Library.

4. Thomas Jefferson was far more renowned than the Wallises and occupied a special place in history. This fame, along with the fact that Jefferson was "an inveterate record keeper and writer of letters," made information about the Hemings family far more accessible. See Gordon-Reed, *Hemingses of Monticello*, 23.

5. Erica Armstrong Dunbar, *Never Caught: The Washingtons' Relentless Pursuit of Their Runaway Slave, Ona Judge* (New York: Simon and Schuster, 2018), xi.

6. Varnum Lansing Collins wrote "Prospect, Near Princeton" (1904); *The Continental Congress at Princeton* (1908); *Early Princeton Printing* (1911); *Princeton* (1914); and *Guide to Princeton: The Town, the University* (1919).

7. George R. Wallace, *Princeton Sketches: The Story of Nassau Hall* (New York: Putnam and Sons, 1893), iv. Wallace describes Johnson among other "old college servants" with half a century's service, but he describes Johnson as "indispensable" and "only" (ibid.).

8. Andrew C. Imbrie, "James Johnson of Princeton: A Biography," *Nassau Literary Magazine* 50, no. 9 (1895): 594–604.

9. Miller, "Jimmy Johnson, D.C.L.," 10.

10. James Olney, "'I was Born': Slave Narratives, Their Status as Autobiography and as Literature," *Callaloo* 20 (Winter 1984): 46–73.

11. *Narrative of the Life of Frederick Douglass, an American Slave, Written by Himself* (Boston: Published at the Anti-Slavery Office, 1845).

12. Solomon Northup, *Twelve Years a Slave* (Auburn, N.Y.: Derby & Miller, 1853).

13. Harriet Jacobs, *Incidents in the Life of a Slave Girl* (Boston: Published for the Author, 1861).

14. Jean Fagan Yellin, *Harriet Jacobs: A Life* (New York: Basic Books, 2004).

15. Christina Accomando, *The Regulations of Robbers: Legal Fictions of Slavery and Resistance* (Columbus: Ohio State University Press, 2001), 115–17, 137.

16. Samuel Ringgold Ward, *Autobiography of a Fugitive Negro: His Anti-Slavery Labours in the United States, Canada, & England* (London: John Snow, 1855).

17. James Watkins, *Narrative of James Watkins, Formerly a "Chattel" in Maryland, U.S.; Containing an Account of His Escape from Slavery, Together with an Appeal on Behalf of Three Millions of Such "Pieces of Property," Still Held under the Standard of the Eagle* (Bolton, Eng.: Kenyon and Abbatt, 1852). The story of Alexander Helmsley is contained in Benjamin Drew, *A North-side View of Slavery: The Refugee: or, The Narratives of Fugitive Slaves in Canada* (Boston: John P. Jewett, 1856), 32–40. Helmsley gained fame as the fugitive claimed in the case of *State v. Sheriff of Burlington County* (1836).

18. Robin W. Winks, "The Making of a Fugitive Slave Narrative—Josiah Henson and Uncle Tom," in *The Slave's Narrative*, edited by Charles Twitchell Davis and Henry Louis Gates Jr. (New York: Oxford University Press, 1991), 112–47.

19. Valerie Smith, *Self-Discovery and Authority in Afro-American Narrative* (Cambridge, Mass.: Harvard University Press, 1987), 36–37.

20. S. Bayard Dod, *Stubble or Wheat? A Story of More Lives Than One* (New York: A. D. F. Randolph, 1888), 68.

21. William Mumford Baker, *His Majesty, Myself* (Boston: Roberts Brothers, 1880).

22. Ibid., 95–98.

23. Jesse Lynch Williams, *The Adventures of a Freshman* (New York: Charles Scribner's Sons, 1889); Williams, *Princeton Stories* (New York: Charles Scribner's Sons, 1916).

24. James Barnes, *A Princetonian: A Story of Undergraduate Life at the College of New Jersey* (New York: G. P. Putnam's Sons, 1899).

25. Joseph Tuisco Wiswall, *Mr. Christopher Katydid (of Casconia): A Tale* (London: Saunders, Otley, 1864).

26. Latta Griswald, *Deering at Princeton* (New York: Macmillan, 1914).

27. See Michel Foucault, *Discipline and Punish: The Birth of the Prison* (London: Allen Lane, 1979).

28. Edwin Mark Norris, *The Story of Princeton* (Boston: Little, Brown, 1917), 5–6; John Rogers Williams, *The Handbook of Princeton* (New York: Grafton, 1905), 100–101.

29. Hageman, *History of Princeton and Its Institutions*, 1:12.

30. Norris, *Story of Princeton*, 101.

31. Six Degrees of Kevin Bacon, also known as the Oracle of Bacon, is based on the concept that any two people on earth are six or fewer acquaintance links apart. In the game, movie fans challenge each other to find the shortest path between any randomly named actor and prolific Hollywood character actor Kevin Bacon. It rests on the assumption that any individual involved in the Hollywood film industry can be linked through his or her film roles to Kevin Bacon in six steps. For an online version of the game, see http://oracleofbacon .org/.

32. See "George Washington to Samuel Stanhope Smith, 24 May 1797," Founders Online, http://founders.archives.gov/documents/Washington/06-01 -02-0123. This letter was published in W. W. Abbot, ed., *The Papers of George Washington*, Retirement Series, vol. 1, *4 March 1797–30 December 1797* (Charlottesville: University Press of Virginia, 1998), 153–54.

33. King Edward VIII of England abdicated the throne to marry U.S. divorcée Wallis Simpson. Simpson's prominent Maryland family was socially intimate with the Wallises, and she, like her father before her, was named in honor of Severn Teackle Wallis, one of Johnson's enslavers.

34. Francis Scott Key maintained a close friendship with U.S. Supreme Court justice Roger Brooke Taney that dated back to their early careers as lawyers in Maryland. The two became in-laws and drew even closer when Taney married Key's sister Ann Key in 1806. See Jefferson Morley, *Snow-Storm in August: Washington City, Francis Scott Key, and the Forgotten Race Riot of 1835* (New York: Doubleday, 2012), 44–50.

35. See, e.g., F. James Davis, *Who Is Black? One Nation's Definition* (University Park: Pennsylvania State University Press, 1991), 145–46.

36. Gina Philogene, "From Race to Culture: The Emergence of African American," in *Representations of the Social: Bridging Theoretical Traditions*, edited by Kay Deaux (Malden, Mass.: Blackwell, 2001), 113, 118.

37. See, e.g., Paul Spickard, *Almost All Aliens: Immigration, Race, and Colonialism in American History and Identity* (New York: Routledge, 2010), 80, which describes European migrants to the United States as forming the "second great panethnicity: the white race." See also Nicholas Faraclas and Marta Viada Bellido de Luna, "Marginalized Peoples, Racialized Slavery and the Emergence of the Atlantic Creoles," in *Agency in the Emergence of Creole Languages: The Role of Women, Renegades, and People of African and Indigenous Descent in the Emergence of the Colonial Era Creoles*, edited by Nicholas Faraclas (Philadelphia: John Benjamins, 2012), 36–37, which describes the creation of a "new Calvinist, capitalist and racialized form of colonization" that relied on strict separation of European-ancestored peoples, who were white, from all others.

38. See George A. Yancey, *Who Is White? Latinos, Asians, and the New Black/ Nonblack Divide* (Boulder, Colo.: Lynne Rienner, 2003), 3–5, 14–15, which argues that although African Americans remain separated, some other racial mi-

norities in the United States, especially Asians and Latinos, may attain majority or white status.

39. Jean Allain, *The Legal Understanding of Slavery: From the Historical to the Contemporary* (Oxford: Oxford University Press, 2012), 4–5.

40. See, e.g., Martin A. Klein, *Slavery and Colonial Rule in French West Africa* (Cambridge: Cambridge University Press, 1998), 15.

1. James Collins of Maryland, and His Escape from Slavery

Epigraph: Andrew C. Imbrie, "James Johnson of Princeton: A Biography," *Nassau Literary Magazine* 50, no. 9 (1895): 594, 595.

1. Andrew C. Imbrie, "James Johnson of Princeton: A Biography," *Nassau Literary Magazine* 50, no. 9 (1895): 594, 595.

2. Ibid.

3. Wilma King, *Stolen Childhood: Slave Youth in Nineteenth-Century America* (Bloomington: Indiana University Press, 2011), 235. King notes that a substantial amount of intrastate slave trade involved young children. Enslaved children were transferred by will, given to newlywed couples, and bequeathed in wills.

4. Ibid.

5. Some have suggested that enslaved children who were sold or transferred were often accompanied by at least one parent. See Marie Jenkins Schwartz, *Born in Bondage: Growing Up Enslaved in the Antebellum South* (Cambridge, Mass.: Harvard University Press, 2009), 165; and Robert William Fogel and Stanley L. Engelman, *Time on the Cross: The Economics of American Negro Slavery* (New York: W. W. Norton and Company, 1995). Herbert Gutman, however, counters Fogel and Engelman's claims that slave children were only rarely sold, hired out, given as a gift, or otherwise transferred without parents. See Herbert G. Gutman, *Slavery and the Numbers Game: A Critique of Time on the Cross* (Urbana: University of Illinois Press, 1975), 9–10. Families were frequently separated as a result of the death of owners and the corresponding need to make legally mandated estate divisions among heirs (ibid., 133–35). Some states did, however, eventually pass laws that barred the sale of small children without their mothers, such as an 1829 Louisiana law that forbade the sale of children under ten without their mothers, and an 1852 Alabama law that proscribed the sale of children under five without their mothers. See Steven Deyle, *Carry Me Back: The Domestic Slave Trade in American Life* (New York: Oxford University Press, 2005), 52. But as Deyle also notes, states in the Upper South had fewer of these prohibitions, and many enslaved children had already been made "orphans" by their owners via separations from parents long before such children came into the hands of slave traders. Michael Tadman writes that separating enslaved families was an integral part of the conduct of the U.S. slave trade and that the slave trade was "custom-built to maximize forcible separations"; see Michael Tadman, *Speculators and Slaves: Masters, Traders, and Slaves in the Old South* (Madison: University of Wisconsin Press, 1989), 141. Tadman calculates that enslaved children in the

Upper South under the age of fourteen had at least a one in three chance of being sold to the Deep South away from parents (ibid., 45). Local sales in the immediate region of the child's home, Tadman asserted, "would have increased an enslaved child's possibility of being separated from parents to one in two" (ibid., 171).

6. Frederick Douglass, *Narrative of the Life of Frederick Douglass: An American Slave* (London: H. G. Collins, 1845), 10.

7. *Baltimore Sun*, December 3, 1839, 1.

8. Philip Wallis (1793–1844) was the father of Philip Custis Wallis, his eldest son.

9. "James Collins Searching for his Brother," Information Wanted Ad, *Christian Recorder* (Philadelphia, Pa.), September 22, 1866, *Last Seen: Finding Family after Slavery*, accessed April 11, 2018, http://www.informationwanted.org/items/show/231.

10. Tera W. Hunter, *Bound in Wedlock: Slave and Free Black Marriage in the Nineteenth Century* (Cambridge, Mass.: Belknap Press of Harvard University Press, 2017).

11. There were several Sarah Harrises in and around Queen Anne's County in this period, but eliminating black and mulatto Sarahs, as well as those who would have been too young to be heads of households before the Civil War, leaves only two likely persons. One was a Sarah Harris born in 1803, living in District 5 of Queen Anne's County, who, in 1870, was a head of household that consisted of two adult children. See Sarah Harris, 1870; Census Place: District 5, Queen Anne's, Maryland; Roll: M593_593; Page: 463B. In 1860 what seems to be the same Sarah Harris appears in the same district with a husband, Robert, and three children, two of whom are also named in the 1870 census cited above. See Sarah Harris, 1860; Census Place: District 5, Queen Anne's, Maryland; Roll: M653_479; Page: 128. A second possibility is Sarah Harris born about 1804, with a husband named Robert. See Sarah Harris, 1860; Census Place: District 1, Queen Anne's, Maryland; Roll: M653_479; Page: 120.

12. James Johnson, 1900; Census Place: Princeton, Mercer, New Jersey; Roll: 982; Page: 3A; Enumeration District: 0054.

13. Allan A. Young, "Age," in *Supplementary Analysis and Derivative Tables: Twelfth Census of the United States, 1900,* edited by Walter Francis Willcox, Allyn Abbott Young et al. (Washington, D.C.: Government Publishing Office, 1906), 130.

14. Lorena Walsh, "The Chesapeake Slave Trade: Regional Patterns, African Origins, and Some Implications," *William and Mary Quarterly* 58 (January 2001): 144; William L. Calderhead, "Slavery in Maryland in the Age of the Revolution, 1775–1790," *Maryland Historical Magazine* 98 (Fall 2003): 311.

15. Transatlantic Slave Database, http://slavevoyages.org/voyages/1RpJDbWa.

16. For a general discussion of the *Clotilde*, see Sylviane A. Diouf, *Dreams of Africa in Alabama: The Slave Ship Clotilda and the Story of the Last Africans Brought*

to America (New York: Oxford University Press, 2007). Although the last surviv-
ior of the Clotilde was believed to be a man named Cudjoe Lewis who died in
1935, recent research suggests that the last survivor from the ship was actually a
woman named Redoshi who died in 1937. See Sandra E. Garcia, "She Survived
Slave Ship, the Civil War and the Depression," *New York Times*, April 3, 2019,
A16.

17. Andrew C. Imbrie, "James Johnson of Princeton: A Biography," *Nassau
Literary Magazine* 50, no. 9 (1895): 594, 597.

18. Barbara J. Fields, *Slavery and Freedom on the Middle Ground: Maryland
during the Nineteenth Century* (New Haven, Conn.: Yale University Press,
1985), 28.

19. Hunter, *Bound in Wedlock*, 13–14.

20. Fields, *Slavery and Freedom on the Middle Ground*, 28–29.

21. The Wallis family was a prominent part of the community in Kent
County in the seventeenth century. The first Maryland Wallis, Samuel, was born
about 1674. He moved to Kent County, where he raised all his children until
his death in 1724. See Guy Wallis, *The Wallis Family of Kent County* (Bristol,
Vt.: [Guy Wallis], 2011). Samuel served twenty-one years as a vestryman for
Shrewsbury Parish, as would many of his descendants; see Shrewsbury Parish
Vestry Records, MSA SC 2513: Shrewsbury Church Collection, microfilm
M339-1, Maryland State Archives, Annapolis (hereafter cited as Maryland State
Archives). He acquired and farmed several tracts of land in Morgan's Creek
Neck and parts of Queen Anne's County that were held by members of the
Wallis family for over one hundred years. He bequeathed a tract of land called
"Partnership," containing nine hundred acres, to his sons Samuel (the father of
Philip Wallis the elder), John, and Hugh; see will of Samuel Wallis, probated
May 9, 1724, Maryland Calendar of Wills, 1645–1743, *Ancestry.com*. A Philip
Wallis advertised over twelve hundred acres for sale near Columbus, Ohio, in
1832. See *Ohio State Journal*, December 5, 1832, 3.

22. Philip Wallis and his son Phillip Custis Wallis moved to Yazoo City, Mississippi, between the 1830s and 1840s. Philip Wallis's son John Samuel moved
to Louisiana, where he became a wholesale merchant and plantation owner. See
Wallis, *Wallis Family of Kent County*, 72.

23. Ibid., 30.

24. Ibid.

25. Ibid.

26. *American & Commercial Daily Advertiser* (Baltimore, Md.), August 26,
1819, 1.

27. For example, Philip Wallis was awarded the prize of $10 for his thor-
oughbred Hunter Skylark at the Easton Cattle Show and Fair in 1827. At the
same show he served on the committee on oxen. See *The American Farmer*,
December 28, 1827, 323. Philip Wallis was frequently listed among owners in
stud books of the time. See, e.g., Richard Mason and Samuel Wyllys Pomeroy,
The Gentleman's New Pocket Farrier (Philadelphia: Grigg & Elliot, 1841), 342,

349. Wallis was noted as a major breeder of horses even years after his death; see William Woodward, "The Thoroughbred Horse in Maryland," *Maryland Historical Magazine* 12 (June 1922): 139–40. A horse belonging to Philip Wallis ran in a Washington, D.C., race in October 1836; see "National Jockey Club Races," *Daily National Intelligencer,* October 3, 1836, 1. In October 1838 his horse Mary Wye ran the Kendall Race Course in Baltimore; see "Kendall Course Races, Fall Meeting, 1838," *Daily National Intelligencer,* October 13, 1838, 4.

28. "Baltimore Races," *Alexandria Gazette,* October 25, 1834, 2.

29. Philip Wallis was named a commissioner of the Real Estate Bank of Baltimore, along with twenty-four other men, by an act of the Maryland State Legislature on March 28, 1836; see "An Act to Incorporate the Real Estate Bank of Baltimore," *Laws Made and Passed by the General Assembly of Maryland* (Annapolis, Md.: Jeremiah Hughes, 1836), chap. 317. The Real Estate Bank was one of two such banks in the state; the other was in Frederick. See Alfred Cookman Bryan, *History of State Banking in Maryland, 1790–1864* (Baltimore, Md.: Johns Hopkins University Press, 1899), 9, 79.

30. *Wheatley v. Wallis,* 3 Har. & J.1 (Md. 1810).

31. Bernard C. Steiner, "James Alfred Pearce," *Maryland Historical Magazine* 16, no. 9 (1921): 332.

32. *Baltimore Sun* (Baltimore, Md.), April 29, 1839, 1. Wallis allegedly made threats against council member Richard J. Cross.

33. *Baltimore Sun,* April 14, 1839, 2.

34. *Republican Star* (Easton, Md.), July 5, 1814, 4. Around the same time Philip Wallis sought to sell several pieces of land that he had apparently inherited from his father's estate. See *Republican Star,* August 30, 1814, 4.

35. *Republican Star,* July 5, 1814, 4.

36. For example, Frederick Douglass was sometimes allowed "the privilege of hiring his time" while enslaved. See Frederick Douglass, *Narrative of the Life of Frederick Douglass: An American Slave* (Dublin: Webb and Chapman, 1846), 101–5. Hiring one's own time was a common practice throughout the slaveholding South, especially in the case of skilled enslaved workers. See Anthony Kaye, *Joining Places: Slave Neighborhoods in the Old South* (Chapel Hill: University of North Carolina Press, 2009), 116–17. But while this may have heralded greater independence for the enslaved in some cases, it did not mean freedom. Slaves hired their time, not their persons; over their persons they had limited control (ibid., 116).

37. Kenneth Cohen, *They Will Have Their Game: Sporting Culture and the Making of the Early American Republic* (Ithaca, N.Y.: Cornell University Press, 2017).

38. Wallis, *Wallis Family of Kent County,* 30.

39. *Delaware Gazette* (Wilmington), May 16, 1814, 4.

40. Ibid.

41. *Republican Star,* May 23, 1815, 4.

42. *Baltimore Patriot*, September 9, 1815, 4. Slaves of Frederick and Stephen Boyer were sold at a sheriff's sale to satisfy liens.

43. Bernard C. Steiner, "Severn Teackle Wallis," *Sewanee Review* 15, no. 1 (1907): 58–74. Severn Teackle Wallis was a great friend of the father of Wallis Warfield Simpson, the Duchess of York. See *Princeton Alumni Weekly*, June 13, 1946, 13; Severn Teackle Wallis, *The Writings of Severn Teackle Wallis*, vol. 1 (Baltimore: John Murphy, 1896), ix.

44. The 1830 census shows that the household of Philip Wallis included one male aged 10–23, one male aged 24–35, one female aged 10–23, one female aged 36–54, and one female under age 10. See Entry for Philip Wallis, Ward 7, Baltimore, Maryland, p. 271, federal manuscript census of 1830, FamilySearch .org, https://familysearch.org/ark:/61903/1:1:XHPS-WVT.

45. Theodore Dwight Weld to Gerrit Smith, form letter, November 28, 1838, in *Letters of Theodore Dwight Weld, Angelina Grimké Weld and Sarah Grimké, 1822–1844*, ed. Gilbert H. Barnes and Dwight L. Dumont, vol. 2 (New York: Appleton-Century, 1934), 717.

46. Isaac Mason, *Life of Isaac Mason as a Slave* (Worcester, Mass.: printed by the author, 1893), 20–22.

47. Ibid., 20.

48. Ibid.

49. Ibid., 62–66. Several Wallis kin, including John Samuel Wallis, Philip Custis Wallis (the sons of Philip and Elizabeth Custis Teackle Wallis), and Philip Wallis, moved south in the 1800s.

50. On November 1, 1864, Maryland was the first of the border states to abolish slavery. This was accomplished with a new state constitution that was enacted by a close vote of the white Maryland men who constituted the general electorate. See Suzanne Ellery Chapelle, *Maryland: A History of Its People* (Baltimore, Md.: Johns Hopkins University Press, 1986), 169.

51. Frederick Douglass, *My Bondage and My Freedom* (New York: Miller, Orton and Mulligan, 1855), 61.

52. Ibid., 62.

53. A common tool that nineteenth-century slave masters used to enforce good behavior in slaves was to make obedience an aspect of religious devotion. Religious instruction to the enslaved frequently focused on obedience, morality, and, although some early teachings to the enslaved denied that they had souls, the possibility of entering heaven through loyalty and obedience to slave masters. See Mia Bay, *The White Image in the Black Mind: African-American Ideas about White People, 1830–1925* (New York: Oxford University Press, 2000), 124–25. Some slave owners romanticized slavery, portraying a system wherein there was mutual affection between the enslaved and the enslaver. This was often done not only as a way to control slaves but also as a way to rationalize enslavement of blacks. Southern newspapers, for example, sometimes printed obituaries of "faithful" slaves that were more glowing than those printed for deceased whites. See Eugene D. Genovese and Elizabeth Fox-Genovese, *Fatal Self-Deception:*

Slaveholding Paternalism in the Old South (New York: Cambridge University Press, 2011), 84.

54. Mark Weiner, *Black Trials: Citizenship from the Beginning of Slavery to the End of Caste* (New York: Alfred A. Knopf, 2004), 4.

55. Anita Aidt Guy, *Maryland's Persistent Pursuit to End Slavery, 1850–1864* (New York: Garland, 1997).

56. Though Douglass stated in his writings that he was owned by Edward Lloyd, Douglass was actually owned by Aaron Anthony, who was an overseer on Lloyd's Wye Plantation. See D. H. Dilbeck, *Frederick Douglass: America's Prophet* (Chapel Hill: University of North Carolina Press, 2018), 12.

57. Ibid., 207.

58. Edward Lloyd V (1779–1834) was the putative owner of Frederick Douglass. Lloyd owned the plantation where Douglass was enslaved during much of his early life. Lloyd was governor of Maryland from 1809 to 1811 and served as a U.S. senator from Maryland from 1819 to 1826.

59. Oswald Tilghman, comp., *History of Talbot County, Maryland, 1661–1861* (Baltimore, Md.: Williams & Wilkins, 1915), 216.

60. Ezekiel Forman Chambers was the maternal uncle of Benjamin Chambers Wickes, Joseph Augustus Wickes, and Peregrine "Pere" Lethbury Wickes, all of whom were students at Princeton in the 1840s and 1850s. For a discussion of the genealogy of the Chambers and Wickes families, see George A. Hanson, *Old Kent: The Eastern Shore of Maryland* (Baltimore, Md.: John P. Des Forges, 1876). Joseph Augustus Wickes was believed to have played a role in betraying Johnson to his master. Ezekiel Forman Chambers served as U.S. senator for Maryland's seventh district in 1826, succeeding Edward Lloyd V, the owner of one of the plantations where slave Frederick Douglass worked as a child.

61. William Still, *The Underground Rail Road: A Record of Facts, Authentic Narratives, Letters, etc.* (Philadelphia: Porter & Coates, 1872), 501.

62. Several fugitive slaves from Maryland who reached freedom provided written accounts of their lives in slavery and their escapes. See James Pennington, *The Fugitive Blacksmith; or, Events in the History of James W. C. Pennington* (London: Charles Gilpin, 1849); Charles Ball, *Fifty Years in Chains, or, the Life of an American Slave* (New York: H. Dayton, 1858); John Thompson, *The Life of John Thompson, a Fugitive Slave* (Worcester, Mass.: John Thompson, 1856); and Noah Davis, *A Narrative of the Life of Rev. Noah Davis, a Colored Man* (Baltimore, Md.: J. F. Weishampel, Jr., 1859).

63. Martha S. Jones, *Birthright Citizens: A History of Race and Rights in Antebellum America* (New York: Cambridge University Press, 2018), 12.

64. Ibid., 13.

65. Entry for Philip Wallis, 1820 U.S. Census; Census, Baltimore Ward 7, Baltimore, Maryland; Page: 353. This census entry shows one free black person and three enslaved persons in the Wallis household.

66. William Henry Siebert, *The Underground Railroad: From Slavery to Freedom* (New York: Macmillan, 1898), vi–vii.

67. Ibid., viii.

68. See, e.g., Sharon Monteith, "Civil Rights Movement Film," in *The Cambridge Companion to American Civil Rights Literature*, edited by Julie Armstrong (New York: Cambridge University Press, 2015); Joseph E. Luders, *The Civil Rights Movement and the Logic of Social Change* (New York: Cambridge University Press, 2010), 56; and Yasuhiro Katagiri, *The Mississippi State Sovereignty Commission: Civil Rights and States' Rights* (Jackson: University of Mississippi Press, 2007), 16–19. Phrases such as "outside agitators," "northern radicals," and "communists" were commonly used during the civil rights era. These phrases were instrumental in shaping behavior and became forms that were embedded in the culture. For a discussion of how such uses of language guide social, legal, and political behavior, see Lolita Buckner Inniss, "A Critical Legal Rhetoric Approach to In Re African-American Slave Descendants Litigation," *Journal of Civil Rights and Economic Development* 24, no. 4 (2010): 649–96.

69. Presbytery of Georgia, "Religious Instruction of the Negroes," *African Repository and Colonial Journal*, November 1844, 332, 336–37.

70. Kate Clifford Larson, *Bound for the Promised Land: Harriet Tubman; Portrait of an American Hero* (New York: Random House, 2004), 30.

71. Ira Berlin, *The Making of African America: The Four Great Migrations* (New York: Viking, 2010).

72. Steiner, "James Alfred Pearce," 332.

73. Ibid.

74. "Wickes-Wallis House," Maryland Historical Trust, Inventory Form for State Historic Sites, June, 1976, https://mht.maryland.gov/secure/medusa/PDF/Kent/K-29.pdf.

75. Steiner, "Severn Teackle Wallis," 59. Philip C. Wallis Jr. was apparently the master of the *Volant*, a steamer that traveled the Mississippi in the 1840s. See *Yazoo City Whig and Political Register*, September 1, 1843, 1.

76. *Easton Gazette* (Easton, Md.), March 7, 1840, 3.

77. Ibid.

78. Entry for P. C. Wallis, Yazoo, Mississippi, p. 321, federal manuscript census of 1840, *FamilySearch.org*, https://familysearch.org/ark:/61903/1:1:XHRL-P35. The P. C. Wallis household consisted of one free white male aged 20–29, one free white female aged 15–19, one free white female under age 5, two male slaves aged 24–35, three male slaves aged 10–23, four male slaves under 10, one female slave aged 36–54, two female slaves aged 24–35, and five female slaves under 23.

79. "Sale of Real Estate," *Sun* (Baltimore, Md.), April 16, 1842, 1.

80. Robert Gilmore vs. Philip Wallis, Elizabeth C. Wallis, Thomas D. Johnston, Josiah Lee, George P. Gover, John Glenn, Charles Simon, Andrew Gregg, James Gregg, John Gregg, Francis H. Smith, Robert M. Proud, Samuel M. Barry, John Hurst, and John W. Walker, Mortgage foreclosure on lots on Charles and Pearl Sts., April 20, 1842, Chancery Papers, Baltimore County Court Maryland

State Archives No.: C 295-2688, http://msa.maryland.gov/msa/refserv/quick ref/html/ba_bcequity.html.

81. *Easton Gazette,* March 7, 1840, 3.

82. John Kennon and Thompson Smith, "Genealogical Aspects of Reported Deaths," *Southwestern Christian Advocate,* November 1, 1844, 43. The *Lucy Walker* was owned by Joseph Vann, a Cherokee Indian who was aboard during the explosion and was killed. See Theda Perdue, *Slavery and the Evolution of Cherokee Society, 1540–1866* (Knoxville: University of Tennessee Press, 1987), 102–3.

83. *Yazoo City Whig* (Yazoo, Miss.), January 3, 1845, http://chronicling america.loc.gov/lccn/sn84020019/1845-01-03/ed-1/seq-2/.

84. Ibid.

85. Ibid.

86. Entry for P. C. Wallis, Yazoo County, Yazoo, Mississippi, p. 85, federal manuscript census of 1850, https://familysearch.org/.

87. Larson, *Bound for the Promised Land,* 28–29.

88. Jeffrey Richardson Brackett, *The Negro in Maryland: A Study of the Institution of Slavery* (Baltimore, Md.: Johns Hopkins University, 1889), 91.

89. Ibid., 66.

90. "An Act to Encourage the More Effectual Apprehending of Runaway Servants and Slaves," in Clement Dorsey, *The General Public Statutory Law and Public Local Law of the State of Maryland, from the Year 1692 to 1839 Inclusive,* vol. 2 (Baltimore, Md.: John D. Toy, 1840), 1115.

91. Brackett, *Negro in Maryland,* 37.

92. Some scholars have noted that the phrase "underground railroad" did not come into regular use until the 1840s, though escaping fugitives had likely used such organized networks before they came to be seen as such. See Eric Foner, *Gateway to Freedom: The Hidden History of the Underground Railroad* (New York: W. W. Norton, 2015), 6–7.

93. Hoang Gia Phan, *Bonds of Citizenship: Law and the Labors of Emancipation* (New York: New York University Press, 2013), 114.

94. Leslie M. Harris, *In the Shadow of Slavery: African Americans in New York City, 1626–1863* (Chicago: University of Chicago Press, 2002), 212.

95. Ibid., 206.

96. Ibid., 212. The Committee of Vigilance generally relied on the tactic of nonresistance, and thus they avoided physical confrontations.

97. William J. Switala, *The Underground Railroad in New York and New Jersey* (Mechanicsburg, Pa.: Stackpole Books, 2006); see also Siebert, *Underground Railroad: From Slavery to Freedom*; and Charles L. Blockson, *The Underground Railroad* (New York: Prentice-Hall, 1987).

98. Joseph A. Boromé, Jacob C. White, Robert B. Ayres, and J. M. McKim, "The Vigilant Committee of Philadelphia," *Pennsylvania Magazine of History and Biography* 92, no. 3 (1968): 320–51.

99. Ibid., 332.

100. Ibid.

101. Andrew Clerk Imbrie to Charlotte Clerk Imbrie, March 10, 1895, Correspondence Home from Princeton, 1891–1895, box 1, folder 20, Andrew C. Imbrie Papers, Princeton University Archives, Department of Rare Books and Special Collections, Princeton University Library.

102. Andrew Clerk Imbrie to Charlotte Clerk Imbrie, March 24, 1895, Correspondence Home from Princeton, 1891–1895, box 1, folder 20, Andrew C. Imbrie Papers, Princeton University Archives, Department of Rare Books and Special Collections, Princeton University Library.

103. Imbrie, "James Johnson of Princeton."

104. Andrew Clerk Imbrie to Charlotte Clerk Imbrie, September 24, 1893, Correspondence Home from Princeton, 1891–1895, box 1, folder 20, Andrew C. Imbrie Papers, Princeton University Archives, Department of Rare Books and Special Collections, Princeton University Library.

105. Andrew C. Imbrie, *Family Record of Andrew Welsh Imbrie and Frances Imbrie*, vol. 1 (n.p.: 1973).

106. Ibid.

107. *Daily Princetonian*, November 23, 1891, 1.

108. Andrew Clerk Imbrie to Charlotte Clerk Imbrie, March 24, 1895, and April 7, 1895, Correspondence Home from Princeton, 1891–1895, box 1, folder 20, Andrew C. Imbrie Papers, Princeton University Archives, Department of Rare Books and Special Collections, Princeton University Library.

109. "An Ex-Slave's Return," *Baltimore Sun*, August 16, 1895, 6.

110. Imbrie, "James Johnson of Princeton."

111. John Thomas Scharf, *History of Delaware, 1608–1688*, vol. 2 (Philadelphia: L. J. Richards, 1888), 766.

112. Ibid., 766–67.

113. "The Princeton Mascot," *Boston Evening Transcript*, August 21, 1902, 8.

114. W. Jeffrey Bolster, *Black Jacks: African American Seamen in the Age of Sail* (Cambridge, Mass.: Harvard University Press, 2009). In the eighteenth and nineteenth centuries, there were both free and enslaved seamen in the Mid-Atlantic. Enslaved seamen were able to capitalize on "their employability and knowledge of white ways and thereby work at the border of slavery and freedom" (ibid., 24). Gerald Mullin estimated that 25 percent of runaway slaves in Virginia between 1706 and 1801 were mariners (quoted in ibid.). See also Jones, *Birthright Citizens*, 21, where she notes that in 1810, 7.4 percent of black heads of household were seamen, and that these men were often sources of regional communication and information.

115. Edward Raymond Turner, *The Negro in Pennsylvania: Slavery—Servitude—Freedom, 1639–1861* (Washington, D.C.: American Historical Association, 1911), 124.

116. Leon F. Litwack, *North of Slavery: The Negro in the Free States* (Chicago: University of Chicago Press, 2009), 51–53.

117. "Navigation of Vessels by Persons of Color," in John H. B. LaTrobe, *The Justices' Practice under the Laws of Maryland* (Baltimore, Md.: Fielding Lucas, Jr., 1847), 238.

118. Ibid.

119. Thomas C. Buchanan, *Black Life on the Mississippi: Slaves, Free Blacks, and the Western Steamboat World* (Chapel Hill: University of North Carolina Press, 2004). Buchanan chronicles how black workers on steamboats linked communities of enslaved and free blacks and aided in escapes. Buchanan notes that both slaves and free blacks did much of the work on steamboats.

120. "An Act to Prevent the Transportation of People of Colour Upon Railroads or Steamboats," in *Laws of Maryland Made and Passed at a Session of Assembly* (Annapolis, Md.: Jeremiah Hughes, 1838), 376.

121. Ibid.

122. Douglass, *Narrative of the Life of Frederick Douglass*, 94–96.

123. Douglass, *My Bondage, My Freedom.*

124. Frederick Douglass, *Life and Times of Frederick Douglass* (Hartford, Conn.: Park, 1882), 245–49. See also David W. Blight, *Frederick Douglass: Prophet of Freedom* (New York: Simon and Schuster, 2018), 80–82.

125. Historian John Muller suggests that James Collins Johnson may, as he claimed, have been invited to escape with Frederick Douglass, and that the plan involving Johnson and Douglass may have been aided by Daniel Lloyd (1812–1875), a son of Douglass's enslaver, Edward Lloyd V.

126. Milton C. Sernett, *North Star Country: Upstate New York and the Crusade for African American Freedom* (Syracuse, N.Y.: Syracuse University Press, 2002), 98–99.

127. Thomas March Clark to John Milton Clapp, September 8, 1835, published online at Spared & Shared 4, http://sparedshared4.wordpress.com/letters/1834-thomas-march-clark-to-john-milton-clapp/.

128. Daniel R. Ernst, "Legal Positivism, Abolitionist Litigation, and the New Jersey Slave Case of 1845," in *Abolitionism and American Law*, edited by John R. McKivigan (New York: Garland, 1999), 103, 105.

129. Stephen B. Weeks, *Southern Quakers and Slavery: A Study in Institutional History* (1896; repr., New York: Bergmann, 1986); Siebert, *Underground Railroad: From Slavery to Freedom.*

130. For an account of James F. Johnson, see Myra B. Armstead Young, *Freedom's Gardener: James F. Brown, Horticulture, and the Hudson Valley in Antebellum America* (New York: New York University Press, 2012).

131. Francis Bazley Lee, *New Jersey as a Colony and as a State: One of the Original Thirteen*, vol. 4 (New York: Publishing Society of New Jersey, 1902), 56. Lee wrote that although it was often said that most blacks in New Jersey were the descendants of fugitive slaves, this was not true except for settlements of blacks in Goulton near Bridgeton, Topetoy Hill on the edge of Mount Holly, and Princeton (ibid., 57).

132. James P. Snell, *History of Hunterdon and Somerset Counties, New Jersey* (Philadelphia: Everts & Peck, 1881), 842–43; *Manual of the Legislature of New Jersey* (Trenton, N.J.: Thomas F. Fitzgerald, 1911), 186.

133. Siebert, *Underground Railroad: From Slavery to Freedom.*

134. Jack Washington, *The Long Journey Home: A Bicentennial History of the Black Community of Princeton, New Jersey, 1776–1976* (Trenton, N.J.: Africa World, 2005).

135. Switala, *Underground Railroad in New York and New Jersey*, 36, 78.

136. "An Ex-Slave's Return," *Baltimore Sun*, August 16, 1895, 6.

2. Princeton Slavery, Princeton Freedom

Epigraph: (First quotation) In that 1836 case, petitioners sought the return of an alleged fugitive slave residing in New Jersey, a man they called Nathan Mead, who called himself Alexander Helmsley. Chief Justice Hornblower of the New Jersey Supreme Court considered the constitutionality of the federal fugitive slave law of 1793 and suggested that the federal government could enforce no part of Article IV other than the Full Faith and Credit Clause. He nevertheless decided in favor of the alleged fugitive, basing his decision on New Jersey's 1826 fugitive slave law. Helmsley later settled in Canada. (Second quotation) Imbrie, "James Johnson of Princeton," 594, 600.

1. Simeon F. Moss, "The Persistence of Slavery and Involuntary Servitude in a Free State (1685–1866)," in *A New Jersey Anthology*, edited by Maxine N. Lurie (New Brunswick, N.J.: Rutgers University Press, 2010), 190–91.

2. Switala, *Underground Railroad in New York and New Jersey*, 29.

3. T. Stephen Whitman, *The Price of Freedom: Slavery and Manumission in Baltimore and Early National Maryland* (Lexington: University Press of Kentucky, 1997), 1.

4. James J. Gigantino II, "'The Whole North Is Not Abolitionized': Slavery's Slow Death in New Jersey, 1830–1860," *Journal of the Early Republic* 34, no. 3 (2014): 411. Gigantino also notes that there was evidence of the underreporting of enslavement.

5. Alvan Stewart, *A Legal Argument Before the Supreme Court of New Jersey at the May Term, 1845, at Trenton for the Deliverance of 4,000 Persons from Bondage* (New York: Finch and Weed, 1845), 26.

6. "An Act for the Gradual Emancipation of Slavery," February 15, 1804, electronically transcribed text of act of the New Jersey State Legislature published by the New Jersey Digital Legal Library, http://njlegallib.rutgers.edu /slavery/acts/A78.html.

7. "Act concerning the Abolition of Slavery," February 22, 1811, electronically transcribed text of act of the New Jersey State Legislature published by the New Jersey Digital Legal Library, http://njlegallib.rutgers.edu/slavery/acts/A83 .html.

8. Ibid.

9. *Ogden v. Price*, 4 Halsted 170 (N.J. Supreme Court, 1827).

10. Ibid., 173.

11. Ibid.

12. "An Act to Abolish Slavery," revision approved April 18, 1846, electronically transcribed text of act of the New Jersey State Legislature published by the New Jersey Digital Legal Library, http://njlegallib.rutgers.edu/slavery/acts/A98 .html.

13. *Thomas Gibbons v. Isaac Morse*, November Term, 1821, 7 N.J.L. 253, accessed May 7, 2016, http://njlegallib.rutgers.edu/slavery/cases/7njl253.html.

14. An Act Respecting Slaves," March 14, 1798, electronically transcribed text of act of the New Jersey State Legislature published by the New Jersey Digital Legal Library, http://njlegallib.rutgers.edu/slavery/acts/A75.html.

15. *Stoutenborough v. Haviland*, in James S. Green, *Reports of the Cases New Jersey Law Reports Argued and Adjudicated in the Supreme Court of Judicature of the State of New Jersey from May Term 1835 to November Term 1836, Inclusive*, vol. 3 (Jersey City, N.J.: Frederick D. Linn, 1876), 266–69.

16. From 1778 to 1837, over forty-five separate revenue acts levied assessments on slaves in New Jersey.

17. "An Act Respecting Slaves," March 14, 1798.

18. *Henry Force v. Elizabeth Haines*, February Term, 1840, 17 N.J.L. 385. The case of Minna is discussed in Hendrik Hartog, *The Trouble with Minna: A Case of Slavery and Emancipation in the Antebellum North* (Chapel Hill: University of North Carolina Press, 2018.)

19. Minna may have found her way back to Henry Force even after everything that had transpired. In the 1840 census, a Henry Force of Woodbridge, Middlesex County, counted among his household a blind female slave aged between thirty-six and fifty-four. See Entry for Henry Force, Woodbridge Township, Middlesex, New Jersey, manuscript federal census for 1840, p. 100. According to the court in *Force v. Haines*, Minna was twenty-nine in 1822 when she was leased to Haines, so in 1840 she would have been about forty-eight.

20. See, e.g., *Township of Chatham v. Canfield*, 8 N.J.L. [3 Wm. Halsted] 52–54 (Sup. Ct. 1824), in which the executors of an estate were held liable for the support of a black pauper on the basis of a provision in the decedent's will. See also *Overseers of Poor of South Brunswick v. Overseers of Poor of East Windsor*, 8 N.J.L. [3 Wm. Halsted] 64–68 (Sup. Ct. 1824), in which South Brunswick sought to remove a pauper slave to East Windsor because his master had lived there before leaving for New York. The court held that East Windsor was not required to support him because he was an unmanumitted slave whose master still had the means to maintain him; see *Overseers of Franklin v. Overseers of Bridgewater*, 20 N.J.L. [Spencer] 567–569 (Sup. Ct. 1846). The ruling in *Overseers of Morris v. Overseers of Warren*, 26 N.J.L. [2 Dutcher] 312 (Sup. Ct. 1857) held that it was not necessary to specify the age of a Negro pauper in an order of

removal to the place of last settlement. An order removing a pauper to Morris Township, where his father had been a slave, was held invalid, since the father had not been legally manumitted there and the child had not been born there.

21. *Overseers of the Poor of Upper Freehold v. Overseers of the Poor of Hillsborough* 13 *N.J.L.* [1 J.S. Green] 289–293 (Sup. Ct. 1833).

22. *Overseers of Poor of Perth Amboy v. Overseers of Poor of Piscataway* 19 N.J.L. 173 (1842).

23. James J. Gigantino, "'The Whole North Is Not Abolitionized': Slavery's Slow Death in New Jersey, 1830–1860," *Journal of the Early Republic* 34, no. 3 (2014): 411.

24. Marion Thompson Wright, "New Jersey Law and the Negro," *Journal of Negro History* 28, no. 2 (1943): 156–99.

25. Joseph Atkinson, *The History of Newark* (Newark, N.J.: Guild, 1878), 239.

26. Ibid.

27. For example, Aaron Burr Sr., the college's second president, purchased a man named Caesar in 1755 shortly before becoming the first college president to occupy Nassau Hall. See Milton Meltzer, *Slavery: A World History* (Boston: Da Capo, 1971), 142. Samuel Finley, the fifth president of Princeton (1761–66), owned six enslaved people when he died in office in 1766. At death Finley's effects included "two negro women, a negro man, and three negro children," along with household furniture, horses, cattle, and books. See William Nelson, ed., *Documents Relating to the Colonial, Revolutionary and Post-Revolutionary History of the State of New Jersey*, vol. 25 (Chesterland, Ohio: General Bookbinding, 1903), vii.

28. That enslaved person was Elizabeth "Betsey" Stockton. Stockton was born a slave in Princeton around 1798. Her mother was a slave who belonged to Robert Stockton. Her father was unknown, but there was some speculation that her father was white, as she was known as a mulatto. While still a child, she came into the ownership of Ashbel Greene, the president of Princeton from 1812 until 1822. See Ashbel Greene and Joseph H. Jones, *The Life of Ashbel Greene* (New York: Robert Carter and Brothers, 1849), 826.

29. As one scholar writes, ideas of high culture, aesthetic sensibilities, taste, and politeness were often closely intertwined with the brutality and inhumanity of slavery. See Simon Gikandi, *Slavery and the Culture of Taste* (Princeton, N.J.: Princeton University Press, 2011), 165–67.

30. Sean Wilentz, "Princeton and the Controversies over Slavery," *Journal of Presbyterian History* 85, no. 2 (2007): 102–11.

31. Beverly C. Tomek, *Colonization and Its Discontents: Emancipation, Emigration, and Antislavery in Antebellum Pennsylvania* (New York: New York University Press, 2012), 15.

32. Archibald Alexander, *A History of Colonization on the Western Coast of Africa* (New York: William S. Martien, 1846), 80.

33. Ibid., 307.

34. James H. Moorhead, *Princeton Seminary in American Religion and Culture*

(Grand Rapids, Mich.: Wm. B. Eerdmans, 2012), 153. See also Tomek, *Colonization and Its Discontents*, cclxv.

35. Not everyone agreed that the faculty at Princeton in the antebellum period was outstanding. One writer observed, in comparing late nineteenth- and early twentieth-century faculty with those who had taught at Princeton earlier in the nineteenth century: "To recruit men of such high quality was no mean task, especially in comparison with their predecessors, the incompetent missionaries and invalid ministers of the mid-19th century." See John D. Davies, "The 'Old' Faculty," *Princeton Alumni Weekly*, November 25, 1960, 6–9. Mid-nineteenth-century Princeton faculty were also described as people who were not fit for "business strife" and who were, it "would seem[,] mostly Princeton alumni who stayed on after graduation, not wanting to go to 'work.'" Princeton was not the only institution to draw heavily from its own graduates for its faculty during its early history. In many of the colleges and universities in the United States, the typical faculty member was a graduate of the college where he taught. See Jack H. Schuster and Martin J. Finkelstein, *The American Faculty: The Restructuring of Academic Work and Careers* (Baltimore, Md.: Johns Hopkins University Press, 2010), 22.

36. Alexander Leitch, *A Princeton Companion* (Princeton, N.J.: Princeton University Press, 1978), 81.

37. James Carnahan, 1820 U.S. Census; Census Place: Georgetown, Washington, District of Columbia; Page 45.

38. Wilder, *Ebony and Ivy*, 263.

39. Nathan Reingold, ed., *The Papers of Joseph Henry: The Princeton Years*, vol. 4 (Washington, D.C.: Smithsonian Institution Press, 1981), 183.

40. James Carnahan, 1840; Princeton, Mercer, New Jersey; Page 42.

41. *The Biblical Repertory and Princeton Review* (Philadelphia: Peter Walker, 1871), 151.

42. William B. Sprague, *Annals of the American Pulpit, or Commemorative Notices of Distinguished American Clergymen of Various Denominations*, vol. 4 (New York: Robert Carter and Brothers, 1858), 737.

43. Albert B. Dod, *Essays, Theological and Miscellaneous* (New York: Wiley and Putnam, 1847), 252.

44. Hageman, *History of Princeton and Its Institutions*, 1:271; Princeton University, *The Princeton Book: A Series of Sketches Pertaining to the History, Organization and Present Condition of Princeton* (Boston: Houghton, Osgood, 1879), 26.

45. James J. Gigantinio II, *The Ragged Road to Abolition* (Philadelphia: University of Pennsylvania Press, 2014), 220. For example, in the 1836 case *State v. The Sheriff of Burlington County*, designated by some historians "the Hornblower Decision," Hornblower wrote, in dicta, that the Fugitive Slave Act of 1793 was unconstitutional.

46. Green argued that slaves were "mere animal[s]" and that freed blacks were little better. He saw free blacks as "an enormous mass of revolting wretchedness and deadly pollution." Quoted in Wilder, *Ebony and Ivy*, 263.

47. Stockton was educated by the Greens and was manumitted around 1817. In 1822 she was sent to serve as a missionary in the Sandwich (Hawaiian) Islands, where she was instrumental in forming the foundations of public education for native Hawaiians. Betsey Stockton chronicled part of her work in Hawaii in a journal, *Betsey Stockton's Journal* (November 20, 1822–July 4, 1823), published at http://www3.amherst.edu/~aardoc/Betsey_Stockton_Journal_1 .html.

48. John Maclean, *History of Princeton: From Its Origin in 1746 to the Commencement of 1854*, vol. 2 (Philadelphia: J. B. Lippincott, 1877), 308.

49. J. Jefferson Looney, "'An Awfully Poor Place': Edward Shippen's Memoir of Princeton in the 1840s," *Princeton University Library Chronicle* 39, no. 1 (1997): 9–10.

50. Thomas Jefferson Wertenbaker, *Princeton, 1746–1896* (Princeton, N.J.: Princeton University Press, 2014), 21. Princeton had been founded using endowment funds from the several early supporters.

51. Ibid., xxi.

52. Princeton University was known as the College of New Jersey from its founding in 1746 until 1896.

53. Wertenbaker, *Princeton*, 21. See also Inniss, "'Southern College Slipped from Its Geographical Moorings.'"

54. See Alfred L. Brophy, *University, Court, and Slave: Pro-Slavery Thought in Southern Colleges and Courts and the Coming of Civil War* (New York: Oxford University Press, 2016), 206–8.

55. Charles Richard Williams, *The Cliosophic Society, Princeton University: A Study of Its History in Commemoration of Its Sesquicentennial Anniversary* (Princeton, N.J.: Princeton University Press, 1916), 35.

56. Ibid.

57. Bruce R. Dane, *A Hideous Monster of the Mind* (Cambridge, Mass.: Harvard University Press, 2009), 68–69.

58. W. Barksdale Maynard, "Princeton in the Confederacy's Service," *Princeton Alumni Weekly*, March 23, 2011, https://paw.princeton.edu/article /princeton-confederacys-service.

59. William Phipps Blake, *History of the Town of Hamden, Connecticut* (Hamden, Conn.: Price, Lee, 1888), 309–10.

60. Robert Field Stockton was a naval officer who rose to the rank of commodore and who is credited later in his career with having successfully negotiated a treaty that eventually led to the founding of Liberia. See Hageman, *History of Princeton and Its Institutions*, 1:326.

61. R. John Brockmann, *Commodore Robert F. Stockton, 1795–1866: Protean Man for a Protean Nation* (Amherst, N.Y.: Cambria, 2009), 58.

62. Thomas Allen Glenn, *Some Colonial Mansions and Those Who Lived in Them: With Genealogies of the Various Families Mentioned*, vol. 1 (Philadelphia: H. T. Coates, 1898), 70–72; 1830 and 1840 Federal Censuses, accessed April 23,

2018, www.ancestry.com.; Alfred Hoyt Bill, Constance M. Greiff, and Walter E. Edge, *A House Called Morven: Its Role in American History, 1701–1954* (Princeton, N.J.: Princeton University Press, 1954), 99.

63. Samuel J. Bayard, *A Sketch of the Life of Commodore Robert F. Stockton . . .* (New York: Derby & Jackson, 1856), 46.

64. Maria Potter Stockton's brother, James Potter, owned escaped enslaved Thomas Sims. In 1851 Sims was arrested in Boston and put on trial for his escape from James Potter's Georgia plantation. Sims was convicted and returned to slavery. See James Buchanan Henry and Christian Henry Scharff, *College as It Is, or, the Collegian's Manual in 1853*, edited by J. Jefferson Looney (Princeton, N.J.: Princeton University Press, 1996), 45.

65. Alexander McQueen Quattlebaum, *Clergymen and Chiefs: A Genealogy of the MacQueen and Macfarlane Families* (Columbia: University of South Carolina Press, 2002), 214.

66. Rachel Caroline Eaton, *John Ross and the Cherokee Indians* (Menasha, Wis.: George Banta, 1914), 19.

67. Clarissa Confer, *The Cherokee Nation in the Civil War* (Norman: University of Oklahoma Press, 2012), 9.

68. Lolita Buckner Inniss, "Cherokee Freedmen and the Color of Belonging," *Columbia Journal of Race and Law* 5, no. 2 (2015): 100–118.

69. The slave revolt started on November 15, 1842, when a group of twenty black slaves owned by the Cherokee escaped and tried to reach Mexico, where slavery had been abolished in 1836. Though the escape failed, it spurred a number of other such slave escapes among the Cherokee. See Tiya Miles, *Ties That Bind: The Story of an Afro-Cherokee Family in Slavery and Freedom* (Berkeley: University of California Press, 2005), 169–71.

70. For example, Andrew J. Polk, a member of the class of 1844 and a cousin to President James K. Polk, spent the Christmas holidays in Philadelphia, about fifty miles away from the college. See John Hope Franklin, *A Southern Odyssey: Travelers in the Antebellum North* (Baton Rouge: Louisiana State University Press, 1977), 69.

71. Edwin Mark Norris, *The Story of Princeton* (Boston: Little, Brown, 1917), 186.

72. See Brophy, *University, Court, and Slave*, 206–8.

73. Charles Richard Williams, *The Cliosophic Society, Princeton University: A Study of Its History in Commemoration of Its Sesquicentennial Anniversary* (Princeton, N.J.: Princeton University Press, 1916), 35.

74. Wright, an 1828 graduate, became a key leader in New York's abolitionist movement. See Eric Foner, *Gateway to Freedom: The Hidden History of America's Fugitive Slaves* (New York: Oxford University Press, 2015), 86.

75. Wright attended the annual meeting of the Literary Society of the Alumni of Nassau Hall, an auxiliary of the Alumni Association of Nassau Hall that was organized in 1832. See C. Peter Ripley, *The Black Abolitionist Papers,*

1830–1846 (Chapel Hill: University of North Carolina Press, 1991), 187. Wright was apparently a former member of the organization. See Lewis Tappan, *The Life of Arthur Tappan* (New York: Hurd and Houghton, 1870), 197.

76. David Brion Davis, *Inhuman Bondage: The Rise and Fall of Slavery in the New World* (New York: Oxford University Press, 2008), 48. See also David E. Swift, *Black Prophets of Justice: Activist Clergy before the Civil War* (Baton Rouge: Louisiana State University Press, 1999), 49.

77. Wright recounted the incident in a letter to Archibald Alexander, one of his former professors at the seminary. See "Fourth Annual Report of the American Anti-Slavery Society, July 1837," *Quarterly Anti-Slavery Magazine* 2 (January 1837): 426.

78. Ibid.

79. Princeton Undergraduate Alumni Index, 1748–1920, http://rbsc .princeton.edu/mudd-dbs/alumni?LNAME=ancrum&FNAME=&YEAR =&qname=ALUMNI&op=Submit. The Ancrums were brothers from Camden, South Carolina; see Mary Chesnut and C. Vann Woodward, *Mary Chesnut's Civil War* (New Haven, Conn.: Yale University Press, 1981), 70.

80. "New and Notable," *Princeton University Library Chronicle* 25, no. 3 (1964): 234.

81. James Carnahan, quoted in "Shameful Outrage at Princeton, N.J.," *Emancipator*, October 27, 1836. Carnahan also denied that any violence had occurred and implied that Wright had himself provoked the attack. The black minister sat down, Carnahan alleged, "while many others unable to find seats, stood during the whole of the discourse" (ibid.).

82. Ibid., 231–32. The student defined lynching as administering thirty-nine lashes with a cowhide, tarring and feathering the man, and setting him adrift in a canoe with a paddle. This could have been a tongue-in-cheek way to refer to more lethal actions, but in the same letter the writer referred to threats that were made to set the man on fire or hang him.

83. John Witherspoon Woods Letters, Student Correspondence and Writings Collection, box 7, folder 10, Princeton University Archives, Department of Rare Books and Special Collections, Princeton University Library. Woods was the grandson of John Witherspoon, the sixth president of Princeton, which made Woods the cousin of Theodosia Ann Mary Prevost, Johnson's rescuer.

84. Ibid.

85. Ibid.

86. "New and Notable," *Princeton University Library Chronicle* 25, no. 3 (1964): 234.

87. Ibid.

88. Ibid., 233.

89. Ibid.

90. Westcott Wilkin, class of 1843, to Sarah Gale Wilkin, February 5, 1841, Student Correspondence and Examination Papers, 1841–1843, box 11, folder 1, Student Correspondence and Writings Collection, Princeton University

Archives, Department of Rare Books and Special Collections, Princeton University Library. Wilkin's father, Samuel Jones Wilkin, was a member of the Princeton class of 1812; his grandfather James Whitney Wilkin was a member of the class of 1785. After Princeton, Wilkin attended law school at Yale and served as a judge in New York and in Minnesota.

91. Ibid.

92. There is no entry in the Princeton alumni database for a Jerry or Gerald Taylor. This may have been a reference to another student surnamed Taylor, or Jerry Taylor may not have been enrolled at the college.

93. John Robert Buhler, "My Microscope," entry dated June 20, 1846, manuscript, Princeton University Rare Books and Special Collections Manuscripts Collection.

94. Ibid.

95. John Robert Buhler, "My Microscope," entry dated June 22, 1846, manuscript, Princeton University Rare Books and Special Collections Manuscripts Collection.

96. Ibid.

97. Edward Wall, *Reminiscences of Princeton College, 1845–1848* (Princeton, N.J.: Princeton University Press, 1914), 31.

98. Ibid.

99. Hageman, *History of Princeton and Its Institutions*, 1:280–81.

100. For instance, William Gulick was the father-in-law of one of Johnson's attorneys, Edward Armstrong. Josiah S. Worth was the jury foreman in Johnson's trial.

101. Ibid.

102. Richard D. Smith, *Princeton* (Charleston, S.C.: Arcadia, 1997), 22–23.

103. The present-day Turning Basin Park is located at 400–401 Alexander Road in Princeton, the spot where many of the businesses of Princeton Basin once stood. As late as the early twentieth century, blacks formed a large part of the Princeton Basin area. For example, in 1899 a black man named Samuel Crews, who according to one press report had "a bad reputation," was shot and killed during a fight with another black man named John Larkin, who reportedly had always "been a steady and hard-working man." Crews was allegedly part of a gang that frequented the area. See "Shot Assailant Dead; Princeton Workman Claims He Killed a Negro in Self-Defense," *New York Times*, July 6, 1899, 2.

104. An advertisement from the July 2, 1839, *Washington Daily National Intelligencer* notes that passengers could travel by train from Philadelphia to Jersey City and that the entire route from Washington, D.C., to New York took six hours and included a steamboat portion at Jersey City, New Jersey.

105. Ibid.

106. Imbrie, "James Johnson of Princeton," 594–604.

107. Entry for Peter Miller, Princeton Township, Mercer County, New Jersey, U.S. manuscript census of 1840, 46, *FamilySearch*, https://familysearch.org/ark

:/61903/1:1:XHYX-26Q, accessed August 24, 2015. The 1880 federal census reported an eighty-three-year-old black male named Peter Miller, born in about 1797, living in the Princeton household of what appears to be a widowed daughter-in-law and grandchildren. It may have been Miller's house in which the family lived; he is described as a laborer and is shown as owning real estate worth $600. See Entry for Peter Miller, Princeton, Mercer County, New Jersey, federal manuscript census of 1880, p. 115, *FamilySearch.org*, https://familysearch .org/ark:/61903/1:1:MN8F-LL7.

108. "Recapitulation of the Aggregate Amount of Each Description of Persons within the District of New Jersey, by Counties and Principle Towns," in *Compendium of the Enumeration and Inhabitants of the United States, as Obtained at the Department of State, from the Returns of the Sixth Census* (Washington, D.C.: Printed by Thomas Allen, 1841), 21–22.

109. Joseph Henry to Elias Loomis, November 29, 1841, in *The Papers of Joseph Henry*, vol. 5, *The Princeton Years, January 1841–December 1843*, edited by Nathan Reingold (Washington, D.C.: Smithsonian Institution Press, 1985), 125–26.

110. Ibid., 226.

111. Ibid., 125–26.

112. According to Edward Shippen, although Parker was sometimes suspected of providing liquor to students, he apparently dealt only in food-stuffs and nonalcoholic beverages. See Edward Shippen, "Some Notes about Princeton," edited by J. Jefferson Looney, *Princeton University Library Chronicle* 59, no. 1 (1997–98): 29.

113. Ibid., 49.

114. Ibid., 29.

115. Ibid., 49.

116. Anthony Simmons willed his property to his wife, Susan Simmons, and several nieces and nephews. Some of the nieces and nephews sued Susan Simmons for part of the estate when she allegedly induced them to sign over some landholdings by telling them (falsely) that they were not entitled to receive any property because their father was an illegitimate child. See *Montgomery v. Simpson*, 31 N.J. 1 (1879).

117. Among the archives at Princeton University is a mortgage held by Anthony Simmons granted by James Brazier. See Brazier, James, Mortgage to Anthony Simmons, 1841, box 2, folder 32, University Land Records, Department of Rare Books and Special Collections, Princeton University Archives, Princeton University Library.

118. Receipt from Anthony Simmons to Princeton for $7.50 in payment for a cord of wood, July 6, 1846, box 2, folder 3, Treasurer's Records, ACS 128, Princeton University Archives.

119. An Anthony Simmons, restaurant owner, is listed as having been born in 1804 in New York to Catherine and John Simmons in the New Jersey Deaths and Burials Index. See Death record for Anthony Simmons, February 5,

1868, New Jersey Deaths and Burials, 1720–1988, *FamilySearch,* https://family
search.org/ark:/61903/1:1:FZCW-Z24, accessed December 12, 2014. A law-
suit by relatives of Simmons (*Montgomery v. Simpson*) indicated that he had died
about March 1, 1868.

120. "Princeton's Colored Cook Dead," *New York Times,* January 26, 1892, 1.
Joline (class of 1775) was the proprietor of the Nassau Inn from 1812 to 1835.
See Varnum Lansing Collins, "Turning Back the Clocks," *Princeton Alumni
Weekly,* April 26, 1929, 857, 862–63.

3. The Betrayal and Arrest of James Collins Johnson

Epigraph: Imbrie, "James Johnson of Princeton," 594, 600.

1. Julia Soon-Joo Lee, *The American Slave Narrative and the Victorian Novel*
(New York: Oxford University Press, 2010), 9–11; Barbara McCaskill, "Intro-
duction," in William Craft, Ellen Craft, *Running a Thousand Miles for Freedom:
The Escape of William and Ellen Craft from Slavery* (Athens: University of Georgia
Press, 1999), viii; Olney, "'I Was Born.'"

2. "True and False Philanthropy," *Nassau Literary Magazine* 9, no. 5 (1845):
185–90.

3. Margaret Abruzzo, "'A Humane Master:—An Obliging Neighbor—A
True Philanthropist': Slavery, Cruelty, and Moral Philosophy," *Princeton University
Library Chronicle* 66, no. 3 (2005): 493–512.

4. Lolita Buckner Inniss, "It's the Hard Luck Life: Women's Moral Luck and
Eucatastrophe in Child Custody Allocation," *Women's Rights Law Reporter* 32
(2010–11): 56. J. R. R. Tolkien coined the term *eucatastrophe* in his discussion of
fairy stories. It refers to a "good catastrophe," the sudden, joyous turn of events
at the end of a story that results in the protagonist's well-being (ibid., 57–58).

5. Hageman, *History of Princeton and Its Institutions,* 1:267.

6. *Maryland Genealogical Bulletin* 21–22 (1980): 174.

7. As late as the 1970s a restored slave cabin that housed an enslaved man,
Sam, born in the 1840s, was present on Cremona Plantation. See "'Sam's
Cabin': Cremona Plantation, Inventory Form for State Historic Sites Survey,"
Maryland State Archives, http://msa.maryland.gov/megafile/msa/stagsere/se1
/se5/026000/026400/026430/pdf/msa_se5_26430.pdf.

8. Richard Henry Spencer, ed., *Genealogical and Memorial Encyclopedia of the
State of Maryland* (New York: American Historical Society, 1919), 239.

9. Probate record for John T. Hawkins, St. Mary's Wills, Liber Jf No 1,
1820–1826; Liber Film No 1, 1826–1840; Liber Gc No. 2, 1840–1857, 269–70,
Maryland Wills and Probate Records, 1604–1998. John Henry Thomas shared
the property with his brother, William Henry Thomas. See also John Martin
Hammond, *Colonial Mansions of Maryland and Delaware* (Philadelphia: J. B. Lippincott, 1914), 244.

10. Office of Dean of the Faculty Records, 1835–1845, Complete and Final
Minutes of Faculty Meetings, 1781–2010, vol. 4, Princeton University Archives,

Department of Rare Books and Special Collections, Princeton University Library, Princeton, New Jersey.

11. Leroy Gresham, "Apropos of Jimmy Johnson," *Princeton Alumni Weekly*, October 4, 1902, 22–23.

12. Ibid.; see also Spencer, *Genealogical and Memorial Encyclopedia of the State of Maryland*, 240–41.

13. Since Severn Teackle Wallis would have been a young lawyer barely thirty years old in 1846, Teackle Wallis Blackiston's may have been named for other family members. Lawrence Buckley Thomas, *The Thomas Book* (New York: Henry T. Thomas Company, 1896), 163. Teackle Wallis Blackiston studied law and began his practice in the office of Severn Teackle Wallis and his uncle John Henry Thomas; see Clayton Coleman Hall, *Baltimore: Biography* (New York: Lewis Historical Publishing Company, 1912), 63.

14. Guy Wallis, *The Wallis Family of Kent County, Maryland* (Kent County, Md.: Guy Wallis, 2011), 45. Severn Teackle Wallis was born on September 8, 1816, to Philip Wallis and Elizabeth Custis Teackle (ibid.). He was named after his paternal grandfather, Severn Teackle. By the 1840s Severn Teackle was an accomplished scholar, so it is possible that Teackle Wallis Blakiston and some other persons born within only a few decades of Severn Teackle Wallis could have been named in his honor. However, numerous other family members born close to the time of the birth of Severn Teackle Wallis were also called Teackle Wallis, suggesting that not all these persons were named for him but for earlier-born Teackle and Wallis ancestors.

15. Entry for John H. Thomas, Free Inhabitants of the 10th Ward of Baltimore City, Maryland, federal manuscript census of 1850, p. 62A, FamilySearch .org.

16. Entry for John Henry Thomas, Inhabitants of the 12th Ward, City of Baltimore, Maryland, federal manuscript census of 1870, p. 27, Ancestry.com. According to this census, John H. Thomas's household included three black servants.

17. "An Act to Authorise S. Teackle Wallis, to Bring Into this State, a Negro Slave therein Mentioned," in *Laws Made and Passed by the General Assembly of the State of Maryland* (Annapolis, Md.: William M'Neir, 1845), n.p., Chapter 164, passed on March 3, 1845, said this: "Be it enacted by the General Assembly of Maryland, That S. Teackle Wallis, Esq'r. of Baltimore city, be and he is hereby authorised to bring into this State a negro slave named Oliver, upon complying with the provisions of the act of eighteen hundred and thirty-nine, chapter fifteen."

18. Maryland State Bar Association, *Report of the Fifteenth Annual Meeting of the Maryland Bar Association* (Baltimore, Md.: Maryland State Bar Association, 1910), 216–17. Cross's brother, Eben Jackson Dickey Cross, also attended Princeton as a member of the class of 1860 (ibid.). Cross's wife, Mary Cabell Porter Breckinridge, also had substantial Princeton family connections. Most noteworthy was the fact that her grandfather, Samuel Miller, was one of the

founding professors at the Princeton Theological Seminary. The woman said to have redeemed James Collins Johnson, Theodosia Ann Mary Prevost, had a Breckinridge brother-in-law, William Lewis Breckinridge, the husband of her sister Frances Prevost, and a Breckinridge uncle by marriage, Joseph Cabell Breckinridge (a member of the class of 1810), the husband of her maternal aunt Mary Clay Smith (the daughter of Samuel Stanhope Smith, a president of the college). Prevost's Breckinridge brother-in-law had taught at Princeton; the nephews attended Princeton and lived with Prevost while they were students there in the 1840s.

19. *Princeton, Sixty-Three: Fortieth-year Book of the Members of the Class of 1863* (Albany, N.Y.: Fort Orange, 1904), 28–29.

20. Gresham, "Apropos Jim Johnson," 22. Gresham, also a lawyer from Baltimore (though he spent much of his life in the ministry), was descended from a slaveholding Georgia family that had relocated to Maryland in the late nineteenth century.

21. Imbrie, "James Johnson of Princeton," 600.

22. Search of surname "Weeks" in Princeton University Undergraduate Alumni Index, 1746–1920, https://rbsc.princeton.edu/databases/undergraduate-alumni-index-part-1.

23. Ibid. William Raymond Weeks, who was born in Brooklyn, Connecticut, was a Presbyterian minister who at one time served at Fourth Presbyterian Church, Newark, New Jersey. On July 11, 1834, Weeks gave a sermon on the sin of slavery. The sermon apparently triggered an anti-abolition riot of a thousand people that damaged the interior and windows of the church. See William Buell Sprague, *Annals of the American Pulpit: Presbyterian*, vol. 4 (New York: Robert Carter and Brothers, 1859), 473–76.

24. William Edward Schenck, *Biography of the Class of 1838 of the College of New Jersey at Princeton, N.J.* (Philadelphia: Jas. B. Rogers, 1889), 150.

25. Nathan Franklin Carter, *The Native Ministry of New Hampshire* (Concord, N.H.: Rumford Printing, 1906), 275.

26. Schenck, *Biography of the Class of 1838*, 151.

27. Ibid.

28. Ibid.

29. College of New Jersey, *Catalogue of the Officers and Students of the College of New Jersey* (Princeton: John Bogart, 1838), 7. Samuel Weeks and John J. Smith lived at 21 West College in the academic year 1837–38.

30. Hanson, *Old Kent*, 98–99.

31. Henry and Scharff, *College as It Is*, 54.

32. Colquitt was governor of Georgia (1877–82) and a two-term U.S. senator from Georgia (1883–94). He served as an officer in the Confederate army, reaching the rank of major general. Colquitt was also the scion of a major slaveholding family. See Lewis Nicholas Wynne, *The Continuity of Cotton: Planter Politics in Georgia, 1865–1892* (Macon, Ga.: Mercer University Press, 1986), 143.

33. Henry Hunter Welles was from Wyalusing, Pennsylvania, and later

became a Presbyterian minister. Albert Welles, *History of the Welles Family in England and Normandy* (New York: Albert Welles, 1876), 190.

34. Bill of exchange signed by John Maclean to College Treasurer J. V. Talmage on March 15, 1844, for payment to Abraham J. Duvant for meals provided to students John Henry Thomas, Joseph Wickes, James Buchanan Smith, Alfred H. Colquitt, and Henry H. Welles, box 2, folder 1, Treasurer's Records, AC 128 Princeton University Archives.

35. The closest common ancestor of Joseph Augustus Wickes (b. 1826), his brother Benjamin Chambers Wickes (b. 1823), and their cousin Simon Wickes (b. 1818), was likely Joseph Wickes (1719–1785). See Hanson, *Old Kent*, 97–99.

36. Ann Fabian, *The Unvarnished Truth: Personal Narratives in Nineteenth-Century America* (Berkeley: University of California Press, 2002), 89–90.

37. Philip Wallis, "The Late Princeton Fugitive Slave Case," *Easton Gazette*, November 18, 1843, 1.

38. These residences are visible in the Fourth District segment of Simon J. Martenet's *Map of Kent County*, 1860, Library of Congress, MSA SC 1213-1-471, http://slavery.msa.maryland.gov/html/mapped_images/ked5.html.

39. James Waddel Alexander wrote that an examination period was occurring during the early days of August and noted his own obligation to conduct an examination on August 7, 1843. He complained that the "hardest work and heaviest examinations come in the heat of summer." See John Hall, ed., *Forty Years' Familiar Letters of James W. Alexander: Constituting, with Notes, a Memoir of His Life* (New York: Scribner and Sons, 1870), 376.

40. James A. Pearce (class of 1856) to Varnum Lansing Collins, July 4, 1916, Wickes, Joseph Augustus, 1917, Undergraduate Alumni Records, box 475, Princeton University Archives, Department of Rare Books and Special Collections, Princeton University Library.

41. In addition to the Wallis-Wickes house, Philip Wallis also inherited from Samuel Wallis the Rebecca Lloyd Anderson House (built circa 1733), which is still on High Street in Chestertown, Maryland. Samuel Wallis, who died in 1807, may have been concerned about Philip Wallis's spending; the elder Wallis stipulated that Philip should not sell the property until he was thirty years old. Philip sold the Anderson house to John Turner in 1829.

42. Wickes House, Chesterton, Maryland, Inventory Form for State Historic Site Survey, Maryland Historical Trust, http://msa.maryland.gov/megafile/msa/stagsere/se1/se5/027000/027700/027762/pdf/msa_se5_27762.pdf. Philip Wallis sold this house as two parcels, the first to William H. Barroll in 1825 and the second to Ezekiel F. Chambers in 1828. Chambers was a member of the extended Wickes family. Barroll was a member of the extended Wallis family.

43. For example, Major Joseph Wickes, who arrived on Kent Island, Maryland, in 1658, became the first slave owner in Kent County, Maryland. See Hanson, *Old Kent*, 90.

44. A process for claiming fugitive slaves had been in place in New Jersey since at least 1798. See "An Act Respecting Slaves," Section 15, published in

Lucius Quintius Cincinnatus Elmer, *A Digest of the Laws of New Jersey* (Bridgeton, N.J.: James M. Newell, 1838), 523.

45. Lucius Quintius Cincinnatus Elmer, *Practical Forms of Proceedings under the Laws of New Jersey* (Bridgeton, N.J.: James M. Newell, 1839), 396–97.

46. Ibid.

47. Ibid.

48. Gresham, "Apropos of Jimmy Johnson," 22–23.

49. *Portland Weekly Advertiser* (Portland, Me.), November 14, 1843, 4.

50. In June 1835 a judgment against Jeffers was issued in favor of William H. Elliott to satisfy the claim. See *Daily National Intelligencer* (Washington, D.C.), June 12, 1885, 1.

51. *Alexandria Gazette*, November 3, 1859, 3. Slave catching was a growing phenomenon in the late eighteenth through the middle decades of the nineteenth century. Blacks, both fugitive and nonfugitive, were in danger of being taken up by organized slave catchers. See Richard Bell, "Kidnappers of Color, the Reverse Underground Railroad, and the Origins of Practical Abolition," *Journal of the Early Republic* 38, no. 2 (2018): 199–230. See also Leslie Harris, *In the Shadow of Slavery: African Americans in New York City, 1626–1863* (Chicago: University of Chicago Press, 2002), 211–12.

52. Key, born in 1779 in Frederick, Maryland, practiced as a lawyer in Maryland and Washington, D.C. He assisted in the conspiracy trial of Aaron Burr Jr. in 1807. Like many of his contemporaries, Key had a complex relationship with slaves and slavery. The Key family was strongly proslavery and owned slaves at their Maryland plantation. In 1800 Key became a slave owner himself, and by 1820 he held twenty enslaved people; see Marc Leepson, *What So Proudly We Hailed: Francis Scott Key, a Life* (New York: Palgrave Macmillan, 2014), 25. Key made scornful reference to enslaved people who had fled to the British during the war of 1812 in the third verse of the poem from which "The Star Spangled Banner" is drawn:

No refuge could save the hireling and slave
From the terror of flight, or the gloom of the grave:
And the star-spangled banner in triumph doth wave,
O'er the land of the free and the home of the brave.

See Robin Blackburn, *The Overthrow of Colonial Slavery, 1776–1848* (New York: Verso, 1988), 288–90.

Francis Scott Key maintained a close friendship with U.S. Supreme Court justice Roger Taney that dated back to their early careers as lawyers in Maryland. Taney, the author of the judicial opinion in *Scott v. Sandford*, 60 U.S. 39 (1857) (declaring the Missouri Compromise unconstitutional), married Key's sister Ann in 1806; see Morley, *Snow-Storm in August*, 43–50. Despite what seemed to be a proslavery point of view, Key also showed some sympathy for slaves. For instance, he represented several enslaved blacks seeking freedom. As a U.S. attorney for the District of Columbia, he argued that over two hundred

Africans who were taken captive on the slave ship *Antelope* should be freed; See Jonathan M. Bryant, *Dark Places of the Earth: The Voyage of Slave Ship* Antelope (New York: W. W. Norton, 2015).

53. Tracy Matthew Milton, *Hanging Henry Gambrill: The Violent Career of Baltimore's Plug Uglies, 1854–1860* (Baltimore: Maryland Historical Society, 2005), 227, 424–25.

54. Ibid., 69, 227–28.

55. On July 4, 1854, Madison Jeffers was severely injured and his ten-year-old son was killed in a train collision. See "Terrible Excitement in Baltimore! Heart-Rending Scene," *Alexandria Gazette*, July 6, 1854, 3; see also John Thomas Scharf, *The Chronicles of Baltimore: Being a Complete History of Baltimore Town* (Baltimore, Md.: Turnbull Brothers, 1874), 545–46; and Melton, *Hanging Henry Gambrill*, 227, 424–25.

56. Jennifer F. Goldsborough, *Silver in Maryland* (Baltimore: Maryland Historical Society, 1983), 261.

57. Jyotsna Sreenivasan, *Poverty and the Government in America: A Historical Encyclopedia*, vol. 1 (Santa Barbara, Calif.: ABC-CLIO, 2009), 123.

58. Charles Lane Venable, *Silver in America, 1840–1940: A Century of Splendor* (Dallas: Dallas Museum of Art, 1995), 148–49.

59. Crandall, the brother of Connecticut abolitionist Prudence Crandall, was prosecuted by U.S. attorney Francis Scott Key. See Leepson, *What So Proudly We Hailed*, 171.

60. Reuben Crandall was charged in 1835 with disseminating antislavery pamphlets in Washington, D.C. See Morley, *Snow-Storm in August*, 127–34. Crandall apparently had a moderate interest in the antislavery movement and came to Washington, D.C., from what had been a thriving New York medical practice in order to attend a patient and lecture in botany. Crandall was arrested when a colleague borrowed from Crandall, read, and then discarded a copy of the *Emancipator*, an antislavery newspaper. A proslavery advocate obtained the discarded paper and gave it to authorities along with information about Crandall. Although Crandall was ultimately acquitted, he spent eight months in prison before his trial, during which time he contracted tuberculosis. The trial itself also took a heavy toll on him. Crandall died eighteen months after his acquittal. See Donald E. Williams Jr., *Prudence Crandall's Legacy: The Fight for Equality in the 1830s, Dred Scott, and Brown v. Board of Education* (Middletown, Conn.: Wesleyan University Press, 2014), 228–31.

61. The Snow Riot was named after Beverly Snow, a successful black restaurateur who became a target of white wrath during the riot. Snow served gourmet food to an exclusive, mostly white clientele. One scholar has asserted that Jeffers was tied to these politically motivated proslavery prosecutions, sometimes at the behest of U.S. attorney Francis Scott Key. See Leepson, *What So Proudly We Hailed*, 171.

62. *United States v. Jeffers*, U.S. Circuit Court for the District of Columbia 1836, 4 Cranch, C.C. 704, quoted in James Brown Scott, ed., *Cases on Inter-*

national Law: Principally Selected from Decisions of English and American Courts (St. Paul, Minn.: West, 1922), 323–25.

63. Morley, *Snow-Storm in August*, 211–20. By 1839 Jeffers was high deputy constable of Baltimore.

64. Jonathan Drake Stevenson, *Memorial and Petition of Colonel J. D. Stevenson of California* (San Francisco: J. R. Brodie, 1886), 81.

65. Wallis, "Late Princeton Fugitive Slave Case," 1.

66. Gresham, "Apropos of Jimmy Johnson," 23.

67. Ibid.

68. Steven Lubet, *The "Colored Hero" of Harpers Ferry: John Anthony Copeland and the War against Slavery* (New York: Cambridge University Press, 2015), 29, 220.

69. Petition of Thomas D. Hogg, Executor, to the Bertie County Court, Petition 21285721, Document Number 7551, North Carolina Department of Archives and History, Records of the North Carolina Supreme Court, Raleigh, North Carolina, https://library.uncg.edu/slavery/petitions/details.aspx?pid =10533.

70. Ibid.

71. Ibid.

72. Gresham, "Apropos of Jimmy Johnson," 23.

73. Varnum Lansing Collins, *Princeton* (New York: Oxford University Press, 1914), 408. Maryland students were prominent in this group. Collins reported that there were sixteen students from Maryland in 1839, eleven in 1842, and twenty-one in 1843.

4. The Fugitive Slave Trial of James Collins Johnson

Epigraph: Quoted in Hageman, *History of Princeton and Its Institutions*, 1:267.

1. Philip Wallis, "The Late Princeton Fugitive Slave Case," *Easton Gazette*, November 18, 1843, 1. Fugitive slave cases, though generally framed as criminal cases, were civil matters that contained many criminal law norms. Hence escapees were typically arrested on warrants and held in municipal custody pending trial, but if adjudged, fugitives were returned to bondage instead of to state incarceration.

2. The inferior courts of common pleas of New Jersey were courts of general jurisdiction that addressed matters relating to the counties where they were located. When a civil case was tried in the inferior court of common pleas, the county clerk recorded the result and issued a formal warrant instructing the sheriff about the legal resolution of the case. Usually the warrant involved the collection of debts, damages, and court fees from one of the parties involved in the suit. The inferior courts of common pleas were abolished in favor of county courts in 1895. See "The Legislation of 1895," *New Jersey Law Journal* 18, no. 4 (1895): 102.

3. Boyce F. Martin Jr., "In Defense of Unpublished Opinions," *Ohio State*

Law Journal 60, no. 1 (1999): 177–97. While some jurists have asserted that the creation of unpublished decisions is a valid response to ballooning numbers of cases wherein issues are repeated, others have expressed the concern that unpublished decisions are sometimes of lower quality and create problems of "predictability, accountability, responsibility, and reviewability." See William L. Reynolds & William M. Richman, "Elitism, Expediency, and the New Certiorari: Requiem for the Learned Hand Tradition," *Cornell Law Review* 81, no. 2 (1996): 273, 284.

4. Frederick G. Kempin Jr., "Precedent and Stare Decisis: The Critical Years, 1800 to 1850," *American Journal of Legal History* 3, no. 1 (1959): 28–54.

5. Steven Wilf, *Law's Imagined Republic: Popular Politics and Criminal Justice in Revolutionary America* (New York: Cambridge University Press, 2010), 108–14.

6. James Kent, *Commentaries on American Law*, 3rd ed. (New York: Clayton & Van Norden, 1836), 476. Kent wrote: "Even a series of decisions are not always conclusive evidence of what is law; and the revision of a decision very often resolves itself into a mere question of expediency, depending upon the consideration of the importance of certainty in the rule, and the extent of property to be affected by a change of it" (ibid.).

7. Henry Scofield Cooley, *A Study of Slavery in New Jersey* (Baltimore, Md.: Johns Hopkins University Press, 1896), 52. One exception to this general rule was in criminal cases where slaves gave evidence against one another.

8. Prior to the Civil War, in all slave states blacks were typically not permitted to testify. This was also the case in some northern states, though there were sometimes exceptions for free blacks. This exception was often tempered by procedural hurdles. In New Jersey, for example, the state Supreme Court held that being black created a presumption of slavery and incompetency that had to be overcome. See *Fox v. Lambson* 8 N.J.L. 275 (1826).

9. Thomas Cobb, *An Inquiry into the Law of Negro Slavery in the United States of America* (Philadelphia: T & J. W. Johnson, 1858), 230.

10. Ibid., 226. The bar on black testimony "is founded not only upon the servile condition of the negro, but also upon his known disposition to disregard the truth."

11. Jeannine Marie DeLombard, *Slavery on Trial: Law, Abolitionism, and Print Culture* (Chapel Hill: University of North Carolina Press, 2009), 76.

12. Ibid., 233. Thomas Cobb wrote what was in its time the comprehensive treatise on the law of black slavery.

13. DeLombard, *Slavery on Trial*, 77. See Ariela J. Gross, *Double Character: Slavery and Mastery in the Antebellum Southern Courtroom* (Athens: University of Georgia Press, 2006).

14. Accomando, *Regulations of Robbers*, 115–17, 137.

15. Ibid., 115.

16. Hageman, *History of Princeton and Its Institutions*, 1:268.

17. Accomando, *Regulations of Robbers*, 135–36.

18. Ibid., 273.

19. Ibid.

20. Lowrey served as a trustee of First Presbyterian Church for one year and as an elder from 1826 to 1845. See Horace Graham Hinsdale, *An Historical Discourse Commemorating the Century of the Completed Organization of the First Presbyterian Church, Princeton, New Jersey* (Princeton, N.J.: Princeton University Press, 1888), 50.

21. Hinsdale, *Historical Discourse Commemorating the Century of the Completed Organization of the First Presbyterian Church*, 50. In 1835 there was a fire at the First Presbyterian Church, and when it was rebuilt in 1837, white members renewed an earlier request that black members form their own church. The black members finally agreed to do so in 1840, when Lowrey, acting for the black members, asked for permission to have a separate communion in their own church. See Hageman, *History of Princeton and Its Institutions*, 1:209.

22. Francis Bazley Lee, *Genealogical and Personal Memorial of Mercer County, New Jersey*, vol. 2 (New York: Lewis, 1907), 487; Hinsdale, *Historical Discourse Commemorating the Century of the Completed Organization of the First Presbyterian Church*, 65.

23. Hageman, *History of Princeton and Its Institutions*, 1:7.

24. Ibid.

25. William C. Alexander headed the College of New Jersey Alumni Association in 1830; see College of New Jersey, *Catalogue of the Officers and Students of the College of New Jersey 1829–1830* (Trenton, N.J.: George Sherman, 1830), 12. See also James Waddel Alexander, *Princeton—Old and New: Recollections of Undergraduate Life* (New York: C. Scribner's Sons, 1898), 89.

26. Hageman, *History of Princeton and Its Institutions*, 1:351–52.

27. Ibid.

28. James Waddel Alexander, *The Life of Archibald Alexander, D.D.: First Professor in the Theological Seminary, at Princeton, New Jersey* (New York: Charles Scribner, 1854), 280. Note that the Waddel family name was frequently spelled "Waddell," even among close members of the family.

29. Robert Olwell, *Masters, Slaves, and Subjects: The Culture of Power in the South Carolina Low Country, 1740–1790* (Ithaca, N.Y.: Cornell University Press, 1998), 155.

30. Ibid.

31. Alexander, *Life of Archibald Alexander*, 280–81.

32. Ibid.

33. Ibid., 281–82.

34. Quoted in Alexander, *History of Colonization on the Western Coast of Africa*, 23.

35. Lefferts A. Loetscher, *Facing the Enlightenment and Pietism: Archibald Alexander and the Founding of Princeton Theological Seminary* (Westport, Conn.: Greenwood, 1983), 56, 83–84, 181. See also Eric Burin, *Slavery and the Peculiar Solution: A History of the American Colonization Society* (Gainesville: University of Florida Press, 2008), 13–14.

36. John Comin and Harold Fredsell, "John Monteith, Pioneer Presbyterian of Detroit," in *Public Education in Michigan*, edited by Gerald L. Poor and Gladys I. Griffin (Mount Pleasant: Division of Field Services, Central Michigan University, 1959), 2. Monteith was one of the founding members of the American Anti-Slavery Society. He was also the first president of and one of the founders of what is now the University of Michigan (ibid., 8). He taught at Hamilton College from 1821 until 1828; see S. H. Cowley, "Notes on the Life of John Monteith," unpublished paper, March 20, 1975, 8–11, http://files.eric.ed.gov/fulltext/ED107169.pdf.

37. Roscoe O. Bonisteel, *John Monteith, First President of the University of Michigan* (Ann Arbor: University of Michigan Press, 1967), 89.

38. Henry Davis, *A Narrative of the Embarrassments and Decline of Hamilton College* (n.p., 1833), 35. Hamilton College was severely stricken by the feud. One year after Monteith left in the spring of 1828, the number of students had declined to nine; it had been 107 in the spring of 1823.

39. Owen W. Muelder, *Theodore Dwight Weld and the American Anti-Slavery Society* (Jefferson, N.C.: McFarland, 2011), 82.

40. Suzanne Flandreau Steel, "A Frontier Library," in *Intellectual Life on the Michigan Frontier: The Libraries of Gabriel Richard and John Monteith*, edited by Leonard A. Coombs and Francis X. Blouin (Ann Arbor, Mich.: Bentley Historical Library, 1985), 211, 214.

41. Edward Armstrong is best known for his editing of an account of the earliest English judicial proceedings in Pennsylvania: *Record of the Court at Upland* (Philadelphia: J. B. Lippincott, 1860).

42. R. F. Williams, *The Members of the Philadelphia Bar, a Complete Catalogue from July, 1776, to July, 1855* (Philadelphia: Decorative Printing House, 1855), 27.

43. *General Catalog of Princeton University, 1746–1906* (Princeton, N.J.: Princeton University Press, 1908), 418.

44. Gulick was the owner of a gristmill in nearby Kingston, New Jersey; see Jeanette K. Muser, *Rocky Hill: Kingston and Griggstown* (Charleston, S.C.: Arcadia, 1998), 5. At one time he was a co-owner of the Nassau Inn; John Henry Hobart, *The Correspondence of John Henry Hobart* (New York: privately printed, 1911), 61. He was also a large-scale landowner and proprietor of a stagecoach line; see A. Van Doren Honeyman, "Two Bedminster Families: McCrea and Henry," *Somerset County Historical Quarterly* 7, no. 2 (1918): 81, 114.

45. Bill of sale of slave named Tom from John Maclean to William Gulick, January 1, 1809, box 1, folder 65, Gulick Family Papers, Manuscripts Division, Department of Rare Books and Special Collections, Princeton University Library.

46. William Beekman Gulick served as a clerk at the Department of the Interior in Washington, D.C., in April 1861, when Confederate troops attempted to take the city; see John Lockwood and Charles Lockwood, *The Siege of*

Washington: The Untold Story of the Twelve Days That Shook the Union (New York: Oxford University Press, 2011), 166.

47. An interesting aspect of the Gulick family in New Jersey is their descent from Anthony Janse van Salee, one of the largest landowners in what is now New York City during the Dutch colonial period. Van Salee is also an ancestor of several prominent U.S. families, including the Vanderbilts and the Whitneys. He was said to be of mixed racial ancestry and was sometimes referred to as black or mulatto. See Carla L. Peterson, *Black Gotham: A Family History of African Americans in Nineteenth-Century New York City* (New Haven, Conn.: Yale University Press, 2011), 40. Some descendants of the Van Salees have denied vehemently that their earliest ancestor in New York was of African heritage. When Jacqueline Kennedy Onassis, a descendant of Van Salee, was confronted with the suggestion that Van Salee had African ancestry, she insisted that the *Van Salees were Jewish, not black.* See Stephanie Rose Bird, *Light, Bright, and Damned Near White: Biracial and Triracial Culture in America* (Westport, Conn.: Greenwood, 2009), 39.

48. *United States v. Holmes*, Circuit Court, E. D. Pennsylvania, 26 F. Cas. 360 (1842).

49. Holmes was indicted under the Crimes Act of 1790, which ordained that "if any seaman, etc. . . . shall commit manslaughter upon the high seas, on conviction, shall be imprisoned not exceeding three years and fined not exceeding one thousand dollars."

50. Brown worked frequently with Robert Purvis, an organizer of the Underground Railroad in Pennsylvania; see Margaret Hope Bacon, *But One Race: The Life of Robert Purvis* (Albany: State University of New York Press, 2012), 71–72, 77–78. In 1857 Purvis and some members of the black community had a falling out with Brown over what was perceived as his betrayal of their interests (ibid., 127–28). In 1836 Brown represented fugitive slave Alexander Helmsley, who had fled Queen Anne's County, Maryland, and faced trial in New Jersey. See *State v. The Sheriff of Burlington*, No. 36286 (N.J. 1836) (unreported decision of New Jersey Court of Errors and Appeals, case records on file at New Jersey State Archives). In the state archives, this case is referred to as *Nathan, Alias Alex. Helmsley v. State* in the Helmsley case file.

51. Philip Wallis, "The Late Princeton Fugitive Slave Case," *Easton Gazette*, November 18, 1843, 1.

52. Hageman, *History of Princeton and Its Institutions*, 1:267.

53. During the early nineteenth century in New Jersey, the designation counselor at law usually signified that a person had been authorized to appear before others in a court of law or equity. Attorneys, in contrast, were not authorized for court appearances but could sign pleadings in common-law courts. New Jersey retained the distinction until 1959. See Walter M. Bastian, "The Profession of Law in England and America: Its Origins and Distinctions," *American Bar Association Journal* 46 (August 1960): 817, 819.

54. Obituary of Samuel Miller Hageman, *Princeton Alumni Weekly*, April 22, 1905, 479; Abraham Van Doren Honeyman, *The Van Doorn Family (Van Doorn, Van Dorn, Van Doren, Etc.) in Holland and America, 1088–1908* (Plainfield, N.J.: Honeyman's Publishing House, 1909), 141.

55. G. Edward White, *Law in American History*, vol. 1, *From the Colonial Years through the Civil War* (New York: Oxford University Press, 2012), 287–88.

56. William D. Popkin, *Evolution of the Judicial Opinion: Institutional and Individual Styles* (New York: New York University Press, 2007), 93.

57. Ibid.

58. Ibid.

59. Hageman, *History of Princeton and Its Institutions*, 1:267.

60. Conway Whittle Sams and Elihu Samuel Riley, *The Bench and Bar of Maryland: A History, 1634–1901*, vol. 2 (Chicago: Lewis, 1901), 372–73.

61. Nancy Isenberg, *Fallen Founder: The Life of Aaron Burr* (New York: Penguin, 2007), 339–40.

62. Steiner, "Severn Teackle Wallis," 58, 71–72. Severn Teackle Wallis was one of several pro-Confederate Maryland legislators who was arrested by federal authorities in 1861. See Robert Brugger, *Maryland: A Middle Temperament* (Baltimore: Johns Hopkins University Press in association with the Maryland Historical Society, 1988), 281.

63. Harry Sythe Cummings was the first black Baltimore city councilman, among other stellar accomplishments during his life. See J. Clay Smith, *Emancipation: The Making of the Black Lawyer, 1844–1944* (Philadelphia: University of Pennsylvania Press, 1999), 145–46.

64. Harry Sythe Cummings and Charles W. Johnson were both graduates of Lincoln University. See David Skillen Bogen, "The First Integration of the University of Maryland School of Law," *Maryland Historical Magazine* 84, no. 1 (1989): 39–41. Two other black students, William Ashbie Hawkins and John L. Dozier, were admitted to the law school, but they were forced out in 1890 because of strong antiblack sentiment (39, 42). After Cummings and Johnson graduated, no other African American students were admitted to the school until a Maryland Court of Appeals decision in 1936 (*Pearson v. Murray*) ruled that the school had to admit them.

65. Steiner, "Severn Teackle Wallis," 62. Steiner extracted this quote from Wallis's address to the University of Maryland Law School in 1869.

66. Ibid.

67. *Prigg v. Pennsylvania*, 16 Peters 539 (1842).

68. Robert M. Cover, *Justice Accused: Antislavery and the Judicial Process* (New Haven, Conn.: Yale University Press, 1975), 195.

69. Ibid., 199.

70. Ibid.

71. See, e.g., Christopher L. M. Eisgruber, "Justice Story, Slavery, and the Natural Law Foundations of American Constitutionalism," *University of Chicago Law Review* 55, no. 1 (1988): 273–327.

72. *Argument of Mr. Hambly, of York, PA, in the Case of Edward Prigg, Plaintiff in Error vs. The Commonwealth of Pennsylvania, Defendant in Error: In the Supreme Court of the United States* (Baltimore, Md.: Lucas & Deaver, 1842), 8.

73. Ibid., 9.

74. Ibid., 8.

75. David G. Smith, *On the Edge of Freedom: The Fugitive Slave Issue in South Central Pennsylvania, 1820–1870* (New York: Fordham University Press, 2014), 94.

76. Barbara Holden-Smith, "Lords of Lash, Loom, and Law: Justice Story Slavery and *Prigg v. Pennsylvania*," *Cornell Law Review* 78, no. 6 (1993): 1086.

77. *Prigg v. Pennsylvania*, 612. For more discussion of Margaret Morgan and the *Prigg* case, see Smith, *On the Edge of Freedom*; and Louis M. Waddell, *To Secure the Blessings of Liberty: Pennsylvania and the Changing U.S. Constitution* (Harrisburg: Pennsylvania Historical and Museum Society, 1986).

78. Howard Jones, *Mutiny on the Amistad: The Saga of a Slave Revolt and Its Impact on American Abolition, Law, and Diplomacy* (New York: Oxford University Press, 1997), 188.

79. *United States v. La Jeune Eugenie, 26 F. Cas.* 832 U.S. App. (1822); *United States v. Schooner Amistad*, 40 U.S. (15 Pet.) 518 (1841). *Amistad* involved the case of the Spanish cargo schooner *La Amistad*, which came aground off the coast of Long Island, New York, in August 1839 with Africans who had been seized from Africa in control of the ship.

80. A revenue cutter was a ship that was part of the U.S. public fleet that helped prevent smuggling of goods and captured Africans. See Irving H. King, *The Coast Guard under Sail: The U.S. Revenue Cutter Service, 1789–1865* (Annapolis, Md.: Naval Institute Press, 1989).

81. *United States v. La Jeune Eugenie*, 846.

82. Ibid., 845.

83. Wendell Bird, *Press and Speech under Assault: The Early Supreme Court Justices, the Sedition Act of 1798, and the Campaign against Dissent* (New York: Oxford University Press, 2016), 473. See also Paul Finkelman, "Story Telling on the Supreme Court: *Prigg v. Pennsylvania* and Justice Story's Judicial Nationalism," *Supreme Court Review* (1994): 247–93.

84. Ibid., 596.

85. Ibid.

86. R. Kent Newmyer, *Supreme Court Justice Joseph Story: Statesman of the Old Republic* (Chapel Hill: University of North Carolina, 1985), 377. See also Henry S. Commager, "Mr. Justice Story," in Gaspar G. Bacon and Arthur N. Holcombe, *The Gaspar G. Bacon Lectures on the Constitution of the United States, 1940–1950* (Boston: Boston University Press, 1953), 31, 44.

87. Smith, *On the Edge of Freedom*, 96. *Dred Scott v. Sandford* was a case involving enslaved man Dred Scott, who sued in Missouri for his freedom after residency in both a free state and a free territory. Scott was victorious in a Missouri trial court. However, the lower court's decision was reversed by the Missouri

Supreme Court. Scott appealed to the U.S. Supreme Court, which ruled against him in a 7-2 decision. See *Dred Scott v. Sandford,* 60 US 393 (1857).

88. Paul Finkelman, "The Taney Court (1836–1864): The Jurisprudence of Slavery and the Crisis of the Union," in *The United States Supreme Court: The Pursuit of Justice,* edited by Christopher L. Tomlins (Boston: Houghton Mifflin Harcourt, 2005), 75, 87.

89. David P. Currie, *The Constitution in the Supreme Court, The First Hundred Years: 1888–1986* (Chicago: University of Chicago Press, 1990), 245n54.

90. Newmyer, *Supreme Court Justice Joseph Story,* 372.

91. H. Robert Baker, *Prigg v. Pennsylvania: Slavery, the Supreme Court, and the Ambivalent Constitution* (Lawrence: University Press of Kansas, 2012), 110–13.

92. Edward Raymond Turner, *The Negro in Pennsylvania: Slavery—Servitude—Freedom, 1639–1861* (Washington, D.C.: American Historical Association, 1911), 197.

93. *National Anti-Slavery Standard,* August 10, 1843.

94. Ibid.

95. Josiah S. Worth was born June 25, 1787, and died June 14, 1854. See *The Trenton Banking Company: A History of the First Century of Its Existence* (Trenton, N.J.: Trenton Banking Company, 1907), 92.

96. Ibid.

97. Thomas F. Fitzgerald and Josephine A. Fitzgerald, *Manual of the Legislature of New Jersey* (Trenton, N.J.: Josephine A. Fitzgerald, 1921), 181.

98. Charles Lanman, *Biographical Annals of the Civil Government of the United States during Its First Century* (Washington, D.C.: James Anglim, 1876), 525.

99. Hageman, *History of Princeton and Its Institutions,* 1:268.

100. Ibid.

101. "Joseph H. Bruere," Class of 1841, box 1, folder 14, Princeton University Class Records, Princeton University Archives, Department of Rare Books and Special Collections, Princeton University Library.

102. College of New Jersey, *Catalogue of the Officers and Students of Princeton University for 1840 and 1841* (Princeton, N.J.: Robert E. Hornor, 1841), 68.

103. Philip Wallis, "The Late Princeton Fugitive Slave Case," *Easton Gazette,* November 18, 1843, 1.

104. Ibid.

105. Ibid.

106. Ibid.

107. Wallis, "Late Princeton Fugitive Slave Case."

108. Ibid. Philip Wallis's letter paints a picture of what might be described as an urban riot.

109. Wallis, "Late Princeton Fugitive Slave Case."

110. Ibid.

111. "The New Jersey Slave Case," *The Constitution* (Middletown, Conn.), August 16, 1843, 2; *Daily Atlas* (Boston, Mass.), August 8, 1843, 1.

112. Stanley Harrold, *Border War: Fighting over Slavery before the Civil War* (Chapel Hill: University of North Carolina Press, 2010), 107–8.

113. Patrick Rael, *Black Identity and Black Protest in the Antebellum North* (Chapel Hill: University of North Carolina Press, 2003), 68.

114. *Daily Atlas*, August 8, 1843, 1.

5. The Rescue of James Collins Johnson

Epigraph: Imbrie, "James Johnson of Princeton," 594, 601.

1. Joseph Henry to Harriet Henry, April 11, 1833, in *The Papers of Joseph Henry*, vol. 2, *November 1832–December 1835: The Princeton Years*, edited by Nathan Reingold (Washington, D.C.: Smithsonian Institution Press, 1975), 57n1.

2. Charles Henry Browning, *Americans of Royal Descent* (Philadelphia: Porter and Coates, 1891), 684–85.

3. *Report of the New York Landmarks Preservation Commission*, "94 Greenwich Street House," June 23, 2009, 3, http://www.nyc.gov/html/lpc/downloads/pdf/reports/94GreenwichstreethouseReportFINAL.pdf.; entry for John Bartow Prevost household, New York Ward 4, New York, New York, p. 726, federal manuscript census of 1800, Ancestry.com.

4. The neighborhood remained popular among New York's elite until the 1850s. Some of the families who lived there were old Yankee and Knickerbocker families like the Whitneys, the Goodhues, and the Suydams. See Eric Homberger, *Mrs. Astor's New York: Money and Social Power in a Gilded Age* (New Haven, Conn.: Yale University Press, 2004), 240.

5. *Report of the New York Landmarks Preservation Commission*.

6. Entry for John Bartow Prevost household, New York Ward 4, New York, New York, p. 726, federal manuscript census of 1800, Ancestry.com.

7. Garret Lansing, *Journal of the Assembly of the State of New York at Their Forty-First Session* (Albany, N.Y.: J. Buel, 1818), 241.

8. Entry for John Bartow Prevost household, federal manuscript census of 1800.

9. Leslie Harris, *In the Shadow of Slavery: African Americans in New York City, 1626–1863* (New Haven, Conn.: Yale University Press, 2004), 1–2. Before the 1827 full termination of slavery in the state, New York had the largest enslaved population outside the South. Harris also notes the discovery in 1991 of an African American burial ground in lower Manhattan. The site, closed in 1790 and in the intervening years covered over by buildings and roads, contained over twenty-thousand bodies of African-ancestored people. Many of those bodies, including the bodies of children, showed signs of hard labor.

10. Edwin G. Burrows and Mike Wallace, *Gotham: A History of New York City to 1898* (New York: Oxford University Press, 1999), 347.

11. Ibid.

12. Walter Barrett, *The Old Merchants of New York City* (New York: Carleton, 1865), 206.

13. Henry Kermit owned two slaves in 1800. See entry for Henry Kermit, New York Ward 2, New York, New York, federal manuscript census of 1800, p. 676, FamilySearch.org, https://familysearch.org. On October 13, 1802, Kermit's black woman slave named Peggy gave birth to a child named Lavina Martin. In a written memorandum of the birth dated June 20, 1803, Kermit wrote that he "abandon[ed]" the child Peggy "according to law. This was a reference to laws permitting slave owners to abandon children to the state. See Birth certificate of Lavina Martin, born October 13, 1802, June 20, 1803, New-York Historical Society, Manuscript Collections Relating to Slavery, Series VII: Legal Documents, 1709–1858, Subseries 1. Birth Certificates, 1800–1818, http://cdm16694.contentdm.oclc.org/cdm/ref/collection/p15052coll5/id/24698.

14. Ronald Bailey, "The Slave(ry) Trade and the Development of Capitalism in the United States," in *The Atlantic Slave Trade*, edited by Joseph E. Inikori and Stanley L. Engerman (Durham, N.C.: Duke University Press, 1992), 205, 215. Bailey asks whether there would have been enough commerce to sustain a trade relationship between the United States and the West Indies without slavery. In 1797 trade with the West Indies in all its various forms constituted one-third of all U.S. foreign commerce. See Stanley Elkins and Eric McKitrick, *The Age of Federalism* (New York: Oxford University Press, 1995), 652.

15. Evelyn Bartow, "The Prevost Family in America," *New York Genealogical and Biographical Record* 13, no. 1 (1882): 28.

16. Samuel Stanhope Smith was known for his theories on the nature of racial difference. See Samuel Stanhope Smith, *An Essay on the Causes of the Variety of Complexion and Figure in the Human Species* (New Brunswick, N.J.: J. Simpson, 1810). Smith is often described as a proponent of black intelligence. For example, he is said to have countered Thomas Jefferson's skepticism that Phyllis Wheatley could have been such an accomplished poet. See Julian D. Mason, "On the Reputation of Phyllis Wheatley, Poet," in *The Poems of Phyllis Wheatley*, edited by Julian D. Mason (Chapel Hill: University of North Carolina Press, 1989), 31. During his time as president of Princeton, Smith became known as something of a religious radical, and he sought to decrease the college curriculum's emphasis on classical education and religion in favor of science. In 1807 Smith expelled three-quarters of the student body for rioting. See Nell Irvin Painter, *The History of White People* (New York: W. W. Norton, 2011), 113–15. The riots were precipitated when one student, Frances D. Cummins, class of 1807, was suspended on March 24, 1807, for harassing townspeople. See Aims McGuinness, "The Great Rebellion of 1807," *Princeton Alumni Weekly* 91 (April 1991): 8, 10.

17. Class of 1818, University Undergraduate Alumni, box 76, Princeton University Archives, Department of Rare Books and Special Collections, Princeton University Library.

18. Bradley J. Longfield, *Presbyterians and American Culture: A History* (Louisville, Ky.: Westminster John Knox, 2013).

19. John Bartow Prevost was the first judge of the Superior Court of the Territory of Orleans from 1804–1808. See Richard N. Côté, *Theodosia Burr Alston: Portrait of a Prodigy* (Mount Pleasant, S.C.: Corinthian Books, 2003), 331. See also Thomas Jefferson to John B. Prevost, July 20, 1804, Tucker-Coleman Collection, Jefferson Papers, Special Collections Research Center, Swem Library, College of William and Mary.

20. Mary-Jo Kline, ed., *Political Correspondence and Public Papers of Aaron Burr*, 2 vols. (Princeton, N.J., 1983), 223–24; Franklin B. Hough, *The New-York Civil List* (Albany, N.Y.: Weed, Parsons, 1858), 428. Prevost is incorrectly listed in Hough as "John P. Prevost."

21. *Ex parte Bollman*, 8 U.S. 75, 2 L. Ed. 554, 1807 U.S. LEXIS 369, 4 Cranch 75 (U.S. 1807). *Bollman* involved the claim that John Bartow Prevost's stepfather, Aaron Burr Jr., had been involved in a treasonous conspiracy against the U.S. government. Some, such as the historian Henry Adams, have asserted that John Bartow Prevost may have helped conceal evidence of Burr's actions. (Burr was later acquitted.) See Henry Adams, *History of the United States of America during the Second Administration of Thomas Jefferson*, vol. 1 (New York: Scribner, 1890), 219, 296, 324. Other information suggests that Prevost knew nothing of Burr's activities and that Burr had not informed Prevost of his plans because Prevost lacked "the requisite discretion." See James Madison, "Report of Bollmans Communication, 23 January 1807," *Founders Online*, National Archives, http://founders.archives.gov/documents/Madison/99-01-02-1325.

22. Mark Fernandez, "Edward Livingston, America and France: Making Law," in *Empires of the Imagination: Transatlantic Histories of the Louisiana Purchase*, edited by Peter J. Kastor and François Weil (Charlottesville: University of Virginia Press, 2009), 279. See also Henry Plauché Dart, "History of the Louisiana Supreme Court," *Louisiana Historical Quarterly* 4, no. 1 (1921): 20–21.

23. Eberhard L. Faber, *Building the Land of Dreams: New Orleans and the Transformation of Early America* (Princeton, N.J.: Princeton University Press, 2015), 135.

24. Gross, *Double Character*, 27–28.

25. Faber, *Building the Land of Dreams*, 127.

26. Dorothy Valentine Smith, "An Intercourse of the Heart: Some Little-Known Letters of Theodosia Burr," *New-York Historical Society Quarterly* 37, no. 1 (1953): 46–47. On hearing that John Bartow Prevost had been named the secretary of a New York City Bank, his half-sister, Theodosia Burr, wrote: "How happy it makes me to hear that you have a salary & are industrious. . . . Will you ever be able to pay your debts? Oh dear brother, that I had a large fortune it should be yours to pay what you owe & make Frances & yourself happy."

27. Fernandez, "Edward Livingston, America and France," 277.

28. Ibid.

29. *The City of New York v. The New York Central Railroad Company*, 199 A.D. 972; 191 N.Y.S. 919; 1921 N.Y. App. Div., 1, 644. Prevost and his wife, Frances Smith Prevost, mortgaged real property to secure $8,000. This case details some of the nineteenth-century history of the land that was the subject of the case, including references to interests of John Bartow Prevost.

30. See *Syndics of Segre v. Brown* in "Cases Argued and Determined in the Supreme Court of Louisiana, Eastern District, June Term, 1813," in Francois-Xavier Martin, *Martin's Reports of Cases Argued and Determined in the Superior Court of the Territory of Orleans and in the Supreme Court of the State of Louisiana* (New Orleans, La.: Samuel L. Stewart, 1846), 421.

31. "Died," *Evening Post* (New York, N.Y.), November 30, 1807, 3.

32. Harold F. Peterson, *Argentina and the United States 1810–1960* (New York: State University of New York, 1964), 38–39, 66–67, 69, 547.

33. Ibid., 38. Prevost sailed on the USS *Ontario*. He was said to have been a political and social favorite of James Monroe. T. C. Elliott, "The Surrender at Astoria in 1818," *Quarterly of the Oregon Historical Society* 19 (March–December 1918): 271, 274.

34. Milton Lomask, *Aaron Burr: The Conspiracy and Years of Exile, 1805–1836* (New York: Farrar, Straus and Giroux, 1982), 44.

35. Both sons graduated from the College of New Jersey in 1818. The graduation for the class would have occurred in the fall of that year.

36. Bartow, "Prevost Family in America," 28. Samuel Stanhope Prevost remained in Latin America after the death of his father. In 1825 he was appointed vice consul to Lima, Peru. He became consul in 1843.

37. Samuel Stanhope Prevost to John Maclean Jr., August 1822, box 2, folder 102, John Maclean, Jr. Papers, Department of Rare Books and Special Collections, Princeton University Archives, Princeton University Library.

38. Felipe Alberto Barreda, *Elespuru* (Buenos Aires: Editorial Lumen, 1957), 77; "National Affairs," *Niles' National Register*, Washington, D.C., November 6, 1841.

39. *The Alsop Claim: The Counter Case of the United States of America for and in Behalf of the Original American Claimants, Versus the Republic of Chile* 15 (Washington, D.C.: U.S. Government Printing Office, 1910), 15.

40. John Bartow Prevost died in 1825 at the age of fifty-eight; see Smith, "Intercourse of the Heart," 53. James Marcus Prevost died in 1829 at the age of twenty-six. Samuel Stanhope Prevost died in 1868 at the age of sixty-four.

41. Lyndon Orr, *Famous Affinities of History: The Romance of Devotion* (New York: Harper & Brothers, 1914), 187; Stephen H. Case and Mark Jacob, *Treacherous Beauty: Peggy Shippen, the Woman behind Benedict Arnold's Plot to Betray America* (Guilford, Conn.: Lyons, 2012), 170.

42. Charles Felton Pidgin, *Theodosia, The First Gentlewoman of Her Time* (Boston: C. M. Clark, 1907), 180–81.

43. Smith, "Intercourse of the Heart," 41, 45.

44. Ibid., 53.

45. Ibid.

46. John Witherspoon Smith was born in 1778 to Samuel Stanhope Smith and his wife, Anne Witherspoon. John Witherspoon Smith graduated from Princeton in 1795.

47. At his death in 1829, John Witherspoon Smith owned a large house and numerous other properties in New Orleans, according to his will. See Samuel Wilson and Bernard Lemann, *New Orleans Architecture: The Lower Garden District* (Gretna, La.: Pelican, 1990), 26–27.

48. Joseph Cabell Breckinridge attended Princeton from 1806 until 1807, when he was expelled for taking part in a campus riot that protested conduct standards. He returned in 1808 and graduated in 1810. See McGuinness, "Great Rebellion of 1807," note 16 above.

49. One source lists a Frances Prevost as a student at the academy during the visit of the Marquis de Lafayette in 1825; *Visit of General Lafayette to the Lexington Female Academy in Lexington, Kentucky* (Lexington, Ky.: John Bradford, 1825), 28. Lafayette Female Academy was originally known as the Lexington Female Academy. Josiah Dunham, the principal of Lexington Female Academy, had invited Lafayette to come to the school. One hundred and fifty students and graduates participated in the program (including, apparently, Frances Prevost). During a speech of welcome to Lafayette, Dunham announced that the school would be renamed in Lafayette's honor. For more discussion of Lafayette's visit, see James Ramage and Andrea S. Watkins, *Kentucky Rising: Democracy, Slavery, and Culture from the Early Republic to the Civil War* (Lexington: University of Kentucky Press, 2011), 14. Lafayette undertook a country-wide tour of the United States in 1825–24, including a visit to the College of New Jersey in 1824, where he received the degree of L.L.D. The degree had been signed by President John Witherspoon in 1790 but had never been sent to Lafayette.

50. Asa Earl Martin, "The Anti-Slavery Movement on Kentucky Prior to 1850" (PhD diss., 1918), 26n39. Note that Breckinridge is often spelled "Breckenridge" across various published sources, including Princeton University records.

51. William Birney, *James G. Birney and His Times* (New York: D. Appleton, 1890), 25.

52. John E. Kleber, *The Encyclopedia of Louisville* (Lexington: University Press of Kentucky, 2001), 724. See also Asa Earl Martin, *The Anti-Slavery Movement in Kentucky Prior to 1850* (Louisville, Ky.: Standard Printing Company, 1918), 129. Breckinridge proposed a plan of gradual emancipation that in many ways resembled the scheme New Jersey adopted (ibid.). He was also an advocate of African colonization; see Lowell H. Harrison, *The Anti-Slavery Movement in Kentucky* (Louisville: University of Kentucky Press, 2015), 56.

53. College of New Jersey, *Catalogue of the Officers and Students of the College of New Jersey, for 1843–1844* (Princeton, N.J.: John T. Robinson, 1844), 724.

54. College of New Jersey, *Catalogue of the Officers and Students of the College of New Jersey, for 1847–1848* (Princeton, N.J.: John T. Robinson, 1848), 102.

55. Smith, "Intercourse of the Heart," 53.

56. Theodosia Burr, Theodosia Prevost's aunt, remarked upon a letter she received from Theodosia Prevost in 1810, but there is no indication of where Theodosia Prevost lived when the letter was sent (ibid.).

57. "Philadelphia, May 15," *New-York Daily Advertiser*, May 16, 1818, 2.

58. John Pintard to Eliza Noel Pintard Davidson, June 22, 1818, in *Letters from John Pintard to His Daughter Eliza Noel Pintard Davidson, 1816–1833*, vol. 1, edited by Dorothy C. Barck (New York: New York Historical Society, 1940), 128–29. John Pintard (1759–1844) began his adult life as a successful and prosperous merchant, thanks to a family inheritance. In 1792 he lost his fortune after participating in Alexander Hamilton's scheme to fund the national debt. Pintard endorsed notes for over $1 million. Pintard had numerous familial connections to Theodosia Prevost, but the closest was apparently through his first cousin, John Marsden Pintard (1744–1810), who was married to Theodosia Prevost's maternal aunt, Elizabeth Smith Pintard.

59. John Pintard to Eliza Noel Pintard Davidson, June 22, 1818, in Barck, *Letters from John Pintard to His Daughter Eliza Noel Pintard Davidson*, 129.

60. Ibid. Pintard wrote of John Bartow Prevost:

If wise & obtainable he ought to stay in S° America in some public character. He wants no talents but application & he cannot condescend to plod for an honest living. There are some characters too lofty, in their own esteem, to submit to vulgar rules of industry & economy. Too proud to labour, they will stoop however to receive pecuniary obligations & to leave their offspring dependent on others. Of all degradations this last is the lowest and I would sooner clean a kennel than not maintain by my own personal labour the children with which God has blessed me. There are different modes & opinions however of Independence. Some are too proud to work & others too proud to live without work.

Pintard may have borne a particular animosity toward Prevost because he appears to have been involved in a real estate deal with Prevost that concerned large mortgages that were eventually foreclosed. See *The City of New York v. The New York Central Railroad Company* (New York Supreme Court 1921), 1, 647. This case detailed some of the nineteenth-century history of the land that was the subject of the case, including references to interests of Prevost and Pintard.

61. "Ann Smith," *Trenton Federalist*, May 12, 1817, 3.

62. Samuel Davies Alexander, *Princeton College during the Eighteenth Century* (New York: Anson D. F. Randolph, 1872), 132.

63. Susan French Smith married Dirck G. Salomons of St. Eustacia, a physician. She moved to St. Eustacia shortly after the marriage but returned to Princeton with her two children when her husband died a few years later in 1815. See H. T. Coates, *Woodhull Genealogy: The Woodhull Family in England and America* (Madison: University of Wisconsin, 1904), 332.

64. Toward the end of her life Susan French Smith Salomons apparently

depended financially on an allowance from her sister, Elizabeth Smith Pintard. See "Letter to John Torrey," December 29, 1841, in *Papers of Joseph Henry*, vol. 5, *January 1841–December 1843, The Princeton Years*, edited by Nathan Reingold (Washington, D.C.: Smithsonian Institution, 1985), 137. According to Joseph Henry, part of Elizabeth Smith Pintard's livelihood came from the "Bayard estate." This may have been a reference to the estate of Judge Samuel Bayard, the husband of Elizabeth Smith Pintard's sister-in-law Martha Pintard Bayard. According to one source, Judge Bayard died on May 12, 1840, leaving a will "with many liberal bequests," but "his estate did not prove adequate to fulfill them all." See Hageman, *History of Princeton and Its Institutions*, 1:228. When this money ceased, Pintard was unable to support her sister, Susan Salomons. Salomons then sought the office of postmaster. See "Letter to John Torrey," December 29, 1841, 137. See also J. Jefferson Looney and Ruth L. Woodward, *Princetonians, 1791–1794: A Biographical Dictionary* (Princeton, N.J.: Princeton University Press, 2016), 210.

65. Elizabeth (Eliza) Smith Pintard, daughter of Dr. Samuel Stanhope Smith, married John Marsden Pintard in 1803; see *New York Evening Post*, May 3, 1803. Her sister, Ann Maria (Smith) Callender, was the wife of Thomas Callender of New York City.

66. Barck, *Letters from John Pintard to his Daughter Eliza Noel Pintard Davidson*, 240.

67. Aaron Burr, *The Private Journal of Aaron Burr during His Residence of Four Years in Europe*, vol. 1 (New York: Harper and Brothers, 1836), 256, 260, 269.

68. Faber, *Building the Land of Dreams*, 127.

69. Peter Force, *The National Calendar and Annals of the United States*, vol. 4 (Washington, D.C.: Davis and Force, 1823), 17.

70. Faber, *Building the Land of Dreams*, 127. See also Kevin J. Hayes, ed., *Jefferson in His Own Time* (Iowa City: University of Iowa Press, 2012), 37.

71. For a discussion of Aaron Burr's treason trial, see R. Kent Newmyer, *The Treason Trial of Aaron Burr: Law, Politics, and the Character Wars of the New Nation* (New York: Cambridge University Press, 2012).

72. Theodosia Ann Mary Prevost's maternal grandmother was Theodosia Stillwell Bartow Prevost, the wife of Aaron Burr Jr. At the time she married Burr, Theodosia Stillwell Bartow Prevost was the widow of British officer James Marcus Prevost. Theodosia Stillwell Bartow Prevost Burr bore a daughter, Theodosia Bartow Burr, in 1783 in Albany, New York. Theodosia Bartow Burr married Joseph Alston, governor of South Carolina, in 1801. On December 30, 1812, Theodosia Bartow Burr Alston set sail on a ship to visit her father and was not heard from again. She was the half-sister of John Bartow Prevost and hence the aunt of Theodosia Ann Mary Prevost.

73. David O. Stewart, *American Emperor: Aaron Burr's Challenge to Jefferson's America* (New York: Simon and Schuster, 2012), 7. Burr believed women to be intellectually equal to men and hung a portrait of Mary Wollstonecraft over his mantel. Not only did Burr advocate education for women, upon his election to

the New York State Legislature, he submitted a bill to allow women to vote. In 1784, as a New York state assemblyman, he unsuccessfully sought to immediately end slavery in that state (ibid.).

74. For instance, when he was in the role of surrogate father to a young visiting French woman, Natalie Delage Sumter, he generously arranged for the payment of all her expenses when she traveled home to France in 1801. See Thomas Tisdale, *A Lady of the High Hills: Natalie Delage Sumter* (Columbia: University of South Carolina Press, 2001), 33.

75. Theodosia Burr wrote in an August 30, 1799, letter to John Bartow Prevost:

> I was not a little surprise & afflicted the other day on seeing our unfortunate brother's farm advertised: sure it will not be sold, it is impossible: it is his all: it would be cruel to deprive him of it. I hope my father has found some means of raising the money: if not what becomes of poor Frederick: you must not fail to write me what has been done for him.

Quoted in Smith, "Intercourse of the Heart," 47.

76. In 1934 Princeton University received as a gift from Edward D. Duffield, class of 1892, a letter to Aaron Burr Jr. from Ashbel Green, the eighth president of the college. Green's letter urged Burr to pay his overdue gift subscription. See "Princeton Bares Woes of Past," *New York Times,* June 24, 1934, N2.

77. "An Unexpected Inheritance," *Baltimore Sun,* October 20, 1858, 1.

78. Ibid.

79. Virgil McClure Harris, *Ancient, Curious and Famous Wills* (London: Stanley Paul, 1912), 342.

80. John Pintard to Eliza Noel Pintard Davidson, April 15, 1817, in Barck, *Letters from John Pintard to His Daughter Eliza Noel Pintard Davidson,* 1:59.

81. Ibid.

82. Hageman, *History of Princeton and Its Institutions,* 1:263–64. Hageman lists Prevost among several "prominent families" who came to Princeton between 1830 and 1840 and took up permanent residence.

83. Joseph Henry to Harriet Henry, April 11, 1833, in *The Papers of Joseph Henry,* vol. 2, *November 1832–December 1835, The Princeton Years,* edited by Nathan Reingold (Washington, D.C.: Smithsonian Institution Press, 1975), 57.

84. Ibid.

85. Somerset County Deeds Book, 519, Somerset County Register of Deeds, Somerville, New Jersey.

86. Thomas Davidson, *The Parthenon Frieze and Other Essays* (London: Kegan, Paul, Trench, 1892), 68.

87. According to notes prepared by Varnum Lansing Collins, Theodosia Prevost lived with a female companion, and the two women were great walkers. See Manuscript Notes on the History of "Jugtown," circa 1927, Varnum Lansing Collins Papers, box 6, folder 5, Department of Rare Books and Special Collections, Princeton University Archives, Princeton University Library.

88. Federal Writers' Project of the Works Progress Administration for the State of New Jersey, *Old Princeton's Neighbors* (Princeton, N.J.: Graphic Arts Press, 1939), 44–45. Some publications have erroneously described the house at 302 Nassau Street as having belonged to Theodosia Stillwell Bartow Prevost Burr, the wife of Aaron Burr. See, e.g., National Register of Historic Places Inventory—Nomination Form for Jugtown Historic District, Princeton, December 1986, 26–27, http://focus.nps.gov/GetAsset?assetID=912dd31c-d911 -4b0a-aa9b-5681192cec84. Theodosia Burr, the most famous of the Theodosias in the Prevost family, died in 1794, long before the house was built. The application also describes the house as having been built in the 1880s or 1890s. Though some renovations may have occurred during this period, the original house was built in the 1830s and was likely the work of Charles Steadman, the famed architect.

89. Varnum Lansing Collins, *Princeton: Past and Present* (Princeton, N.J.: Princeton University Press, 1931), 161.

90. Ibid.

91. Somerset County Deeds Book T, 206.

92. In 1840 R. E. Horner, as executor of Jesse Scott, sold land to Miss Prevost. See Mercer County Deeds, Book B, p. 645. From 1888 to 1897 the Red House was the home of Evelyn College for Women. See Collins, *Princeton: Past and Present*, 143, 144: "The red house, occupied from 1888 to 1897 by Evelyn College for Women which had a lively existence much enjoyed by Princeton undergraduates with introductions and social inclinations, was built by Miss Prevost and was her residence for many years" (ibid.).

93. J. W. Otley and J. Keily, *Map of Mercer County, New Jersey Entirely from Original Surveys*, Camden, N.J., L. van der Veer, 1849. This map was produced by J. W. Otley and J. Keily. See Historic Maps Collection, Firestone Memorial Library, Princeton, New Jersey. It is available online at the Library of Congress website: https://www.loc.gov/item/2004629246/.

94. John Maclean Jr. was a member of the College of New Jersey faculty for fifty years, serving successively as tutor, professor, vice president, and tenth president. His was one of the longest associations in Princeton's history. He was the son of the first professor of chemistry, John Maclean Sr., and was born in Princeton and lived there most of his life. Maclean attended the college and graduated as a member of the class of 1816. He then attended the Princeton Theological Seminary and earned a divinity degree. Maclean began his career in the college as a tutor in Greek at the age of eighteen. He became a full professor at twenty-three, vice president at twenty-nine, and president at fifty-four. Maclean was apparently very popular among students and alumni, especially southerners. As one student observed: "His character was so well known, and he was so popular in the South, that it was said of him in the Civil War, that he could have gone anywhere in the Confederacy unchallenged." See Edward Wall, *Reminiscences of Princeton College, 1845–1848* (Princeton, N.J.: Princeton University Press, 1914), 7.

95. Theodora Prevost to John Maclean Jr., October 21, 1852, box 2, folder 103 (Prevost, Theodosia, 1852–1855), John Maclean, Jr. Papers, Department of Rare Books and Special Collections, Princeton University Archives, Princeton University Library.

96. Ibid.

97. Dellenbusch, Edward, February 12, 1859, John Maclean, Jr. Papers, box 1, folder 68, Princeton University Archives, Department of Rare Books and Special Collections, Princeton University Library.

98. Ibid.

99. In 1841 Stanhope Prevost married Maria Mauricia Moreyra Abella-fuertes Querejazu of Peru, a member of several politically and economically elite Peruvian families; see Ulrich Mücke, *Political Culture in Nineteenth-Century Peru: The Rise of the Partido Civil 72* (Pittsburgh: University of Pittsburgh Press, 2004). Within twelve years, the couple had six children: John (Juan) Francis Prevost-Moreyra, born 1843; Henry (Enrique) Stanhope Prevost-Moreyra, born November 1846; Charles (Carlos) Augustus Prevost-Moreyra, born April 1848; Louis (Luis) Eugene Prevost-Moreyra, born August 1849; Mary Ann (Mariana) Theodosia Prevost Moreyra, born July 1851; and Francis (Francesca) Prevost, born 1853. See Bartow, "Prevost Family in America," 28. Two more children were born after 1853; see Browning, *Americans of Royal Descent*, 685.

100. Theodosia Prevost to John McClean Jr., November 24, 1855, box 2, folder 103, John Maclean, Jr. Papers, Department of Rare Books and Special Collections, Princeton University Archives, Princeton University Library.

101. Ibid. The child was likely Louis (Luis) Eugene Prevost-Moreyra, who was six years old in 1855. See Bartow, "Prevost Family in America," 28.

102. Prevost's will listed her address as High Bridges in New Barbadoes and stated that she had purchased the house from Hannah Maria Knapp. See Last Will and Testament and Codicil of Theodosia Prevost, probated December 28, 1864, Liber I, 496–98, New York Wills and Probate Records, 1659–1999, Ancestry.com.

103. Entry for Eleanor Provost [Prevost], Free Inhabitants in the Town of Hackensack in the County of Bergen, State of New Jersey, p. 74, federal manuscript census of 1860, FamilySearch.org.

104. Last Will and Testament and Codicil of Theodosia Prevost, probated December 28, 1864, Liber I, 496–98, New York Wills and Probate Records, 1659–1999, Ancestry.com.

105. Platt was a New York lawyer. See George Lewis Platt, *The Platt Lineage: A Genealogical Research and Record* (New York: Thomas Whitaker, 1891), 44. He was the partner of John M. Bowers in a New York law firm. See "Sudden Death of James N. Platt," *New York Times*, June 17, 1894, 2. Platt, who never married, left an estate of more than $1 million. See "Will of James N. Platt," *New York Times*, July 8, 1894, 1.

106. Last Will and Testament and Codicil of Theodosia Prevost, New Jersey Index of Wills, Inventories, Etc., vol. 1, Ancestry.com.

107. Frances Caroline Prevost Breckinridge had twelve children with her husband, William L. Breckinridge. See Alexander Brown, *The Cabells and Their Kin* (New York: Houghton Mifflin, 1895), 512.

108. Browning, *Americans of Royal Descent*, 685.

109. "John Bartow Breckinridge," Class of 1843 (undated), box 1, folder 16, Princeton University Class Records, Department of Rare Books and Special Collections, Princeton University Archives, Princeton University Library.

110. College of New Jersey, *Catalogue of the Officers and Students of the College of New Jersey 1842–1843*, 5. Prevost's nephew Marcus Prevost Breckinridge, class of 1854, also boarded with Prevost during his years at the college.

111. Stephanie E. Jones-Rogers, *They Were Her Property* (New Haven, Conn.: Yale University Press, 2019), xii.

112. Ibid.

113. Hageman, *History of Princeton and Its Institutions*, 1:268.

114. Ibid., 23. Castle Howard, near the Millstone River, was on the road from Princeton to Kingston.

115. "Captain Thomas Lavender," *Friends' Review*, February 27, 1869, 419.

116. Doughty was apparently the first Quaker in the area to free a slave. In 1797 he freed his twenty-eight-year-old enslaved man Caesar Foster. Doughty was also instrumental in the passage of New York's emancipation act. See Ethan Allen Doughty, "The Doughty Family of Long Island," *New York Genealogical and Biographical Record* 43, no. 4 (1912): 323.

117. "Captain Thomas Lavender."

118. Ibid., 420.

119. Arthur Edwin Bye, "Stony Brook Meeting at Princeton," *Friends' Intelligencer*, October 31, 1914, 669.

120. Prison Discipline Society, *Reports of the Prison Discipline Society, Boston*, vol. 3 (Boston: T. R. Marvin, 1855), 501, 598.

121. "An Act to Incorporate the Princeton Mutual Fire Insurance Company," 1856, Chapter 85, *Acts of the Eightieth Legislature of the State of New Jersey* (New Brunswick, N.J.: A. R. Speer, 1856), 168.

122. "Captain Thomas Lavender," 420.

123. Ibid., 418.

124. Philip Wallis, "The Late Fugitive Slave Case," *Easton Gazette*, November 18, 1843, 1.

125. "British Officers and American Credit," *Daily National Intelligencer*, August 8, 1843, 3.

126. A. D. Paterson, ed., "The Fugitive Slave Case," *The Anglo American: A Journal of Literature, News, Politics, the Drama, Fine Arts, Etc.*, August 12, 1843, 383. *The Anglo American* was a summary of U.S. news; its report on Johnson's case cited the *Philadelphia Gazette* as its source.

127. Joseph Henry to Harriet Henry, August 1843, in Reingold, *Papers of Joseph Henry*, 5:379.

128. Ibid.

129. Joseph Henry to Elias Loomis, November 29, 1841, in Reingold, *Papers of Joseph Henry*, 125–26.

130. Michael F. Conlin, "Joseph Henry's Smithsonian during the Civil War," in *An Uncommon Time: The Civil War and the Northern Home Front*, edited by Paul Alan Cimbala and Randall M. Miller (New York: Fordham University Press, 2002), 189, 191.

131. "The Slave Case in New Jersey," *Sun* (Baltimore, Md.), August 7, 1843, 2.

132. Miller, "Jimmy Johnson, D.C.L.," 10.

133. Edward Raymond Turner, *The Negro in Pennsylvania: Slavery, Servitude, Freedom, 1639–1861* (Washington, D.C.: American Historical Association, 1911), 197.

6. Johnson's Princeton Life after the Trial

Epigraph: Imbrie, "James Johnson of Princeton," 594, 601.

1. Washing Receipts for Winter 1843–1844, box 2, folder 1, Treasurer's Records, AC 128, Princeton University Archives, Department of Rare Books and Special Collections, Princeton University Library. Here a person called "James Collins" is shown as a payee; this was likely James Collins Johnson.

2. Inniss, "'Southern College Slipped from Its Geographical Moorings.'" Prior to 1794, college rules were silent on student servants. Beginning that year, students were forbidden to employ their own private servants at the college, though nothing seemed to forbid them from employing or boarding servants or enslaved people off campus (ibid., 243).

3. The use of the word *servant* in Princeton rule compilations did not eliminate the possibility of enslaved attendants. Many enslavers employed euphemisms such as "my servant," "my Negro," "my people," or "my boy, girl, man, or woman" instead of the more starkly accurate "slave." See, e.g., Robert Manson Myers, *A Georgian at Princeton* (New York: Harcourt Brace Jovanovich, 1976). Myers gives an account of letters exchanged between April 17, 1850, through June 24, 1852, by Charles Colcock Jones Sr. and his wife, Mary, and their son Charles Jr., a member of the Princeton class of 1852. Charles Jr. wrote in reference to his family's enslaved people: "Picked out a small beef for the people" (ibid., 196) and "Our object is to secure bacon to our people" (ibid., 295). But even if Princeton student rules were read as prohibitions on bringing slaves to campus, it is possible that such provisions were ignored, as were some other provisions of the college rules. For instance, though students were also forbidden to keep firearms at the college for much of the college's history, this prohibition was routinely flouted, as gun-bearing Princetonians were regularly noted. See J. Jefferson Looney, "'An Awfully Poor Place': Edward Shippen's Memoir of the College of New Jersey in the 1840s," *Princeton University Library Chronicle* 39, no. 1 (1997): 28–30. See also entry for February 5, 1844, Faculty Minutes, 1835–1845, Office of Dean of the Faculty Records, Princeton Uni-

versity Archives, Department of Rare Books and Special Collections, Princeton University Library.

4. Henry and Scharff, *College as It Is*, 68.

5. Students frequently used a product called Camphine, the trade name for an illuminating oil distilled from turpentine (ibid., 70). Camphine was about 20 percent cheaper than other burning fluids, but it was more flammable than other oils. Students prepared tightly wound balls of cotton yarns dipped in Camphine that they set on fire and tossed back and forth while wearing gloves. Professor Joseph Henry wrote that "*Fire Balls* are made every 4th of July by the students. They purchase nearly a barrel of the Spirits of turpentine and steep with it balls of cotton wick until they are perfectly saturated." See Nathan Reingold, ed., *The Papers of Joseph Henry*, vol. 2, *November 1832–December 1835: The Princeton Years* (Washington, D.C.: Smithsonian Institution Press, 1975), 422. See also James W. Alexander Jr., *Princeton—Old and New* (New York: Scribner, 1899), 46.

6. Henry and Scharff, *College as It Is*, 58.

7. Ibid. Even with the inconveniences of the smoke and soot, rooms in Nassau Hall were "considered the swell residences" during this period. See Edward Shippen, "Some Notes about Princeton," *Princeton University Library Chronicle* 59, no. 1 (1997): 46.

8. Henry and Scharff, *College as It Is*, 68.

9. Ibid.

10. Ibid.

11. Ibid.

12. Richard D. Smith, *Princeton University* (Charleston, S.C.: Arcadia, 2015), 19.

13. The back campus area was burned down once each session; Henry and Scharff, *College as It Is*, 135. For instance, in 1846 there was a massive burning of the back campus privies; see Wertenbaker, *Princeton*, 243. Burning or exploding privies was apparently a common practice in the early history of the nation's other older colleges and universities. See, e.g., David Alexander Lockmiller, *Scholars on Parade: Colleges, Universities, Costumes and Degrees* (New York: Macmillan, 1969), 80, for the early nineteenth-century burning of privies at what is now Brown University. See also James Axtell, *Wisdom's Workshop: The Rise of the Modern University* (Princeton, N.J.: Princeton University Press, 2016), 188.

14. Nicholas L. Syrett, *The Company He Keeps: A History of White College Fraternities* (Chapel Hill: University of North Carolina Press, 2009), 69; Henry and Scharff, *College as It Is*, 54; Alexander, *Princeton—Old and New*, 89.

15. "'Way Back When," *Daily Princetonian*, March 9, 1940, 2.

16. See note 119, "Gansvoort and Black Jim," *Nassau Rake*, June 27, 1854, 3.

17. See Miller, "Jimmy Johnson, D.C.L.," 10, in which Miller suggests that Johnson was "willing to do jobs obnoxious to local workmen in those preplumbing days (and so gaining the permanent nickname of 'James Odoriferous')."

18. W. E. B. Du Bois, *The Philadelphia Negro: A Social Study* (Philadelphia: University of Pennsylvania Press, 2010), 487.

19. Leslie M. Harris, *In the Shadow of Slavery: African Americans in New York City, 1626–1863* (Chicago: University of Chicago Press, 2004), 80. Harris discusses the limited availability of jobs for black workers in the early emancipation era in New York City, noting that "many of the jobs that black workers held were the ones that white workers feared and despised" (ibid.).

20. Leon F. Litwack, *North of Slavery* (Chicago: University of Chicago Press, 2009), 157.

21. The relatively gentle treatment of white servants is part of what Ariela Gross described as the belief among southern men that all white men were equals, and that only blacks were part of the "mudsill class." See Gross, *Double Character*, 49.

22. Robert Manson Myers, ed., *A Georgian at Princeton* (New York: Harcourt Brace Jovanovich, 1976), 73.

23. Daniel Roland Fusfeld and Timothy Mason Bates, *The Political Economy of the Urban Ghetto* (Carbondale: Southern Illinois University Press, 1984), 286.

24. Sheila Tully Boyle and Andrew Bunie, *Paul Robeson: The Years of Promise and Achievement* (Amherst: University of Massachusetts Press, 2005), 16.

25. Ibid.

26. David R. Roediger, *The Wages of Whiteness: Race and the Making of the American Working Class* (New York: Verso Books, 1999), 147. See, e.g., Phyllis F. Field, *The Politics of Race in New York: The Struggle for Black Suffrage in the Civil War Era* (Ithaca, N.Y.: Cornell University Press, 2009), 40–41.

27. Barnet Schecter, *The Devil's Own Work: The Civil War Draft Riots and the Fight to Reconstruct America* (New York: Walker Publishing, 2009), 37. See also John Gabriel, *Whitewash: Racialized Politics and the Media* (New York: Routledge, 2002), 51.

28. "Scenes in Country Life in Western New-Jersey Number Two," *New York Daily Times*, July 22, 1853, 2.

29. Ibid.

30. Ibid.

31. For example, in 1928, a black prisoner who escaped custody in Middlesex County, New Jersey, complained that he had been removed from a jail where he was serving his sentence and "rented out" as a worker at a nearby farm. See "Peonage Condition Reported in Jersey: Escaped Prisoner Says He Was Hired Out, Beaten and Starved," *New York Amsterdam News*, August 1, 1928, 3. Even as late as 1940, there were allegations that New Jersey farmers and labor contractors used a peonage system that recruited blacks from the South, paid them low wages, and housed them in poor conditions. See Brian Darnton, "'Peonage' on Farms in New Jersey Charged," *New York Times*, August 1, 1940, 17.

32. Entry for James Collins, Free Inhabitants of Princeton Township in the County of Mercer, State of New Jersey, p. 50, manuscript federal census for 1850, Ancestry.com.

33. Leigh Fought, *Women in the World of Frederick Douglass* (New York: Oxford University Press, 2017), 2. Moreover, the practice of not speaking about women in such accounts was often entrenched in later historical writings that uncritically followed the lead of their predecessors in ignoring the women surrounding male subjects (ibid.).

34. Samuel H. Preston and Michael R. Haines, *Fatal Years: Child Mortality in Late Nineteenth-Century America* (Princeton, N.J.: Princeton University Press, 2014), 50.

35. Ibid., 50–57.

36. Ibid., 94. Although some research has determined that child mortality was as much as 89 percent higher for blacks than for whites, Preston and Haines found that such assessments relied on a data set that was largely focused on urban dwellers and thus overstated the trend for rural-dwelling blacks, who typically faced less chance of infant mortality. Preston and Haines calculated overall national child mortality to be 58 percent higher for blacks than whites.

37. Entry for Thomas Collins, District 1, County of Dorchester, State of Maryland, p. 23, manuscript federal census for 1870, Ancestry.com.

38. Death record for Phillis Johnson, July 17, 1852, Princeton, New Jersey, Deaths and Burials Index, 1798–1971, Ancestry.com. A black woman named Phillis Johnson died August 28, 1843, in nearby Ewing and was buried in Trenton, New Jersey. Presbyterian Historical Society; Philadelphia, Pennsylvania; Session/Register_Baptisms, Deaths_1857-1864, Ancestry.com. While this 1843 decedent may have been Johnson's Phillis, it is unlikely, since this is also the period surrounding his fugitive slave trial, and none of the numerous press accounts mention her death. Moreover, given Johnson's propensity for marriage, it is more likely that Johnson's Phillis died in 1852 and that only some six months later he remarried. Most persuasively, the 1850 census shows a Maryland-born, black James Collins living in Princeton with a Maryland-born Phillis Collins. In his interview with Imbrie, Johnson said that his wife was buried in town, but he did not indicate which cemetery. See Imbrie, "James Johnson of Princeton," 594, 597.

39. Marriage of James Johnson and Catherine McCrea, December 23, 1852, New Jersey Department of State, Marriage Records, May 1848–May 1878, Princeton, Mercer County, Book T, page 226, FamilySearch.org.

40. Ibid.

41. Princeton Theological Seminary Alumni Association and Joseph Heatly Dulles, *Necrological Reports and Annual Proceedings of the Alumni Association of Princeton Theological Seminary*, vol. 3 (Princeton, N.J.: C. S. Robinson and Company, 1900), 146–47. Duffield was a professor of mathematics and mechanics at Princeton. He was also an ordained Presbyterian minister who graduated from Princeton Seminary in 1848 and was closely associated with the Second Presbyterian Church in Princeton.

42. Entry for James Johnson, Free Inhabitants in the Princeton Township in

the County of Mercer, State of New Jersey, p. l, federal manuscript census for 1860, Ancestry.com.

43. Some education was available for blacks as early as the 1830s in Princeton as a result of the work of Betsey Stockton at District School number 6 in Princeton Township and at a Sabbath school for black children. See Joan N. Burstyn and Women's Project of New Jersey, *Past and Promise: Lives of New Jersey Women* (Syracuse, N.Y.: Syracuse University Press, 1996), 89. The Witherspoon Street School for Colored Children educated the black children of Princeton from 1858 until the Princeton Public Schools were integrated in 1948. The school was originally in the building at 184 Witherspoon Street, a short distance away from Johnson's home.

44. Entry for James Johnson, Inhabitants in the Borough of Princeton, County of Mercer, State of New Jersey, p. 18, federal manuscript census of 1870, Ancestry.com.

45. Until the late 1800s, 30 percent of women married in their teens. See Albert E. McCormick Jr., *Historical Demography through Genealogies: Explorations into Pre-1900 American Population Issues* (Bloomington, Ind.: iUniverse, 2011), 7.

46. Anna Bustill Smith, *Reminiscences of Colored People of Princeton, New Jersey* (n.p., 1913), 13.

47. Entry for Malon Sorter, Free Inhabitants of Princeton Township in the County of Mercer, State of New Jersey, p. 37, federal manuscript census of 1850, Ancestry.com.

48. Thomas D. Snyder, ed., *120 Years of American Education: A Statistical Portrait* (Washington, D.C.: U.S. Department of Education, 1993), 31.

49. New Jersey Department of Education, *Annual Report of the Board of Education and the Superintendent of Public Instruction of New Jersey, with Accompanying Documents, for the School Year Ending June 30, 1895*, Part 2 (Trenton, N.J.: John L. Murphy, 1894), 154. Princeton High School did not admit blacks until 1919, after a black resident of the town threatened to sue if his child was not permitted to attend high school in town. See Boyle and Bunie, *Paul Robeson*, 28.

50. Corinne T. Field, *The Struggle for Equal Adulthood* (Chapel Hill: University of North Carolina Press, 2014), 89–90.

51. Ibid. A Sarah D. Gordon was born on September 4, 1879, to a father named William S. Gordon and a mother whose maiden name was Sortor, according to New Jersey birth records; "New Jersey Births and Christenings Index, 1660–1931," Ancestry.com. However, she is listed as white, an assessment that may have been based on the census taker's visual inspection of the child and/or her parents. Both Emily and William were designated as mulattos in some accounts, and they may have been very light-skinned. Sarah may have died young. A Sarah M. D. Gordon is recorded as having died on October 22, 1881, at the age of two years, one month. See New Jersey, Deaths and Burials Index, 1798–1971, Ancestry.com.

52. Record of birth of Gordon son, June 4, 1887, District of Columbia, District of Columbia Births and Christenings, 1830–1955, Ancestry.com.

This database is a compilation of records of the Family History Center of the Church of Jesus Christ of Latter-day Saints.

53. Ibid.

54. Entry for William Gordon, Borough of Princeton, County of Mercer, State of New Jersey, p. 29, federal manuscript census of 1870, Ancestry.com; "William S. Gordon," National Park Service, The Civil War, https://www.nps .gov/civilwar/search-sailors-detail.htm?sailorId=GOR0016.

55. Entry for Annie Gordon, Borough of Princeton, County of Mercer, State of New Jersey, p. 29, federal manuscript census of 1870, Ancestry.com.

56. Smith, *Reminiscences of Colored People of Princeton*, 6.

57. Jack Washington, *Bicentennial History of the Black Community of Princeton, New Jersey, 1776–1976* (Trenton, N.J.: Africa World, 2005), 91.

58. Death record for William S. Gordon, 1891, District of Columbia Deaths, 1874–1961, FamilySearch.org.

59. William S. Gordon Pension File, U.S. Civil War Pension Index, *General Index to Pension Files, 1861–1934*, Ancestry.com.

60. Death record for Emily W. Gordon, age 40, August 9, 1895, Princeton, New Jersey, New Jersey Deaths and Burials Index, 1798–1971, Ancestry.com.

61. William S. Gordon Pension File.

62. Claire Prechtel-Kluskens, "Anatomy of a Union Civil War Pension File," *National Geographic Society Magazine* 34, no. 3 (2008): 42.

63. Death record for Cath. Johnson, June 22, 1880, in New Jersey, Deaths, 1670–1988, FamilySearch.org.

64. Ibid.

65. Macdonald was a graduate of the College of New Jersey class of 1871 and a graduate of the University of Pennsylvania medical school in 1875. See "Deaths," *Journal of the American Medical Association* 58, no. 11 (March 16, 1912): 797.

66. Francis Bazley Lee, *Genealogical and Personal Memorial of Mercer County, New Jersey*, vol. 2 (New York: Lewis, 1907), 613.

67. Ibid.

68. State of New Jersey, *Fifteenth Annual Report of the Board of Health* (Trenton, N.J.: John L. Murphy, 1891), 327. Macdonald was one of seven physicians listed in Princeton in 1891, eleven years after the death of Catherine McCrea Johnson.

69. Entry for Cathrine [*sic*] Johnson, wife of James Johnson, Borough of Princeton, County of Mercer, State of Princeton, p. 21, federal manuscript census of 1880, Ancestry.com.

70. John Cruser, administrator of the estate of Joseph Scott, to James C. Johnson, December 25, 1851, Book of Deeds, Mercer County, page 337.

71. Entry for James Collins, federal manuscript census of 1850.

72. See, e.g., Carroll Davidson Wright, *Outline of Practical Sociology: With Special Reference to American Conditions* (New York: Longmans, Green, 1899), 232.

73. Alexander, *Princeton—Old and New*, 88.

74. Ibid.

75. Henry and Scharff, *College as It Is*, 66.

76. Ibid., 56.

77. Frank B. Everitt, "Class Notes, Class of 1886," *Princeton Alumni Weekly*, April 23, 1948, 13.

78. Princeton University, *Quadragesimal Record, Class of '75, Princeton University* (Princeton, N.J.: Princeton University Press, 1915), 35.

79. Washing Receipts for Winter 1843–1844.

80. Receipt to John Maclean from James Collins Johnson, September 9, 1852, box 2, folder 6, Office of the Treasurer Records, AC128, Department of Rare Books and Special Collections, Princeton University Library, Princeton, New Jersey.

81. Receipt to the College of New Jersey from James Johnson, December 19, 1852, box 2, folder 6, Office of the Treasurer Records, AC128, Department of Rare Books and Special Collections, Princeton University Library, Princeton, New Jersey.

82. Record of the marriage of Catherine McCrea and James Johnson.

83. Untitled and undated sketch, box 2, folder 4, University Land Records, Department of Rare Books and Special Collections, Princeton University Library, Princeton, New Jersey.

84. Ibid. The sketch also includes the property owner on the north side of Johnson, Richard Oakham, a black man. Oakham once served as a witness in a case in which his testimony was rejected because he could not produce a certificate of manumission; see Christopher Phillips and Jason L. Pendleton, eds., *The Union on Trial: The Political Journals of Judge William Barclay Napton* (Columbia: University of Missouri Press, 2005), 12. Next to Oakham's land on the sketch is an area labeled "Black Burying Ground." That area is now part of Princeton Cemetery.

85. Davison, "Chap 19th, A Visit to the Colored People of Princeton."

86. Diana Williams, "Can Quadroon Balls Represent Acquiescence or Resistance?" in *Gendered Resistance: Women, Slavery, and the Legacy of Margaret Garner*, edited by Mary E. Frederickson and Delores M. Walter (Urbana: University of Illinois Press, 2013), 115, 119.

87. Ibid., 119.

88. Davison, "Chap 19th, A Visit to the Colored People of Princeton," 1.

89. Ibid.

90. William Simpson was born around 1833. He is shown is the 1860 census as being employed in real estate, which comports with Davison's descriptions of his property ownership. See Entry for William Simpson, Free Inhabitants in the Princeton Township in the County of Mercer, State of New Jersey, p. l, federal manuscript census of 1860, Ancestry.com.

91. Davison, "Chap. 19th, A Visit to the Colored People of Princeton," 4.

92. Ibid.

93. Ibid.

94. Ibid., 7.

95. Ibid.

96. Entry for William Simpson, Free Inhabitants in the Princeton Township in the County of Mercer.

97. Imbrie, "James Johnson of Princeton," 601–2.

98. Entry for James Johnson, Free Inhabitants in the Princeton Township in the County of Mercer, State of New Jersey, p. 1, federal manuscript census of 1860, Ancestry.com.

99. Alexander, *Princeton—Old and New*, 90.

100. This name is variously spelled as "Anetta," "Annett," "Annette," and "Annetta" in census and other historical documents. I use the first spelling in my own writing for consistency.

101. Entry for Anetta Johnson, Ward 2, Princeton Borough, Mercer County, New Jersey, p. 3, federal manuscript census of 1900, Ancestry.com.

102. Entry for Annett Warden, Fifth Ward, Baltimore City, State of Maryland, p. 186, federal manuscript census of 1870, Ancestry.com. Annett Warden is shown here as born 1843, in residence with several persons surnamed Webb.

103. George F. Bragg, *Men of Maryland* (Baltimore, Md.: Church Advocate, 1914), 123; Harrison Webb and Ann Webb, Free Inhabitants of Columbia, County of Lancaster, State of Pennsylvania, p. 16, federal manuscript census of 1850, Ancestry.com.

104. Ibid.

105. It is worth noting, however, that as early as 1815, in *Kitty v. Chittier*, a Pennsylvania federal district court recognized that children born to a fugitive slave mother after her flight to Pennsylvania had an independent claim to freedom that did not rest on the status of their mother. See Richard S. Newman, *The Transformation of American Abolitionism: Fighting Slavery in the Early Republic* (Chapel Hill: University of North Carolina Press, 2002), 77–78.

106. Entry for Harrison Webb, Schedule L, Free Inhabitants of 8th Ward, Baltimore City, County of Baltimore, State of Maryland, p. 568, federal manuscript census of 1860, FamilySearch.org.

107. St. James was the first black Episcopal church south of the Mason-Dixon Line and the third black Episcopal congregation established in the nation. See Bragg, *Men of Maryland*, 86, 123–24.

108. Eric Gardner, *Unexpected Places: Relocating Nineteenth-Century African American Literature* (Jackson: University Press of Mississippi, 2010), 85. Webb was a member of the Galbreth Lyceum, one of several black educational and debating clubs in Baltimore. Founded in 1852 and named for the Reverend George Galbreth, a minister in the AME Zion Church, the lyceum featured a library; sponsored lectures and debates and lessons on grammar, rhetoric, logic, and composition; and later published a newspaper. See Joseph Brown, "'To Bring Out the Intellect of the Race': An African American Freedmen's Bureau Agent in Maryland," *Maryland Historical Magazine* 104, no. 4 (2009): 380, 398.

109. Bragg, *Men of Maryland*, 124.

110. Brown, "'To Bring Out the Intellect of the Race,'" 374, 398; listing for Rev. Harrison H. Webb, *Wood's Baltimore City Directory 1872* (Baltimore, Md.: John W. Woods, 1872), p. 401, *U.S. City Directories, 1822–1995*, Ancestry.com.

111. Will of Harrison Holmes Webb, Maryland Wills and Probate Records, Will Books, Liber J.h.b 45, 1878–1879, 106.

112. Entry for Jordan Warden, Inhabitants in the Fifth Ward, Baltimore City, State of Maryland, p. 186, federal manuscript census of 1870, FamilySearch.org.

113. Listing for Annetta Warden, *Sheriff and Taylor's Baltimore City Directory for 1885* (Harrisburg, Pa.: Patriot, [1885]), 684, *U.S. City Directories, 1822–1995*, Ancestry.com.

114. Listing for Annette Warden, *R. L. Polk Co's Baltimore City Directory for 1894* (Baltimore, Md.: Nichols, Killam, & Maffitt, 1894), 770, *U.S. City Directories, 1822–1995*, Ancestry.com.

115. Alexander, *Princeton—Old and New*, 90.

116. "An Ex-Slave's Return," *Baltimore Sun*, August 16, 1895, 6.

117. Hunter, *Bound in Wedlock*, 298. Blacks married and remarried at rates equal to and sometimes greater than whites.

118. Death record for Emily W. Gordon.

119. "Gansvoort and Black Jim," *Nassau Rake*, June 27, 1854, 3.

120. This may have been a reference to Henry Sanford Gansevoort, class of 1855.

121. *Nassau Rake*, 1859, 92.

122. Ibid.

123. Ibid.

124. Alexander, *Princeton—Old and New*, 88.

125. College of New Jersey Class of 1872, *Essays and Reviews on Subjects, Consequential and Insignificant* (New York: D. Appleton, 1869), 68.

126. Ibid., 94.

127. Ibid.

128. Geneviève Fabre, "Performing Freedom: Negro Election Celebrations as Political and Intellectual Resistance in New England, 1740–1850," in *Celebrating Ethnicity and Nation: American Festive Culture from the Revolution to the Early Twentieth Century*, edited by Genevieve Fabre, Jürgen Heideking, and Kai Dreisbach (New York: Berghahn Books, 2001), 91–92.

129. Hageman, *History of Princeton and Its Institutions*, 1:292.

130. Ibid.

131. Ibid., 1:292–93.

132. Edwin Mark Norris, *The Story of Princeton* (Boston: Little, Brown, 1917), 190.

133. Ibid.

134. John Maclean, "The Recent Riot at Princeton College," *New York Times*, September 24, 1861.

135. Iver Bernstein, *The New York City Draft Riots* (New York: Oxford University Press, 1990), 13.

136. "Another Day of Rioting," *New York Times*, July 18, 1863.

137. Ibid.

138. Hageman, *History of Princeton and Its Institutions*, 1:300.

139. Ibid.

140. Ibid., 308. Black regiments were not issued official flags that distinguished them as distinct regiments, but special flags were often presented to them nonetheless. A series of seven Pennsylvania regimental flags was created by David Bustill Bowser, a black artist in Philadelphia. Bowser was an ancestor of Maria Bustill Robeson, the mother of native Princetonian Paul Robeson. Many of the black regimental flags were decorated with allegorical scenes that combined the black experience with the history of the broader United States. The flag of the Sixth Regiment in Pennsylvania showed Columbia, the personification of liberty, speaking to a soldier in combat gear while a black girl applauds. See Philip R. N. Katcher, *Flags of the American Civil War*, vol. 3, *State and Volunteer* (Oxford: Osprey, 1993), 40.

141. Edward A. Miller, *The Black Civil War Soldiers of Illinois: The Story of the Twenty-Ninth U.S. Colored Infantry* (Columbia: University of South Carolina Press, 1998), 19.

142. Ibid.

143. "Trial of James Lewis for the Murder of James Rowland," 1863, box 354, folder 8, Historical Subject Files Collection, Princeton University Archives, Department of Rare Books and Special Collections, Princeton University Library.

144. For more on Richard T. Greener, the first black graduate at Harvard College, see Werner Sollors, Caldwell Titcomb, and Thomas A. Underwood, *Blacks at Harvard: A Documentary History of African-American Experience at Harvard and Radcliffe* (New York: New York University Press, 1993), 37. For Richard Henry Green, the first black graduate of Yale University, see Ariel Kaminer, "Discovery Leads Yale to Revise a Chapter of Its Black History," *New York Times*, March 4, 2014, A14.

145. James Axtell, *The Making of Princeton University: From Woodrow Wilson to the Present* (Princeton, N.J.: Princeton University Press, 2006), 144. Another source suggests that there may have been earlier black graduates who passed as white. Maurine Rothschild, "*Frances O. Grant*, Interview," in *The Black Woman Oral History Project*, vol. 4, edited by Ruth Edmonds Hill (Westport, Conn.: Meckler, 1991), 377. In dismissing Woodrow Wilson's policies discouraging the attendance of black students, Grant asserted that "a great many Negroes" knew "two or three students who had gone through Princeton as white" (ibid.).

146. Robert Bridges, "Undergraduate Life in the Seventies," *Princeton Alumni Weekly*, January 23, 1931, 375, 377.

147. Ibid., 377.

148. Ibid.

149. W. E. B. Du Bois, *The College-Bred Negro* (Atlanta: Atlanta University Press, 1900), 36.

150. Ibid.

151. "Colored Instructor Dead," *New York Times*, January 4, 1903, 22.

152. Ibid.

153. Ibid.

154. Victor O. Freeburg, *William Henry Welch at Eighty: A Memorial Record of Celebrations around the World in His Honor* (New York: Milbank Memorial Fund, 1930), 69.

155. John Starr, *Hospital City: The Story of the Men and Women of Bellevue* (New York: Crown, 1957), 134.

156. "Colored Instructor Dead."

157. "White and Black Married: How a Young Farmer Wooed and Won an Old Negro's Daughter," *New York Times*, April 9, 1887, 5.

158. The other two are Connecticut and New Hampshire. See Fay Botham, *Almighty God Created the Races: Christianity, Interracial Marriage, and American Law* (Chapel Hill: University of North Carolina Press, 2009), 52–53.

159. Entry for Cornelius Van Tilburg, Raritan Township, Middlesex County, New Jersey, p. 11, federal manuscript census for 1900, Ancestry.com.

160. Entry for Cornelius Van Tilburgh, Piscataway Township, Middlesex County, New Jersey, p. 13A, federal manuscript census for 1910, Ancestry.com.

161. Sourland Mountain extends from the Delaware River at Lambertville to the western end of Hillsborough Township near the community of Neshanic, through Montgomery Township and into Hopewell Township in Mercer County.

162. "Miscegenation in New Jersey: A Colony of Ignorant Black and White People, Their Mode of Life," *New York Times*, May 27, 1879, 2.

163. An example is Sylvia Dubois, a black woman from the Sourland Mountain area who lived and worked in Princeton for decades. Dubois worked for many years in the home of Louis Tulane, the father of Paul Tulane, who founded Tulane University in New Orleans. Dubois cared for Paul Tulane when he was a small child. She later worked for Victor Tulane, Paul's brother. Dubois seems to have taken great pains to tell an interviewer who asked about her years with the Tulanes in Princeton that Victor Tulane was a "great man and a good man" who "used his servants well," that Paul Tulane was a nice boy, Madam Tulane was a good woman, and "all the servants liked 'em." See Cornelius Wilson Larison, *Silvia Dubois: A Biografy of the Slave Who Whipt Her Mistress and Ganed Her Freedom*, edited by Jared Lobdell (1883; repr., New York: Oxford University Press, 1988), 70.

164. "The Black and White Inhabitants of Sourland Mountain," *New York Times*, January 2, 1880, 5.

165. *Nassau Rake*, June.

166. *Nassau Rake*, June 1858, 26.

167. Ibid.

168. "Collins on the Stand," *Sun*, July 18, 1895.

169. "Two Princeton Students Shot," *New York Times*, June 8, 1895, 3; "The

Ohl Murder Trial Defense in Opening Sets Up Justifiable Homicide," *Trenton Evening Times*, July 17, 1895. At one point Downes denied being present during the incident.

170. "Collins Tells His Story," *New York Times*, July 18, 1895, 9. The article noted that among the observers at the trial were Mary Brown Wanamaker Warburton, the then-newlywed wife of Barclay Warburton, publisher of the *Philadelphia Evening Telegraph*, and Anne Tracy Morgan, the youngest daughter of wealthy financier John Pierpont Morgan.

171. "Frederick P. Ohl Is Dead," *New York Times*, June 13, 1895, 5.

172. "Murderer Freed, Will Work Here," *Trenton Times*, October 16, 1909.

173. "Postscript to a Letter from F. H. Braislin, September 16, 1892," Braislin, Frank Howard, 1894; Undergraduate Alumni Records, box 223, Princeton University Archives, Department of Rare Books and Special Collections, Princeton University Library.

174. Ibid.

175. Ibid.

176. *Princeton Press*, May 16, 1896.

177. Ibid.

178. Entries for James Johnson and Anetta Johnson, Princeton Township, Mercer County, New Jersey, p. 3, federal manuscript census of 1900, Ancestry .com.

179. "The pathetic case of 'Uncle Dicky Redding' is shown in one of the photographs. There he sits in the wreck of a building which he formerly owned, still allowed to remain by the kindness of the present owner, because it would break the old man's heart to even know that his house belonged to another. It was sold for taxes—a little assistance at that time might have pre-served what is really a valuable property to the old man." See New Jersey State Conference of Social Work, *Proceedings of the New Jersey Conference of Charities and Corrections: Tenth Annual Meeting* (Trenton, N.J.: MacRellish and Quigley, 1911), 250.

180. Entry for Anetta Johnson, Princeton Township, Mercer County, New Jersey, p. 3, federal manuscript census of 1900, Ancestry.com. Anetta's occupa-tion is listed as dressmaker.

181. Martin Duberman, *Paul Robeson: A Biography* (New York: Open Road Media, 2014), 567. Alexander "Ting" Robert Taylor Jr. was the son of Alex-ander Robert Taylor Sr. and Anetta V. Webb. Anetta V. Webb was the daughter of Harrison Homes Webb Jr. and the niece of Anetta Webb Warden Johnson, the last wife of James Collins Johnson. A nephew of Alexander "Ting" Robert Taylor reported that the nickname Ting was bestowed because his uncle "always had change jingling in his pockets" (telephone interview with George H. Taylor Jr., June 15, 2015).

182. William Drew Robeson was born into slavery on the Robeson plan-tation in Cross Road Township, Martin County, North Carolina. He escaped slavery in his midteens and fled north, where he first settled in Pennsylvania and

then joined the Union Army during the Civil War. Robeson attended college at Lincoln University, and then married Maria Bustill, a member of a prominent black, white, and Native American mixed-race family. The elder Robeson served as minister of Witherspoon Presbyterian Church from 1880 until 1901. See Duberman, *Paul Robeson*, 567–70. Though Robeson was highly popular among his black parishioners, many white Princetonians resented his advocacy for black rights in Princeton and caused him to be removed from his Princeton pulpit. See Boyle and Bunie, *Paul Robeson*, 16.

183. William Hudnut, "Class Notes," *Princeton Alumni Weekly*, October 9, 1959, 16.

184. Ibid.

185. Philip Yale Nicholson, *Labor's Story in the United States* (Philadelphia, Pa.: Temple University Press, 2004), 131. Millions of workers, farmers, and businesses lost jobs and businesses.

186. Imbrie, "James Johnson of Princeton," 602.

187. Hunter at 223.

188. Philip Sheldon Foner, ed., *Paul Robeson Speaks: Writings, Speeches, and Interviews, 1918–1974* (New York: Citadel, 1978), 201.

189. New Jersey State Conference of Social Work, *Proceedings of the New Jersey Conference of Charities*, 250. The conference reported that "there are at present no paupers in Princeton; that is, no poor supported entirely by the town. There are but ten cases now receiving assistance from this town, eight of these are colored, two are Italians."

190. Greene roomed with the family of Charlotte Martins, also an employee of the library. Charlotte Martins's grandfather was from the West Indies and may have been black or mixed race. See Heidi Ardizzone, *An Illuminated Life: Belle Da Costa Greene's Journey from Prejudice to Privilege* (New York W. W. Norton, 2007), 63–65.

191. Ibid., 69.

192. Susie J. Pak, *Gentleman Bankers: The World of J. P. Morgan* (Cambridge, Mass.: Harvard University Press, 2013), 45–46; J. Clay Smith, *Emancipation: The Making of the Black Lawyer, 1844–1944* (Philadelphia: University of Pennsylvania Press, 1999), 46.

193. Pak, *Gentleman Bankers*, 46.

194. Ibid.

195. Ibid.

196. "Aged Princeton Negro Dead," *New York Times*, July 23, 1902, 9; "Princeton Old Vendor Dead," *Cleveland Plain Dealer*, July 23, 1902, 2; "Death Notice, James Johnson," *St. Albans Daily Messenger* (Vt.), July 23, 1902, 2; "'Jimmie' Is Dead: Fruit Vender and Mascot of Princeton College Passes Away," *Trenton Evening Times*, July 23, 1902, 3.

197. In the October 1902 *Princeton Alumni Weekly*, letters appeared recalling Johnson. See, e.g., Leroy Gresham '92, "Apropos of Jimmy Johnson," *Princeton Alumni Weekly*, October 4, 1902, 22–23. One alumnus, a member of the class

of 1886, recalled Johnson in an article published over forty years after Johnson's death; see Miller, "Jimmy Johnson, D.C.L.," 10.

198. Smith, *Reminiscences of Colored People of Princeton*, 9–10.

199. Ibid., 10.

200. Smith, *Legendary Locals of Princeton*, 75. Though Johnson is the only person named on his tombstone, there are other persons entombed at the site. Cemetery records show that a lot with four graves was purchased in 1902 when James Collins Johnson died. Anetta Johnson died on February 8, 1913, and was buried in this same lot on February 10, 1913. There is a note on the interment record for Anetta, indicating "grave of first wife in same plot." It is hard to envision that either of Johnson's other two known wives, Phillis, who died in 1852, and Catherine, who died in 1880, would have been moved from another plot and reinterred here so many years after their deaths. This leaves open the possibility that Johnson may indeed have had four wives, as some sources claimed. An interment record for a Caroline J. Webb is shown in this same plot also. She died on December 8, 1919, and was buried on December 10. Her record shows her buried in the lot with James and "Mrs. Johnson." See Linda Gilmore and Nassau Presbyterian Church, "Re: Johnson Family in Princeton Cemetery," e-mail to author, January 9, 2019. The reference to Caroline J. Webb may indicate Clara J. Webb, a sister of Johnson's wife Anetta, who is shown in some census records living with Anetta during the latter's residency in Princeton before and after the death of James Collins Johnson in 1902, and during Anetta's residency in Maryland before coming to Princeton.

201. Entry for Annetta Johnson, Princeton Borough, Mercer County, New Jersey, p. 7A, federal manuscript census for 1910, Ancestry.com.

202. Smith, *Reminiscences of Colored People of Princeton*, 10.

203. Ibid.

Conclusion

Epigraph: Alexander, *Princeton—Old and New*, 89.

1. Gordon-Reed, *Hemingses of Monticello*, 23.

2. Pierre Nora, "Between History and Memory: *Les Lieux des Mémoire*," in "Memory and Counter-Memory, special issue, *Representations* 26 (Spring 1989): 7–24.

3. Mark Auslander has written about how slavery in the context of universities raises issues about the contrast between idealized utopian memorial spaces and the underclass life African-ancestored peopled who were enslaved in the university context often experience. See Mark Auslander, "The Other Side of Paradise: Glimpsing Slavery in the University's Utopian Landscapes," *Southern Spaces*, May 13, 2010, http://www.southernspaces.org/2010/other-side-paradise-glimpsing-slavery-universitys-utopian-landscapes.

4. Alexander, *Princeton—Old and New*, 89.

5. "U.N.C. Chancellor Apologizes for History of Slavery at Chapel Hill,"

New York Times, October 13, 2018, https://www.nytimes.com/2018/10/13/us/unc-carolina-apologize-slavery.html.

6. Alfred Brophy, "Forum on Slavery and Universities: Introduction," *Slavery and Abolition* 39, no. 2 (2018): 229–35.

7. Ibid., 231.

8. Adeel Hassan, "Georgetown Students Agree to Create Reparations Fund," *New York Times*, April 12, 2019, https://www.nytimes.com/2019/04/12/us/georgetown-reparations.html.

9. "Glasgow University to Pay Reparations for 200 Million Pounds Extracted from Region," November 25, 2018, http://jamaica-gleaner.com/article/lead-stories/20181125/updated-glasgow-university-pay-reparations-ps200m-extracted-region?fbclid=IwAR1oRNcGdAt8dFj2uyKWo0IwwG6YcRX7Id BuPqHT-0KpP2-y__Fiqc1xm6c.

10. Brophy, "Forum on Slavery and Universities."

Acknowledgments

Epigraph: Simon Leys, "The Imitation of Our Lord Don Quixote," *New York Review of Books*, June 11, 1998, 32.

1. Michel de Certeau, *The Practice of Everyday Life*, translated by Steven Rendall (Berkeley: University of California Press, 1984), xxi.

Bibliography

Archives and Libraries

Department of Rare Books and Special Collections, Princeton University Library

> Andrew C. Imbrie Papers
> Gulick Family Papers
> John Maclean, Jr. Papers
> Office of Dean of the Faculty Records
> Princeton University Class Records
> Treasurer's Records
> Undergraduate Alumni Records

Filson Historical Society, Louisville, Kentucky

> John Wesley Hunt Papers

Maryland State Archives, Annapolis, Maryland

> Mrs. Ford K. Brown Collection
> Shrewsbury Church Collection

Schlesinger Library, Radcliffe Institute, Harvard University

> Ann Maria Davison Papers, 1814–1866

Special Collections Research Center, Earl Gregg Swem Library, College of William and Mary, Williamsburg, Virginia

> Tucker-Coleman Papers, 1664–1945

Newspapers

African Repository and Colonial Journal
Alexandria Gazette
Baltimore Patriot

Baltimore Sun
Boston Evening Transcript
Daily National Intelligencer
Delaware Gazette (Wilmington)
Easton Gazette (Easton, Md.)
Evening Post (New York, N.Y.)
Friends' Intelligencer
National Anti-Slavery Standard
New-York Daily Advertiser
New York Evening Post
New York Times
Niles' National Register (Washington, D.C.)
The Pennsylvania Gazette
Princeton Alumni Weekly
Princeton Press
Princetonian
Republican Star (Easton, Md.)
Stevens Point Journal (Wis.)
The Sun (Baltimore, Md.)
The Yazoo City Whig (Yazoo, Miss.)
Yazoo City Whig and Political Register

Published Sources

Abruzzo, Margaret. "'A Humane Master—an Obliging Neighbor—a True Philanthropist': Slavery, Cruelty, and Moral Philosophy." *Princeton University Library Chronicle* 66, no. 3 (2005) 493–512.

Accomando, Christina. *The Regulations of Robbers: Legal Fictions of Slavery and Resistance.* Columbus: Ohio State University Press, 2001.

Adams, Henry. *History of the United States of America during the Second Administration of Thomas Jefferson.* Vol. 1. New York: Scribner, 1890.

Alexander, Archibald. *A History of Colonization on the Western Coast of Africa.* New York: William S. Martien, 1846.

Alexander, James Waddel. *The Life of Archibald Alexander, D.D.: First Professor in the Theological Seminary, at Princeton, New Jersey.* New York: Charles Scribner, 1854.

———. *Princeton—Old and New: Recollections of Undergraduate Life.* New York: C. Scribner's Sons, 1898.

Alexander, Samuel Davies. *Princeton College during the Eighteenth Century.* New York: Anson D. F. Randolph and Company, 1872.

Allen, Jody L. "Thomas Dew and the Rise of Proslavery Ideology at William & Mary." *Slavery and Abolition* 39, no. 2 (2018): 267–79.

American Tract Society. *The Happy Negro.* In *Tracts Published by the New England Tract Society*, vol. 1, 49–52. Andover, Mass.: Flagg and Gould, 1814.

Ardizzone, Heidi. *An Illuminated Life: Belle Da Costa Greene's Journey from Prejudice to Privilege.* New York: W. W. Norton, 2007.

Argument of Mr. Hambly, of York, PA, in the Case of Edward Prigg, Plaintiff in Error vs. The Commonwealth of Pennsylvania, Defendant in Error: In the Supreme Court of the United States. Baltimore, Md.: Lucas & Deaver, 1842.

Armstrong, Edward, ed. *Record of the Court at Upland.* Philadelphia: J. B. Lippincott, 1860.

Axtell, James. *The Making of Princeton University: From Woodrow Wilson to the Present.* Princeton, N.J.: Princeton University Press, 2006.

———. *Wisdom's Workshop: The Rise of the Modern University.* Princeton, N.J.: Princeton University Press, 2016.

Bacon, Margaret Hope. *But One Race: The Life of Robert Purvis.* Albany: State University of New York Press, 2012.

Bailey, Ronald. "The Slave(ry) Trade and the Development of Capitalism in the United States: The Textile Industry in New England." In *The Atlantic Slave Trade: Effects on Economies, Societies, and Peoples in Africa, the Americas, and Europe,* edited by Joseph E. Inikori and Stanley L. Engerman, 205–46. Durham, N.C.: Duke University Press, 1992.

Baker, H. Robert. *Prigg v. Pennsylvania: Slavery, the Supreme Court, and the Ambivalent Constitution.* Lawrence: University Press of Kansas, 2012.

Baker, William Mumford. *His Majesty, Myself.* Boston: Roberts Brothers, 1880.

Ball, Charles. *Fifty Years in Chains, or, the Life of an American Slave.* New York: H. Dayton, 1858.

Baptist, Edward. *The Half Has Never Been Told: Slavery and the Making of American Capitalism.* New York: Basic Books, 2012.

Barck, Dorothy C., ed. *Letters from John Pintard to His Daughter Eliza Noel Pintard Davidson, 1816–1833.* Vol. 1. New York: New York Historical Society, 1940.

Barreda, Felipe Alberto. *Elespuru.* Buenos Aires: Editorial Lumen, 1957.

Barrett, Walter [Joseph A. Scoville]. *The Old Merchants of New York City.* New York: Carleton, 1865.

Bartow, Evelyn. "The Prevost Family in America." *New York Genealogical and Biographical Record* 13, no. 1 (1882): 27–28.

Bastian, Walter M. "The Profession of Law in England and America: Its Origins and Distinctions." *American Bar Association Journal* 46 (August 1960): 817–20.

Bay, Mia. *The White Image in the Black Mind: African-American Ideas about White People, 1830–1925.* New York: Oxford University Press, 2000.

Berlin, Ira. *The Making of African America: The Four Great Migrations.* New York: Viking, 2010.

Bernstein, Iver. *The New York City Draft Riots.* New York: Oxford University Press, 1990.

Bird, Stephanie Rose. *Light, Bright, and Damned Near White: Biracial and Triracial Culture in America.* Westport, Conn.: Greenwood, 2009.

Bird, Wendell. *Press and Speech under Assault: The Early Supreme Court Justices, the Sedition Act of 1798, and the Campaign against Dissent.* New York: Oxford University Press, 2016.

Birney, William. *James G. Birney and His Times.* New York: D. Appleton, 1890.

Blackburn, Robin. *The Overthrow of Colonial Slavery, 1776–1848.* New York: Verso, 1988.

Blake, William Phipps. *History of the Town of Hamden, Connecticut.* Hamden, Conn.: Price, Lee, 1888.

Blight, David W. *Frederick Douglass: Prophet of Freedom.* New York: Simon and Schuster, 2018.

Blockson, Charles L. *The Underground Railroad.* New York: Prentice-Hall, 1987.

Bogen, David Skillen. "The First Integration of the University of Maryland School of Law." *Maryland Historical Magazine* 84, no. 1 (1989): 39–49.

Bolster, W. Jeffrey. *Black Jacks: African American Seamen in the Age of Sail.* Cambridge, Mass.: Harvard University Press, 2009.

Bonisteel, Roscoe O. *John Monteith, First President of the University of Michigan.* Ann Arbor: University of Michigan Press, 1967.

Boromé, Joseph A., Jacob C. White, Robert B. Ayres, and J. M. McKim. "The Vigilant Committee of Philadelphia." *Pennsylvania Magazine of History and Biography* 92, no. 3 (1968): 320–51.

Botham, Fay. *Almighty God Created the Races: Christianity, Interracial Marriage, and American Law.* Chapel Hill: University of North Carolina Press, 2009.

Boulukos, George. *The Grateful Slave: The Emergence of Race in Eighteenth-Century British and American Culture.* Cambridge: Cambridge University Press, 2008.

Boyd, Kendra, Miya Carey, and Christopher Blakley. "Old Money: Rutgers University and the Political Economy of Slavery in New Jersey." In *Scarlet and Black: Slavery and Dispossession in Rutgers History, Volume 1,* edited by Marisa J. Fuentes and Deborah Gray White, 43–57. New Brunswick, N.J.: Rutgers University Press, 2016.

Boyle, Sheila Tully, and Andrew Bunie. *Paul Robeson: The Years of Promise and Achievement.* Amherst: University of Massachusetts Press, 2005.

Brackett, Jeffrey Richardson. *The Negro in Maryland: A Study of the Institution of Slavery.* Baltimore, Md.: Johns Hopkins University, 1889.

Bradley, Stefan M. "The Southern-Most Ivy: Princeton University from Jim Crow Admissions to Anti-Apartheid Protests, 1794–1969." *American Studies* 51, nos. 3–4 (2010): 109–30.

Bragg, George F. *Men of Maryland.* Baltimore, Md.: Church Advocate, 1914.

Brophy, Alfred L. *University, Court, and Slave: Pro-Slavery Thought in Southern Colleges and Courts and the Coming of Civil War.* New York: Oxford University Press, 2016.

———. "Forum on Slavery and Universities: Introduction." *Slavery and Abolition* 39, no. 2 (2018): 229–35.

Brown, Alexander. *The Cabells and Their Kin.* New York: Houghton Mifflin, 1895.

Brown, Joseph. "'To Bring Out the Intellect of the Race': An African American Freedmen's Bureau Agent in Maryland." *Maryland Historical Magazine* 104, no. 4 (2009): 374–401.

Brown, William Wells. *Narrative of William W. Brown, a Fugitive Slave.* Boston: Anti-Slavery Office, 1847.

Browning, Charles Henry. *Americans of Royal Descent.* Philadelphia: Porter and Coates, 1891.

Brugger, Robert. *Maryland: A Middle Temperament.* Baltimore, Md.: Johns Hopkins University Press in association with the Maryland Historical Society, 1988.

Buchanan, Thomas C. *Black Life on the Mississippi: Slaves, Free Blacks, and the Western Steamboat World.* Chapel Hill: University of North Carolina Press, 2004.

Burin, Eric. *Slavery and the Peculiar Solution: A History of the American Colonization Society.* Gainesville: University of Florida Press, 2008.

"The Burning of Nassau Hall." *Journal of Presbyterian History* 4, no. 8 (1908): 364.

Burr, Aaron. *The Private Journal of Aaron Burr during His Residence of Four Years in Europe.* Vol. 1. New York: Harper and Brothers, 1836.

Burrows, Edwin G., and Mike Wallace. *Gotham: A History of New York City to 1898.* New York: Oxford University Press, 1999.

Burstyn, Joan N., and Women's Project of New Jersey. *Past and Promise: Lives of New Jersey Women.* Syracuse, N.Y.: Syracuse University Press, 1996.

Burton, Antoinette. "'Small Stories' and the Promise of New Narratives." In *Contesting Archives: Finding Women in the Sources,* edited by Nupur Chaudhuri, Sherry J. Katz, and Mary Elizabeth Perry, vii–x. Urbana: University of Illinois Press, 2010.

Byfield, Mary, Francis Joseph Hogan, and New-York Religious Tract Society. *The Happy Negro: To Which Is Added, the Grateful Negro.* Children's Books, 2nd series. Vol. 18. New York: New-York Religious Tract Society, 1825.

Calderhead, William L. "Slavery in Maryland in the Age of the Revolution, 1775–1790." *Maryland Historical Magazine* 98 (Fall 2003): 303–24.

"Captain Thomas Lavender." *Friends' Review,* February 27, 1869, 419–20.

Carter, Nathan Franklin. *The Native Ministry of New Hampshire.* Concord, N.H.: Rumford Printing.

Case, Stephen H., and Mark Jacob. *Treacherous Beauty: Peggy Shippen, the Woman behind Benedict Arnold's Plot to Betray America.* Guilford, Conn.: Lyons, 2012.

Certeau, Michel de. *The Practice of Everyday Life.* Translated by Steven Rendall. Berkeley: University of California Press, 1984.

Chapelle, Suzanne Ellery. *Maryland: A History of Its People.* Baltimore, Md.: Johns Hopkins University Press, 1986.

Chesnut, Mary, and C. Vann Woodward. *Mary Chesnut's Civil War.* New Haven, Conn.: Yale University Press, 1981.

"Class Begins to Paint Picture of Princeton's Ties to Slavery." *Princeton Alumni Weekly,* May 15, 2013. https://paw.princeton.edu/article/class-begins-paint -picture-princeton%E2%80%99s-ties-slavery.

Coates, H. T. *Woodhull Genealogy: The Woodhull Family in England and America.*
Madison: University of Wisconsin, 1904.

Cobb, Thomas. *An Inquiry into the Law of Negro Slavery in the United States of America.* Philadelphia: T & J.W. Johnson, 1858.

College of New Jersey. *Catalogue of the Officers and Students of the College of New Jersey, 1829–1830.* Trenton, N.J.: George Sherman, 1830.

———. *Catalogue of the Officers and Students of Princeton University, for 1840 and 1841.* Princeton, N.J.: Robert E. Hornor, 1841.

———. *Catalogue of the Officers and Students of the College of New Jersey, for 1842–1843.* Princeton, N.J.: John T. Robinson, 1843.

———. *Catalogue of the Officers and Students of the College of New Jersey, for 1843–1844.* Princeton, N.J.: John T. Robinson, 1844.

———. *Catalogue of the Officers and Students of the College of New Jersey, for 1847–'48.* Princeton, N.J.: John T. Robinson, 1848.

———. *Laws of the College of New Jersey.* Princeton, N.J.: Chas. S. Robinson, 1870.

———. *Laws of the College of New Jersey: Revised, Amended, and Adopted by the Board of Trustees.* Princeton, N.J.: The Board, 1875.

College of New Jersey Class of 1872. *Essays and Reviews on Subjects, Consequential and Insignificant.* New York: D. Appleton, 1869.

Collins, Varnum Lansing. *The Continental Congress at Princeton.* Princeton, N.J.: University Library, 1908.

———. *Early Princeton Printing.* Princeton, N.J.: Princeton University Press, 1911.

———. *Guide to Princeton: The Town, the University.* Princeton, N.J.: Princeton University Press, 1919.

———. *Princeton.* New York: Oxford University Press, 1914.

———. *Princeton: Past and Present.* Princeton, N.J.: Princeton University Press, 1931.

———. "Prospect, near Princeton." *Princeton University Bulletin* 15, no. 3 (1904): 164–82.

———. "Turning Back the Clocks." *Princeton Alumni Weekly,* April 26, 1929, 857–64.

Comin, John, and Harold Fredsell. "John Monteith, Pioneer Presbyterian of Detroit." In *Public Education in Michigan,* edited by Gerald L. Poor and Gladys I. Griffin, 1–21. Mount Pleasant: Division of Field Services, Central Michigan University, 1959.

Commager, Henry S. "Mr. Justice Story." In *The Gaspar G. Bacon Lectures on the Constitution of the United States, 1940–1950,* Gaspar G. Bacon and Arthur N. Holcombe. Boston: Boston University Press, 1953.

Conlin, Michael F. "Joseph Henry's Smithsonian during the Civil War." In *An Uncommon Time: The Civil War and the Northern Home Front,* edited by Paul Alan Cimbala and Randall M. Miller, 189–213. New York: Fordham University Press, 2002.

Cooley, Charles Horton. "The Development of Sociology at Michigan." In *Sociological Theory and Social Research: Being Selected Papers of Charles Horton Cooley*, 3–14. New York: Henry Holt, 1930.

Cooley, Henry Scofield. *A Study of Slavery in New Jersey*. Baltimore, Md.: Johns Hopkins University Press, 1896.

Côté, Richard N. *Theodosia Burr Alston: Portrait of a Prodigy*. Mount Pleasant, S.C.: Corinthian Books, 2003.

Cover, Robert M. *Justice Accused: Antislavery and the Judicial Process*. New Haven, Conn.: Yale University Press, 1975.

Currie, David P. *The Constitution in the Supreme Court: The First Hundred Years, 1888–1986*. Chicago: University of Chicago Press, 1990.

Dain, Bruce R. *A Hideous Monster of the Mind*. Cambridge, Mass.: Harvard University Press, 2009.

Dantas, Mariana L. R. *Black Townsmen: Urban Slavery and Freedom in the Eighteenth-Century Americas*. New York: Palgrave Macmillan, 2008.

Dart, Henry Plauché. "The History of the Supreme Court of Louisiana." *Louisiana Historical Quarterly* 4, no. 1 (1921): 14–71.

Davidson, Thomas. *The Parthenon Frieze and Other Essays*. London: Kegan, Paul, Trench, 1892.

Davis, David Brion. *Inhuman Bondage: The Rise and Fall of Slavery in the New World*. New York: Oxford University Press, 2008.

Davis, Henry. *A Narrative of the Embarrassments and Decline of Hamilton College*. n.p., 1833.

Davis, Matthew L., ed. *The Private Journal of Aaron Burr, during His Residence of Four Years in Europe; with Selections from His Correspondence*. Vol. 1. New York: Harper and Brothers, 1836.

Davis, Noah. *A Narrative of the Life of Rev. Noah Davis, a Colored Man*. Baltimore, Md.: J. F. Weishampel Jr., 1859.

Deetz, Kelley Fanto. "Finding Dignity in a Landscape of Fear: Enslaved Women and Girls at the University of Virginia." *Slavery and Abolition* 39, no. 2 (2018): 251–66.

DeLombard, Jeannine Marie. *Slavery on Trial: Law, Abolitionism, and Print Culture*. Chapel Hill: University of North Carolina Press, 2009.

Deyle, Steven. *Carry Me Back: The Domestic Slave Trade in American Life*. New York: Oxford University Press, 2005.

Documents Relating to the Colonial History of the State of New Jersey. Vol. 8. Westminster, Md.: Heritage Books, 2008.

Dorsey, Clement. *The General Public Statutory Law and Public Local Law of the State of Maryland, from the Year 1692 to 1839 Inclusive*. Vol. 2. Baltimore, Md.: John D. Toy, 1840.

Doty, Ethan Allen. "The Doty Family of Long Island." *New York Genealogical and Biographical Record* 43 (1912): 312–24.

Douglass, Frederick. *Life and Times of Frederick Douglass*. Hartford, Conn.: Park, 1882.

————. *My Bondage and My Freedom*. 1855; repr., Urbana: University of Illinois Press, 1987.

————. *Narrative of the Life of Frederick Douglass: An American Slave*. London: H. G. Collins, 1845.

Doughty, Ethan Allen. "The Doughty Family of Long Island." *New York Genealogical and Biographical Record* 43, no. 4 (1912): 273–87.

Dowling, Elizabeth. *A Slave in the White House: Paul Jennings and the Madisons*. New York: Palgrave Mcmillan, 2012.

Drew, Benjamin. *A North-side View of Slavery: The Refugee: or, The Narratives of Fugitive Slaves in Canada*. Boston: John P. Jewett, 1856.

Du Bois, W. E. B. *The College-Bred Negro*. Atlanta: Atlanta University Press, 1900.

————. *The Philadelphia Negro: A Social Study*. Philadelphia: University of Pennsylvania Press, 2010.

————. *The Suppression of the African Slave-Trade to the United States of America, 1638–1870*. New York: Longmans, Green, 1904.

Duberman, Martin. *Paul Robeson: A Biography*. New York: Open Road Media, 2014.

Dunbar, Erica Armstrong. *Never Caught: The Washingtons' Relentless Pursuit of Their Runaway Slave, Ona Judge*. New York: Simon and Schuster, 2018.

Edgeworth, Maria. "The Grateful Negro." In vol. 3 of *Popular Tales*. London: J. Johnson, 1811.

Eisgruber, Christopher L. M. "Justice Story, Slavery, and the Natural Law Foundations of American Constitutionalism." *University of Chicago Law Review* 55, no. 1 (1988): 273–327.

Elkins, Stanley, and Eric McKitrick. *The Age of Federalism*. New York: Oxford University Press, 1995.

Elliott, T. C. "The Surrender at Astoria in 1818." *Quarterly of the Oregon Historical Society* 19 (March 1918–December 1918): 271, 274.

Elmer, Lucius Quintius Cincinnatus. *Practical Forms of Proceedings under the Laws of New Jersey*. Bridgeton, N.J.: James M. Newell, 1839.

Ernst, Daniel R. "Legal Positivism, Abolitionist Litigation, and the New Jersey Slave Case of 1845." In *Abolitionism and American Law*, edited by John R. McKivigan, 103–31. New York: Garland, 1999.

Faber, Eberhard L. *Building the Land of Dreams: New Orleans and the Transformation of Early America*. Princeton, N.J.: Princeton University Press, 2015.

Fabre, Geneviève. "Performing Freedom: Negro Election Celebrations as Political and Intellectual Resistance in New England, 1740–1850." In *Celebrating Ethnicity and Nation: American Festive Culture from the Revolution to the Early Twentieth Century*, edited by Genevieve Fabre, Jürgen Heideking, and Kai Dreisbach, 91–123. New York: Berghahn Books, 2001.

Faderman, Lillian. *Surpassing the Love of Men: Romantic Friendship and Love between Women from the Renaissance to the Present*. New York: William Morrow, 1981.

Faubion, James D. *The Ethics of Kinship: Ethnographic Inquiries*. Lanham, Md.: Rowan and Littlefield, 2001.

Federal Writers' Project of the Works Progress Administration for the State of New Jersey. *Old Princeton's Neighbors*. Princeton, N.J.: Graphic Arts, 939.

Ferguson, Robert A. *Law and Letters in American Culture*. Cambridge, Mass.: Harvard University Press, 1984.

Fernandez, Mark. "Edward Livingston, America and France: Making Law." In *Empires of the Imagination: Transatlantic Histories of the Louisiana Purchase*, edited by Peter J. Kastor and François Weil, 268–98. Charlottesville: University of Virginia Press, 2009.

Field, Corinne T. *The Struggle for Equal Adulthood*. Chapel Hill: University of North Carolina Press, 2014.

Field, Phyllis F. *The Politics of Race in New York: The Struggle for Black Suffrage in the Civil War Era*. Ithaca, N.Y.: Cornell University Press, 2009.

Fields, Barbara J. *Slavery and Freedom on the Middle Ground: Maryland during the Nineteenth Century*. New Haven, Conn.: Yale University Press, 1985.

Finkelman, Paul. "Chief Justice Hornblower of New Jersey and the Fugitive Slave Law of 1793." In *Slavery and the Law*, edited by Paul Finkelman, 113–41. Lanham, Md.: Rowan and Littlefield, 2001.

———. "Story Telling on the Supreme Court: *Prigg v. Pennsylvania* and *Justice Story's* Judicial Nationalism." *Supreme Court Review* (1994): 247–93.

———. "The Taney Court (1836–1864): The Jurisprudence of Slavery and the Crisis of the Union." In *The United States Supreme Court: The Pursuit of Justice*, edited by Christopher L. Tomlins, 75–102. Boston: Houghton Mifflin Harcourt, 2005.

Fitzgerald, Thomas F., and Josephine A. Fitzgerald. *Manual of the Legislature of New Jersey*. Trenton, N.J.: Josephine A. Fitzgerald, 1921.

Fogel, Robert William, and Stanley L. Engelman. *Time on the Cross: The Economics of American Negro Slavery*. New York: W. W. Norton, 1995.

Foner, Eric. *Gateway to Freedom: The Hidden History of America's Fugitive Slaves*. New York: Oxford University Press, 2015.

Foner, Philip Sheldon, ed. *Paul Robeson Speaks: Writings, Speeches, and Interviews, 1918–1974*. New York: Citadel, 1978.

Force, Peter. *The National Calendar and Annals of the United States*. Vol. 4. Washington, D.C.: Davis and Force, 1823.

Foucault, Michel. *Discipline and Punish: The Birth of the Prison*. Translated by Alan Sheridan. New York: Vintage Books, 1995.

Fought, Leigh. *Women in the World of Frederick Douglass*. New York: Oxford University Press, 2017.

Franklin, John Hope. *A Southern Odyssey: Travelers in the Antebellum North*. Baton Rouge: Louisiana State University Press, 1977.

Franklin, John Hope, and Loren Schweninger. *Runaway Slaves: Rebels on the Plantation*. New York: Oxford University Press, 2000.

Freeburg, Victor O. *William Henry Welch at Eighty: A Memorial Record of Cele-brations Around the World in His Honor*. New York: Milbank Memorial Fund, 1930.

Fusfeld, Daniel Roland, and Timothy Mason Bates. *The Political Economy of the Urban Ghetto*. Carbondale: Southern Illinois University Press, 1984.

Gabriel, John. *Whitewash: Racialized Politics and the Media*. New York: Routledge, 2002.

Gardner, Eric. *Unexpected Places: Relocating Nineteenth-Century African American Literature*. Jackson: University Press of Mississippi, 2010.

General Catalog of Princeton University, 1746–1906. Princeton, N.J.: Princeton University Press, 1908.

Genovese, Eugene D., and Elizabeth Fox-Genovese. *Fatal Self-Deception: Slaveholding Paternalism in the Old South*. New York: Cambridge University Press, 2011.

Gigantino, James J., II. *The Ragged Road to Abolition: Slavery and Freedom in New Jersey, 1775–1865*. Philadelphia: University of Pennsylvania Press, 2014.

———. "'The Whole North Is Not Abolitionized': Slavery's Slow Death in New Jersey, 1830–1860." *Journal of the Early Republic* 34, no. 3 (2014): 411–37.

Gilmore, Linda, and Nassau Presbyterian Church. "Re: Johnson Family in Princeton Cemetery." E-mail message to author, January 9, 2019.

Gordon-Reed, Annette. *The Hemingses of Monticello: An American Family*. New York: W. W. Norton, 2008.

Greene, Evarts Boutell, Virginia D. Harrington, and Columbia University Council for Research in the Social Sciences. *American Population before the Federal Census of 1790*. Baltimore, Md.: Genealogical, 1993.

Gresham, Leroy. "Apropos of Jimmy Johnson." *Princeton Alumni Weekly*, October 4, 1902, 22–23.

Gross, Ariela. *Double Character: Slavery and Mastery in the Antebellum Southern Courtroom*. Athens: University of Georgia Press, 2006.

Gutman, Herbert G. *Slavery and the Numbers Game: A Critique of Time on the Cross*. Urbana: University of Illinois Press, 1975.

Guy, Anita Aidt. *Maryland's Persistent Pursuit to End Slavery, 1850–1864*. New York: Garland, 1997.

Hageman, John Frelinghuysen. *History of Princeton and Its Institutions*. 2 vols. Philadelphia: J. B. Lippincott, 1879.

Hall, John, ed. *Forty Years' Familiar Letters of James W. Alexander: Constituting, with Notes, a Memoir of His Life*. New York: Scribner and Sons, 1870.

Hamilton, Sylvia. "Naming Names, Naming Ourselves: A Survey of Early Black Women in Nova Scotia." In *We're Rooted Here and They Can't Pull Us Up: Essays in African Canadian Women's History*, edited by Peggy Bristow, 13–40. Toronto: University of Toronto Press, 1994.

Hammond, John Martin. *Colonial Mansions of Maryland and Delaware*. Phila-delphia: J. B. Lippincott, 1914.

Hanson, George A. *Old Kent: The Eastern Shore of Maryland*. Baltimore, Md.: John P. Des Forges, 1876.

Harris, Leslie M. *In the Shadow of Slavery: African Americans in New York City, 1626–1823*. Chicago: University of Chicago Press, 2003.

Harris, Virgil McClure. *Ancient, Curious, and Famous Wills*. London: Stanley Paul, 1912.

Harrison, Lowell H. *The Anti-Slavery Movement in Kentucky*. Louisville: University of Kentucky Press, 2015.

Harrison, Samuel Alexander. *History of Talbot County, Maryland, 1661–1861*. Vol. 1. Baltimore, Md.: Williams and Wilkins, 1915.

Harrold, Stanley. *Border War: Fighting over Slavery before the Civil War*. Chapel Hill: University of North Carolina Press, 2010.

Hartog, Hendrik. *The Trouble with Minna: A Case of Slavery and Emancipation in the Antebellum North*. Chapel Hill: University of North Carolina Press, 2018.

Hayes, Kevin J., ed. *Jefferson in His Own Time*. Iowa City: University of Iowa Press, 2012.

Henry, James Buchanan, and Christian Henry Scharff. *College as It Is, or, the Collegian's Manual in 1853*. Introduction by J. Jefferson Looney. Princeton, N.J.: Princeton University Libraries, 1996.

Hicks, Cheryl D. *Talk with You like a Woman: African American Women, Justice, and Reform in New York*. Chapel Hill: University of North Carolina Press, 2010.

Hicks, Paul DeForest. *Joseph Henry Lumpkin: Georgia's First Chief Justice*. Athens: University of Georgia Press, 2002.

Hinsdale, Horace Graham. *An Historical Discourse Commemorating the Century of the Completed Organization of the First Presbyterian Church, Princeton, New Jersey*. Princeton, N.J.: Princeton University Press, 1888.

Hobart, John Henry. *The Correspondence of John Henry Hobart*. New York: privately printed, 1911.

Hodges, Graham Russell. *Black New Jersey: 1664 to the Present Day*. New Brunswick, N.J.: Rutgers University Press, 2018.

———. *Root and Branch: African Americans in New York and East Jersey, 1613–1863*. Chapel Hill: University of North Carolina Press, 1999.

Hodges, Graham Russell, and Alan Edward Brown. *"Pretends to Be Free": Runaway Slave Advertisements from Colonial and Revolutionary New York and New Jersey*. New York: Garland, 1994.

Holden-Smith, Barbara. "Lords of Lash Loom and Law: Justice Story Slavery and *Prigg v. Pennsylvania*." *Cornell Law Review* 78, no. 6 (1993): 1086–151.

Honeyman, A[braham] Van Doren. "Two Bedminster Families: McCrea and Henry." *Somerset County Historical Quarterly* 7, no. 2 (1918): 81–118.

———. *The Van Doorn Family (Van Doorn, Van Dorn, Van Doren, Etc.) in Holland and America, 1088–1908*. Plainfield, N.J.: Honeyman's Publishing House, 1909.

Hough, Franklin B. *The New-York Civil List*. Albany, N.Y.: Weed, Parsons, 1858.

Hudnut, William H., III. "Samuel Stanhope Smith, Enlightened Conservative." *Journal of the History of Ideas* 17, no. 4 (1956): 540–55.

Hunter, Tera W. *Bound in Wedlock: Slave and Free Black Marriage in the Nineteenth Century.* Cambridge, Mass.: Belknap Press of Harvard University Press, 2017.

Imbrie, Andrew C. *Family Record of Andrew Welsh Imbrie and Frances Imbrie.* Vol. 1. n.p.: 1973.

———. "James Johnson of Princeton: A Biography." *Nassau Literary Magazine* 50, no. 9 (1895): 594–604.

Inniss, Lolita Buckner. "Cherokee Freedmen and the Color of Belonging." *Columbia Journal of Race & Law* 5, no. 2 (2015): 100–118.

———. "A Critical Legal Rhetoric Approach to In Re African-American Slave Descendants Litigation." *Journal of Civil Rights and Economic Development* 24, no. 4 (2010): 649–96.

———. "A Fugitive Slave in Princeton." *Princeton Alumni Weekly* 117, no. 2 (October 5, 2016): 27–30.

———. "It's the Hard Luck Life: Women's Moral Luck and Eucatastrophe in Child Custody Allocation." *Women's Rights Law Reporter* 32, no. 1 (2010–11): 56–80.

———. "James Collins Johnson: The Princeton Fugitive Slave." https://slavery .princeton.edu/stories/james-collins-johnson (accessed November 2017).

———. "'A Southern College Slipped from Its Geographical Moorings': Slavery at Princeton." *Slavery and Abolition* 39, no. 2 (2018): 236–50.

Isenberg, Nancy. *Fallen Founder: The Life of Aaron Burr.* New York: Penguin, 2007.

Jones, Howard. *Mutiny on the Amistad: The Saga of a Slave Revolt and Its Impact on American Abolition, Law, and Diplomacy.* New York: Oxford University Press, 1997.

Jones, Martha. *Birthright Citizens: A History of Race and Rights in Antebellum America.* New York: Cambridge University Press, 2018.

Jones-Rogers, Stephanie E. *They Were Her Property: White Women Slave Owners in the American South.* New Haven, Conn.: Yale University Press, 2019.

Jordan, Ryan P. *Slavery and the Meetinghouse: The Quakers and the Abolitionist Dilemma, 1820–1865.* Bloomington: Indiana University Press, 2007.

Kapur, Ratna. "'Faith' and the 'Good' Liberal: The Construction of Female Sexual Subjectivity in Anti-Trafficking Discourse." In *Sexuality and the Law: Feminist Engagements,* edited by Vanessa Munro and Carl Franklin Stychin, 223–58. New Delhi: Sage, 2007.

Karabel, Jerome. *The Chosen: The Hidden History of Admission and Exclusion at Harvard, Yale, and Princeton.* Boston: Houghton Mifflin Harcourt, 2006.

Katagiri, Yasuhiro. *The Mississippi State Sovereignty Commission: Civil Rights and States' Rights.* Jackson: University of Mississippi Press, 2007.

Katcher, Philip R. N. *Flags of the American Civil War.* Vol. 3, *State and Volunteer.* Oxford: Osprey, 1993.

Kempin, Frederick G., Jr. "Precedent and Stare Decisis: The Critical Years, 1800 to 1850." *American Journal of Legal History* 3, no. 1 (1959): 28–54.

Kent, James. *Commentaries on American Law*. 3rd ed. New York: Clayton & Van Norden, 1836.

Kerridge, Ronald D. "Answering 'The Trumpet to Discord': Southerners at the College of New Jersey, 1820–1860, and Their Careers." Senior thesis, Princeton University, 1984.

King, Irving H. *The Coast Guard under Sail: The U.S. Revenue Cutter Service, 1789–1865.* Annapolis, Md.: Naval Institute Press, 1989.

King, Wilma. *Stolen Childhood: Slave Youth in Nineteenth-Century America.* Bloomington: Indiana University Press, 2011.

Kleber, John E. *The Encyclopedia of Louisville.* Lexington: University Press of Kentucky, 2001.

Kline, Mary-Jo, ed. *Political Correspondence and Public Papers of Aaron Burr.* 2 vols. Princeton, N.J. Princeton University Press, 1983.

Kulikoff, Allan. *Tobacco and Slaves: The Development of Southern Cultures in the Chesapeake, 1680–1800.* Chapel Hill: University of North Carolina Press, 1986.

Lanman, Charles. *Biographical Annals of the Civil Government of the United States during Its First Century.* Washington, D.C.: James Anglim, 1876.

Lansing, Garret. *Journal of the Assembly of the State of New York at Their Forty-First Session.* Albany, N.Y.: J. Buel, 1818.

Larison, Cornelius Wilson. *Silvia Dubois: A Biografy of the Slave Who Whipt Her Mistress and Ganed Her Freedom.* Edited by Jared Lobdell. 1883; repr., New York: Oxford University Press, 1988.

Larson, Kate Clifford. *Bound for the Promised Land: Harriet Tubman; Portrait of an American Hero.* New York: Random House, 2004.

LaTrobe, John H. B. *The Justices' Practice under the Laws of Maryland.* Baltimore, Md.: Fielding Lucas, Jr., 1847.

Laws Made and Passed by the General Assembly of Maryland. Annapolis, Md.: Jeremiah Hughes, 1836.

Laws of Maryland Made and Passed at a Session of Assembly. Annapolis, Md.: Jeremiah Hughes, 1838.

Lee, Francis Bazley. *Genealogical and Personal Memorial of Mercer County, New Jersey.* Vol. 2. New York: Lewis, 1907.

———. *New Jersey as a Colony and as a State: One of the Original Thirteen.* Vol. 4. New York: Publishing Society of New Jersey, 1903.

Leepson, Marc. *What So Proudly We Hailed: Francis Scott Key, a Life.* New York: Palgrave Macmillan, 2014.

A Legal Argument Before the Supreme Court of the State of New Jersey at the May Term, 1845, at Trenton for the Deliverance of 4,000 Persons from Bondage. New York: Finch and Weed, 1845.

Leitch, Alexander. *A Princeton Companion.* Princeton, N.J.: Princeton University Press, 2015.

Levinson, Sanford. *Written in Stone: Public Monuments in Changing Societies.* Durham, N.C.: Duke University Press, 2018.

Link, Arthur S. *The Papers of Woodrow Wilson.* Vol. 19, *1909–1910.* Princeton, N.J.: Princeton University Press, 1975.

Litwack, Leon F. *North of Slavery: The Negro in the Free States.* Chicago: University of Chicago Press, 2009.

Lockmiller, David Alexander. *Scholars on Parade: Colleges, Universities, Costumes and Degrees.* New York: Macmillan, 1969.

Lockwood, John, and Charles Lockwood. *The Siege of Washington: The Untold Story of the Twelve Days That Shook the Union.* New York: Oxford University Press, 2011.

Loetscher, Lefferts A. *Facing the Enlightenment and Pietism: Archibald Alexander and the Founding of Princeton Theological Seminary.* Westport, Conn.: Greenwood, 1983.

Lomask, Milton. *Aaron Burr: The Conspiracy and Years of Exile, 1805–1836.* New York: Farrar, Straus and Giroux, 1982.

Longfield, Bradley J. *Presbyterians and American Culture: A History.* Louisville, Ky.: Westminster John Knox, 2013.

Looney, J. Jefferson. "'An Awfully Poor Place': Edward Shippen's Memoir of the College of New Jersey in the 1840s." *Princeton University Library Chronicle* 39, no. 1 (1997): 8–57.

Looney, J. Jefferson, and Ruth L. Woodward. *Princetonians, 1791–1794: A Biographical Dictionary.* Princeton, N.J.: Princeton University Press, 2016.

Lubet, Steven. *The "Colored Hero" of Harpers Ferry: John Anthony Copeland and the War against Slavery.* New York: Cambridge University Press, 2015.

Luders, Joseph E. *The Civil Rights Movement and the Logic of Social Change.* New York: Cambridge University Press, 2010.

Maclean, John. *History of the College of New Jersey, from Its Origin in 1746 to the Commencement of 1854.* New York: J. B. Lippincott, 1877.

Manual of the Legislature of New Jersey. Trenton, N.J.: Thomas F. Fitzgerald, 1911.

Mappen, Marc. *Jerseyana: The Underside of New Jersey History.* New Brunswick, N.J.: Rutgers University Press, 1992.

Marshall, Kenneth H. *Manhood Enslaved: Bondmen in Eighteenth- and Early Nineteenth-Century New Jersey.* Rochester, N.Y.: University of Rochester Press, 2011.

Martin, Asa Earl. *The Anti-Slavery Movement in Kentucky Prior to 1850.* Louisville, Ky.: Standard Printing Company of Louisville, 1918.

———. "The Anti-Slavery Movement in Kentucky Prior to 1850." PhD diss., 1918.

Martin, Boyce F., Jr. "In Defense of Unpublished Opinions." *Ohio State Law Journal* 60, no. 1 (1999): 177–97.

Martin, Francois-Xavier. *Martin's Reports of Cases Argued and Determined in the Superior Court of the Territory of Orleans and in the Supreme Court of the State of Louisiana.* New Orleans, La.: Samuel L. Stewart, 1846.

Mason, Isaac. *Life of Isaac Mason as a Slave.* Worcester, Mass.: self-published, 1893.

Mason, Julian D. "On the Reputation of Phyllis Wheatley, Poet." In *The Poems of Phyllis Wheatley*, edited by Julian D. Mason, 23–34. Chapel Hill: University of North Carolina Press, 1989.

Maxcy, Virgil. *Laws of Maryland.* Vol. 1. Baltimore, Md.: Philip H. Nicklin, 1811.

Maynard, William Barksdale. *Woodrow Wilson: Princeton to the Presidency.* New Haven, Conn.: Yale University Press, 2014.

Mazureau, Etienne. "George Matthews: President of the Supreme Court of Louisiana." *Louisiana Historical Quarterly* 4 (January–October 1921): 154–88.

McCormick, Albert E. *Historical Demography through Genealogies: Explorations into Pre–1900 American Population Issues.* Bloomington, Ind.: iUniverse, 2011.

McManus, Edgar J. *A History of Negro Slavery in New York.* Syracuse, N.Y.: Syracuse University Press, 2001.

McSherry, James. *A History of Maryland: From Its First Settlement in 1634, to the Year 1848.* Baltimore, Md.: John Murphy, 1849.

Mellick, Andrew. *The Story of an Old Farm.* Somerville, N.J.: Union-Gazette, 1889.

Meltzer, Milton. *Slavery: A World History.* Boston: DaCapo, 1971.

Miller, Edward A. *The Black Civil War Soldiers of Illinois: The Story of the Twenty-Ninth U.S. Colored Infantry.* Columbia: University of South Carolina Press, 1998.

Miller, Marion Mills. "Jimmy Johnson, D.C.L.: Reminiscences of an Alumnus on [a] Famous Character of the Nineties." *Princeton Alumni Weekly*, April 23, 1948, 10.

Minor, DoVeanna S. Fulton, and Reginald H. Pitts. Introduction to *Speaking Lives, Authoring Texts: Three African American Women's Oral Slave Narratives*, edited by DoVeanna S. Fulton Minor and Reginald H. Pitts, 1–38. Albany: State University of New York Press, 2012.

Monteith, Sharon. "Civil Rights Movement Film." In *The Cambridge Companion to American Civil Rights Literature*, edited by Julie Armstrong, 123–42. New York: Cambridge University Press, 2015.

Moorhead, James H. *Princeton Seminary in American Religion and Culture.* Grand Rapids, Mich.: Wm. B. Eerdmans, 2012.

Morley, Jefferson. *Snow-Storm in August: Washington City, Francis Scott Key, and the Forgotten Race Riot of 1835.* New York: Doubleday, 2012.

Moss, Simeon F. "The Persistence of Slavery and Involuntary Servitude in a Free State (1685–1866)." In *A New Jersey Anthology*, edited by Maxine N. Lurie. New Brunswick, N.J.: Rutgers University Press, 2010.

Mücke, Ulrich. *Political Culture in Nineteenth-Century Peru: The Rise of the Partido Civil 72.* Pittsburgh: University of Pittsburgh Press, 2004.

Muelder, Owen W. *Theodore Dwight Weld and the American Anti-Slavery Society.* Jefferson, N.C.: McFarland, 2011.

Mulcahy, Linda. *Legal Architecture: Justice, Due Process, and the Place of Law.* New York: Routledge, 2010.

Mulder, John M. *Woodrow Wilson: The Years of Preparation*. Princeton, N.J.: Princeton University Press, 2015.

Muser, Jeanette K. *Rocky Hill: Kingston and Griggstown*. Charleston, S.C.: Arcadia, 1998.

Myers, Robert Manson. *A Georgian at Princeton*. New York: Harcourt Brace Jovanovich, 1976.

New Jersey Department of Education. *Annual Report of the Board of Education and the Superintendent of Public Instruction of New Jersey, with Accompanying Documents, for the School Year Ending June 30, 1895*. Part 2. Trenton, N.J.: John L. Murphy, 1894.

New Jersey State Conference of Social Work. *Proceedings of the New Jersey Conference of Charities: Tenth Annual Meeting*. Trenton, N.J.: MacCrellish and Quigley, 1911.

Newman, Richard S. *The Transformation of American Abolitionism: Fighting Slavery in the Early Republic*. Chapel Hill: University of North Carolina Press, 2002.

Newmyer, R. Kent. *Supreme Court Justice Joseph Story: Statesman of the Old Republic*. Chapel Hill: University of North Carolina Press, 1985.

———. *The Treason Trial of Aaron Burr: Law, Politics, and the Character Wars of the New Nation*. New York: Cambridge University Press, 2012.

Nicholson, Philip Yale. *Labor's Story in the United States*. Philadelphia: Temple University Press, 2004.

Nora, Pierre. "Between History and Memory: *Les Lieux des Mémoire*." In "Memory and Counter-Memory," special issue, *Representations* 26 (Spring 1989): 7–24.

Nora, Pierre, and Lawrence D. Kritzman. *Realms of Memory: Conflicts and Divisions*. Vol. 1. New York: Columbia University Press, 1996.

Norris, Edwin Mark. *The Story of Princeton*. Boston: Little, Brown, 1917.

O'Brien, Michael. *Conjectures of Order: Intellectual Life and the American South*. Chapel Hill: University of North Carolina Press, 2004.

Olwell, Robert. *Masters, Slaves, and Subjects: The Culture of Power in the South Carolina Low Country, 1740–1790*. Ithaca, N.Y.: Cornell University Press, 1998.

Orr, Lyndon. *Famous Affinities of History: The Romance of Devotion*. New York: Harper & Brothers, 1914.

Painter, Nell Irvin. *Creating Black Americans: African-American History and Its Meanings, 1619 to the Present*. New York: Oxford University Press, 2006.

———. *The History of White People*. New York: W. W. Norton, 2011.

Pak, Susie J. *Gentleman Bankers: The World of J. P. Morgan*. Cambridge, Mass.: Harvard University Press, 2013.

Palmer, Edgar. "A New Princeton-Town." *Princeton Alumni Weekly*, September 26, 1936, 31–33.

Paterson, A. D., ed. "The Fugitive Slave Case." *The Anglo American: A Journal of Literature, News, Politics, the Drama, Fine Arts, Etc.*, August 12, 1843, 383.

Paynter, John H. "The Fugitives of the Pearl." *Journal of Negro History* 1, no. 3 (1916): 243–64.

Pennington, James W. C. *The Fugitive Blacksmith; or, Events in the History of James W. C. Pennington.* 3rd ed. London: C. Gilpin, 1850.

Peterson, Carla L. *Black Gotham: A Family History of African Americans in Nineteenth-Century New York City.* New Haven, Conn.: Yale University Press, 2011.

Peterson, Harold F. *Argentina and the United States, 1810–1960.* New York: State University of New York, 1964.

Phan, Hoang Gia. *Bonds of Citizenship: Law and the Labors of Emancipation.* New York: New York University Press, 2013.

Phillips, Christopher, and Jason L. Pendleton, eds. *The Union on Trial: The Political Journals of Judge William Barclay Napton.* Columbia: University of Missouri Press, 2005.

Pidgin, Charles Felton. *Theodosia, the First Gentlewoman of Her Time.* Boston: C. M. Clark, 1907.

Platt, George Lewis. *The Platt Lineage: A Genealogical Research and Record.* New York: Thomas Whitaker, 1891.

Poole, Robert M. *On Hallowed Ground: The Story of Arlington National Cemetery.* New York: Bloomsbury, 2009.

Popkin, William D. *Evolution of the Judicial Opinion: Institutional and Individual Styles.* New York: New York University Press, 2007.

Prechtel-Kluskens Claire. "Anatomy of a Union Civil War Pension File." *National Geographic Society Magazine* 34, no. 3 (2008): 42.

Preston, Samuel H., and Michael R. Haines. *Fatal Years: Child Mortality in Late Nineteenth-Century America.* Princeton, N.J.: Princeton University Press, 2014.

Princeton, Sixty-Three: Fortieth-Year Book of the Members of the Class of 1863. Albany, N.Y.: Fort Orange, 1904.

Princeton Theological Seminary Alumni Association and Joseph Heatly Dulles. *Necrological Reports and Annual Proceedings of the Alumni Association of Princeton Theological Seminary.* Vol. 3. Princeton, N.J.: C. S. Robinson and Company, 1900.

Princeton University. *Laws of the College of New Jersey: Revised, Amended and Adopted by the Board of Trustees, January 1851.* Princeton, N.J.: J. T. Robinson, 1851.

———. *Quadragesimal Record, Class of '75, Princeton University.* Princeton, N.J.: Princeton University Press, 1915.

Princeton University Trustees. *By-Laws of the Board of Trustees of the College of New Jersey.* New York: Polhemus, 1876.

———. *Report of the Trustee Committee on Woodrow Wilson's Legacy.* Princeton, N.J.: Princeton University, 2016.

Princeton University and New Jersey. *Charter of the College of New Jersey, with*

Amendments, and the Laws of New Jersey Relative to the College. Newark, N.J.: The College Press, 1868.

Rael, Patrick. *Black Identity and Black Protest in the Antebellum North.* Chapel Hill: University of North Carolina Press, 2003.

Ramage, James, and Andrea S. Watkins. *Kentucky Rising: Democracy, Slavery, and Culture from the Early Republic to the Civil War.* Lexington: University of Kentucky Press, 2011.

Raum, John O. *The History of New Jersey: From Its Earliest Settlement to the Present Time, including a Brief Historical Account of the First Discoveries and Settlement of the Country.* Philadelphia: J. E. Potter, 1877.

Reingold, Nathan, ed. *The Papers of Joseph Henry.* Vol. 2, *November 1832– December 1835: The Princeton Years.* Washington, D.C.: Smithsonian Institution Press, 1975.

———. *The Papers of Joseph Henry.* Vol. 5, *January 1841–December 1843: The Princeton Years.* Washington, D.C.: Smithsonian Institution, 1985.

Reynolds, William L., and William M. Richman. "Elitism, Expediency, and the New Certiorari: Requiem for the Learned Hand Tradition." *Cornell Law Review* 81, no. 2 (1996): 273–342.

Ricord, F. W., ed. *History of Union County, New Jersey.* 2 vols. Newark, N.J.: East Jersey History, 1897.

Ripley, C. Peter. *The Black Abolitionist Papers, 1830–1846.* Chapel Hill: University of North Carolina Press, 1991.

Roediger, David R. *The Wages of Whiteness: Race and the Making of the American Working Class.* New York: Verso Books, 1999.

Rothschild, Maurine. "Frances O. Grant, Interview." In *The Black Woman Oral History Project*, vol. 4, edited by Ruth Edmonds Hill. Westport, Conn.: Meckler, 1991.

Rowland, Dunbar, ed. *Official Letter Books of W. C. C. Claiborne, 1801–1816.* Vol. 4. Jackson, Miss.: State Department of Archives and History, 1917.

Ryerson, Edgerton. *The Loyalists of America and Their Times: From 1620 to 1816.* Vol. 1. Toronto: William Briggs, 1880.

Sams, Conway Whittle, and Elihu Samuel Riley. *The Bench and Bar of Maryland: A History, 1634–1901.* Vol. 2. Chicago: Lewis, 1901.

Scharf, John Thomas. *Baltimore City and County, from the Earliest Period to the Present Day.* Baltimore, Md.: L. H. Everts, 1881.

———. *History of Delaware, 1608–1688.* Vol. 2. Philadelphia: L. J. Richards, 1888.

Schecter, Barnet. *The Devil's Own Work: The Civil War Draft Riots and the Fight to Reconstruct America.* New York: Walker, 2009.

Schenck, William Edward. *Biography of the Class of 1838 at the College of New Jersey at Princeton, N.J.* Philadelphia: Jas. B. Rogers, 1889.

Schwartz, Marie Jenkins. *Born in Bondage: Growing Up Enslaved in the Antebellum South.* Cambridge, Mass.: Harvard University Press, 2009.

Scott, James C. *Domination and the Arts of Resistance: Hidden Transcripts.* New Haven, Conn.: Yale University Press, 1990.

Seabrook, Lorraine, and Jack Seabrook. *Hopewell Valley.* Charleston, S.C.: Arcadia, 2000.

Sernett, Milton C. *North Star Country: Upstate New York and the Crusade for African American Freedom.* Syracuse, N.Y.: Syracuse University Press, 2002.

Shippen, Edward. "Some Notes about Princeton." *Princeton University Library Chronicle* 59, no. 1 (1997): 15–57.

Siebert, William Henry. *The Underground Railroad: From Slavery to Freedom.* New York: Macmillan, 1898.

Slaughter, Thomas P. *Bloody Dawn: The Christiana Riot and Racial Violence in the Antebellum North.* New York: Oxford University Press, 1994.

Smith, Anna Bustill. *Reminiscences of Colored People of Princeton, New Jersey.* n.p., 1913.

Smith, David G. *On the Edge of Freedom: The Fugitive Slave Issue in South Central Pennsylvania, 1820–1870.* New York: Fordham University Press, 2014.

Smith, Dorothy Valentine. "An Intercourse of the Heart: Some Little-Known Letters of Theodosia Burr." *New-York Historical Society Quarterly* 37, no. 1 (1953): 43–56.

Smith, J. Clay. *Emancipation: The Making of the Black Lawyer, 1844–1944.* Philadelphia: University of Pennsylvania Press, 1999.

Smith, Richard D. *Legendary Locals of Princeton.* Charleston, S.C.: Arcadia, 2014.

———. *Princeton University.* Charleston, S.C.: Arcadia, 2015.

Smith, Samuel Stanhope. *An Essay on the Causes of the Variety of Complexion and Figure in the Human Species.* New Brunswick, N.J.: J. Simpson, 1810.

Smith, Valerie. *Self-Discovery and Authority in Afro-American Narrative.* Cambridge, Mass.: Harvard University Press, 1987.

Snell, James P. *History of Hunterdon and Somerset Counties, New Jersey.* Philadelphia: Everts & Peck, 1881.

———. *History of Sussex and Warren Counties, New Jersey.* Philadelphia: Everts & Peck, 1881.

Snyder, Thomas D., ed. *120 Years of American Education: A Statistical Portrait.* Washington, D.C.: U.S. Department of Education, 1993.

Soderland, Jean R. *Quakers and Slavery: A Divided Spirit.* Princeton, N.J.: Princeton University Press, 1985.

Sollors, Werner, Caldwell Titcomb, and Thomas A. Underwood. *Blacks at Harvard: A Documentary History of African-American Experience at Harvard and Radcliffe.* New York: New York University Press, 1993.

Spencer, Richard Henry, ed. *Genealogical and Memorial Encyclopedia of the State of Maryland.* New York: American Historical Society, 1919.

Sprague, William Buell. *Annals of the American Pulpit: Presbyterian.* Vol. 4. New York: Robert Carter and Brothers, 1859.

Starr, John. *Hospital City: The Story of the Men and Women of Bellevue.* New York: Crown, 1957.

State of New Jersey. *Fifteenth Annual Report of the Board of Health.* Trenton, N.J.: John L. Murphy, 1891.

Steel, Suzanne Flandreau. "A Frontier Library." In *Intellectual Life on the Michigan Frontier: The Libraries of Gabriel Richard & John Monteith*, edited by Leonard A. Coombs and Francis X. Blouin, 211–35. Ann Arbor, Mich.: Bentley Historical Library, 1985.

Steiner, Bernard C. "Severn Teackle Wallis." *Sewanee Review* 15, no. 1 (1907): 58–74.

Stern, Simon. "Forensic Oratory and the Jury Trial in Nineteenth-Century America." *Comparative Legal History* 3, no. 7 (2015): 293–306.

Stewart, Alvan. *A Legal Argument before the Supreme Court of New Jersey at the May Term, 1845, at Trenton for the Deliverance of 4,000 Persons from Bondage.* New York: Finch and Weed, 1845.

Stewart, David O. *American Emperor: Aaron Burr's Challenge to Jefferson's America.* New York: Simon and Schuster, 2012.

Still, William. *The Underground Rail Road: A Record of Facts, Authentic Narratives, Letters, etc.* Philadelphia: Porter & Coales, 1872.

Svejda, George J., and United States Office of Archeology and Historic Preservation Division of History. *History of the Star-Spangled Banner from 1814 to the Present.* Washington, D.C.: Division of History, Office of Archeology and Historic Preservation, 1969.

Swift, David E. *Black Prophets of Justice: Activist Clergy before the Civil War.* Baton Rouge: Louisiana State University Press, 1999.

Switala, William J. *The Underground Railroad in New York and New Jersey.* Mechanicsburg, Pa.: Stackpole Books, 2006.

Synnott, Marcia Graham. *Student Diversity at the Big Three: Changes at Harvard, Yale, and Princeton since the 1920s.* New Brunswick, N.J.: Transaction, 2013.

Syrett, Nicholas L. *The Company He Keeps: A History of White College Fraternities.* Chapel Hill: University of North Carolina Press, 2009.

Tadman, Michael. *Speculators and Slaves: Masters, Traders, and Slaves in the Old South.* Madison: University of Wisconsin Press, 1989.

Tanner, Edwin P. *The Province of New Jersey, 1664–1738.* New York: Columbia University, 1908.

Tappan, Lewis. *The Life of Arthur Tappan.* New York: Hurd and Houghton, 1870.

Taslitz, Andrew E. *Reconstructing the Fourth Amendment: A History of Search and Seizure, 1789–1868.* New York: New York University Press, 2006.

Thompson, John. *The Life of John Thompson, a Fugitive Slave.* Worcester, Mass.: John Thompson, 1856.

Tilghman, Oswald. *History of Talbot County, Maryland, 1661–1861.* Baltimore, Md.: Williams & Wilkins, 1915.

Tisdale, Thomas. *A Lady of the High Hills: Natalie Delage Sumter*. Columbia: University of South Carolina Press, 2001.

Tomek, Beverly C. *Colonization and Its Discontents: Emancipation, Emigration, and Antislavery in Antebellum Pennsylvania*. New York: New York University Press, 2012.

Turner, Edward Raymond. *The Negro in Pennsylvania: Slavery—Servitude— Freedom, 1639–1861*. Washington, D.C.: American Historical Association, 1911.

VanderVelde, Lea. *Mrs. Dred Scott: A Life on Slavery's Frontier*. New York: Oxford University Press, 2009.

Waddell, Louis M. *To Secure the Blessings of Liberty: Pennsylvania and the Changing U.S. Constitution*. Harrisburg: Pennsylvania Historical and Museum Society, 1986.

Wall, Edward. *Reminiscences of Princeton College, 1845–1848*. Princeton, N.J.: Princeton University Press, 1914.

Wallace, George R. *Princeton Sketches: The Story of Nassau Hall*. New York: Putnam and Sons, 1893.

Wallis, Guy. *The Wallis Family of Kent County*. Bristol, Vt.: [Guy Wallis], 2011.

Walsh, Lorena. "The Chesapeake Slave Trade: Regional Patterns, African Origins, and Some Implications." *William and Mary Quarterly* 58 (January 2001): 139–70.

Washington, Jack. *Bicentennial History of the Black Community of Princeton, New Jersey, 1776–1976*. Trenton, N.J.: Africa World, 2005.

———. *The Long Journey Home: A Bicentennial History of the Black Community of Princeton, New Jersey, 1776–1976*. Trenton, N.J.: Africa World, 2005.

———. *The Quest for Equality: Trenton's Black Community, 1890–1965*. Trenton, N.J.: Africa World, 1993.

Watkins, James. *Narrative of the Life of James Watkins, Formerly a "Chattel" in Maryland, U.S.: Containing an Account of His Escape from Slavery, Together with an Appeal on Behalf of Three Millions of Such "Pieces of Property," Still Held under the Standard of the Eagle*. Bolton, Eng.: Kenyon and Abbatt, 1852.

Weeks, Stephen Beauregard. *Southern Quakers and Slavery: A Study in Institutional History*. Baltimore, Md.: Johns Hopkins, 1896.

Weiner, Mark. *Black Trials: Citizenship from the Beginning of Slavery to the End of Caste*. New York: Alfred A. Knopf, 2004.

Wertenbaker, Thomas Jefferson. *Princeton, 1746–1896*. 1946; repr., Princeton, N.J.: Princeton University Press, 2014.

White, G. Edward. *Law in American History*. Vol. 1, *From the Colonial Years through the Civil War*. New York: Oxford University Press, 2012.

Whitehead, William A. *East Jersey under the Proprietary Governments: A Narrative of Events Connected with the Settlement and Progress of the Province, Until the Surrender of the Government to the Crown in 1703*. 2nd ed. Newark, N.J.: M. R. Dennis, 1875.

Wilder, Craig Steven. *Ebony and Ivy: Race, Slavery, and the Troubled History of America's Universities*. New York: Bloomsbury, 2013.

Wilentz, Sean. "Princeton and the Controversies over Slavery." *Journal of Presbyterian History* 85, no. 2 (2007): 102–11.

Wilf, Steven. *Law's Imagined Republic: Popular Politics and Criminal Justice in Revolutionary America*. New York: Cambridge University Press, 2010.

Williams, Charles Richard. *The Cliosophic Society, Princeton University: A Study of Its History in Commemoration of Its Sesquicentennial Anniversary*. Princeton, N.J.: Princeton University Press, 1916.

Williams, Diana. "Can Quadroon Balls Represent Acquiescence or Resistance?" In *Gendered Resistance: Women, Slavery, and the Legacy of Margaret Garner*, edited by Mary E. Frederickson and Delores M. Walter, 115–32. Urbana: University of Illinois Press, 2013.

Williams, Donald E., Jr. *Prudence Crandall's Legacy: The Fight for Equality in the 1830s, Dred Scott, and Brown v. Board of Education*. Middletown, Conn.: Wesleyan University Press, 2014.

Williams, John Rogers. *The Handbook of Princeton*. New York: Grafton, 1905.

Williams, R. F. *The Members of the Philadelphia Bar, a Complete Catalogue from July, 1776, to July, 1855*. Philadelphia: Decorative Printing House, 1855.

Wilson, Samuel, and Bernard Lemann. *New Orleans Architecture: The Lower Garden District*. Gretna, La.: Pelican, 1990.

Winks, Robin W. "The Making of a Fugitive Slave Narrative—Josiah Henson and Uncle Tom." In *The Slave's Narrative*, edited by Charles Twitchell Davis and Henry Louis Gates Jr., 112–47. New York: Oxford University Press, 1991.

Witherspoon, J., and J. Rodgers. *The Works of the Rev. John Witherspoon, D.D. L.L.D. Late President of the College, at Princeton New-Jersey*. 3 vols. Philadelphia: William W. Woodward, 1801.

Wolinetz, Gary K. "New Jersey Slavery and the Law." *Rutgers Law Review* 50 (1998): 2227–58.

Wood, Arthur Evans. *Some Unsolved Social Problems of a University Town*. Ann Arbor, Mich.: C. W. Graham, 1920.

Woodson, Carter G. *The Negro in Our History*. Washington, D.C.: Associated Press, 1922.

Wong, Edlie L. *Neither Fugitive nor Free: Atlantic Slavery, Freedom Suits, and the Legal Culture of Travel*. New York: New York University Press, 2009.

Wright, Carroll Davidson. *Outline of Practical Sociology: With Special Reference to American Conditions*. New York: Longmans, Green, 1899.

Wright, Marion Thompson. *The Education of Negroes in New Jersey*. New York: Bureau of Publications, Teachers' College, Columbia University, 1941.

———. "New Jersey Laws and the Negro." *Journal of Negro History* 28, no. 2 (1943): 156–99.

Yentsch, Anne Elizabeth. *A Chesapeake Family and Their Slaves: A Study in Historical Archaeology*. New York: Cambridge University Press, 1994.

Young, Allan A. "Age." In *Supplementary Analysis and Derivative Tables: Twelfth Census of the United States, 1900*, edited by Walter Francis Willcox, Allyn Abbott Young, et al. Washington, D.C.: Government Publishing Office, 1906.

Young, Myra B. Armstead. *Freedom's Gardener: James F. Brown, Horticulture, and the Hudson Valley in Antebellum America*. New York: New York University Press, 2012.

Index

abolitionism: Breckinridge family and, 89, 183n52; Burr and, 186n73; Monteith and, 74; in New Jersey, 41–42, 51; Prevost and, 95; reputation of, 35; slave catchers and, 65; Story and, 80; in the town of Princeton, 34–35

Abraham (man enslaved by Phillip Wallis), 19

ACS. *See* American Colonization Society

African colonization, 28, 73. *See also* American Colonization Society; Liberia

African-descended persons, African Americans. *See* blacks

African Lane. *See* Witherspoon Street

African Methodist Episcopal (AME) church, 36

agency: criminal versus civic, 70; slaves and, 24

Alexander, Archibald, 43, 72–73

Alexander, James Waddel, 72–73, 113, 129, 168n39

Alexander, Joseph Addison, 73

Alexander, William Cowper, 43, 72–74

alienation, slavery and, 10

Allain, Jean, 10

Allen, Jody L., 137n5

Alston, Joseph, 185n72

Alston, Theodosia Bartow Burr, 88, 91, 181n26, 185n72, 186n75

American Anti-Slavery Society, 74, 82

American Colonization Society (ACS), 42–44, 73

American Party, 65

American Presbyterian Church, 42

American Whig Society, 49

Amistad case, 80, 177n79

Ancrum, Thomas James, 50–51

Ancrum, William Alexander, 50–51

Anderson, Maria, 59

Anderson (Rebecca Lloyd) House, 168n41

Antelope, 170n52

Anthony, Aaron, 151n56

apprenticeships, 39; Jeffers and, 65

Armstrong, Edward, 72, 74–75, 174n41

Ashmore, John, 78

Ashmore, Margaret, 78–79

Ashmun Institute, 72

Askin, Frank, 75

Astor, John Jacob, 85

Auslander, Mark, 203n3

Babcock, student, 115*f*

Baker, William Mumford, 5

Lolita Buckner Inniss, J.D., LL.M., Ph.D., is a professor of law at Southern Methodist University Dedman School of Law, where she serves as the Senior Associate Dean for Academic Affairs and where she was an inaugural Robert G. Storey Distinguished Faculty Fellow. Her research addresses historic, geographic, metaphoric, and visual norms of law, especially in the context of race, gender, and comparative constitutionalism.

ESE SELECT TITLES FROM EMPIRE STATE EDITIONS

Mark Naison and Bob Gumbs, *Before the Fires: An Oral History of African American Life in the Bronx from the 1930s to the 1960s*

Robert Weldon Whalen, *Murder, Inc., and the Moral Life: Gangsters and Gang-busters in La Guardia's New York*

Joanne Witty and Henrik Krogius, *Brooklyn Bridge Park: A Dying Waterfront Transformed*

Sharon Egretta Sutton, *When Ivory Towers Were Black: A Story about Race in America's Cities and Universities*

Pamela Hanlon, *A Wordly Affair: New York, the United Nations, and the Story behind Their Unlikely Bond*

Britt Haas, *Fighting Authoritarianism: American Youth Activism in the 1930s*

David J. Goodwin, *Left Bank of the Hudson: Jersey City and the Artists of 111 1st Street*. Foreword by DW Gibson

Nandini Bagchee, *Counter Institution: Activist Estates of the Lower East Side*

Carol Lamberg, *Neighborhood Success Stories: Creating and Sustaining Affordable Housing in New York*

Susan Celia Greenfield (ed.), *Sacred Shelter: Thirteen Journeys of Homelessness and Healing*

Elizabeth Macaulay Lewis and Matthew M. McGowan (eds.), *Classical New York: Discovering Greece and Rome in Gotham*

Susan Opotow and Zachary Baron Shemtob (eds.), *New York after 9/11*

Andrew Feffer, *Bad Faith: Teachers, Liberalism, and the Origins of McCarthyism*

Colin Davey with Thomas A. Lesser, *The American Museum of Natural History and How It Got That Way*. Foreword by Kermit Roosevelt III

Wendy Jean Katz, *Humbug: The Politics of Art Criticism in New York City's Penny Press*

For a complete list, visit www.fordhampress.com/empire-state-editions.